TAKING PARIS

TAKING PARIS

THE EPIC BATTLE FOR THE CITY OF LIGHTS

MARTIN DUGARD

CALIBER

CALIBER

An imprint of Penguin Random House LLC
penguinrandomhouse.com

Copyright © 2021 by Martin Dugard
Penguin supports copyright. Copyright fuels creativity, encourages diverse voices, promotes
free speech, and creates a vibrant culture. Thank you for buying an authorized edition of this
book and for complying with copyright laws by not reproducing, scanning, or distributing
any part of it in any form without permission. You are supporting writers and allowing
Penguin to continue to publish books for every reader.

DUTTON and the D colophon are registered trademarks of Penguin Random House LLC.

Maps by Chris Erichson

LIBRARY OF CONGRESS CATALOGING-IN-PUBLICATION DATA

Names: Dugard, Martin, author.
Title: Taking Paris: The epic battle for the city of lights / by Martin Dugard.
Other titles: Epic battle for the city of lights
Description: [New York]: Caliber, [2021] | Includes index.
Identifiers: LCCN 2021017300 (print) | LCCN 2021017301 (ebook) |
ISBN 9780593183083 (hardcover) | ISBN 9780593183106 (ebook)
Subjects: LCSH: World War, 1939–1945—Campaigns—France—Paris. |
World War, 1939–1945—France—Paris. | Paris (France)—History—1940–1944. |
France—History—German occupation, 1940–1945.
Classification: LCC D762.P3 D77 2021 (print) |
LCC D762.P3 (ebook) | DDC 940.54/214361—dc23
LC record available at https://lccn.loc.gov/2021017300
LC ebook record available at https://lccn.loc.gov/2021017301

Printed in the United States of America
1 3 5 7 9 10 8 6 4 2

BOOK DESIGN BY TIFFANY ESTREICHER

For Monique Dugard Lewis,
who once called Paris home

Between survival and victory there are many stages.
—WINSTON CHURCHILL

PROLOGUE

The war resumes on a Friday.

"German planes swarmed all over Western Europe," the *New York Times* reports in this morning's edition, "to the outskirts of Paris and London today in complete disregard of neutral borders."

Air-raid warnings wail in Paris as Heinkel and Dornier bombers zoom low in formation. The morning air is cool as antiaircraft guns open fire. Tens of thousands of Parisians dutifully walk and run to the Métro tunnels at Madeleine, Place des Fêtes, and République. Taking the stairs to the underground railway platforms, they wait for the all clear, enduring dank air, no running water, and a frustrating lack of *toilettes*.

But these thousands are the minority in a city of 3 million people. The rest of Paris sees no need to cease making breakfast, sipping coffee, making love, and otherwise preparing for a three-day holiday weekend.

By 8:00 a.m. it is over. "Paris's air alarm lasted an hour and fifty-two minutes," notes the *Times*. "Anti-aircraft batteries fired furiously. Streaking past Paris, the planes continued on to the sea."

Then Paris goes back to normal, the citizens once again marching down into the Métro—this time to catch the train for work.

The sirens sound again at 4:55 in the afternoon, but Parisians remain calm and even blasé as the *drôle de guerre*—"funny war"—seems to be ending. Or, as the British call it, putting a spin on the French translation: the "phony war." For the eight months since Germany invaded Poland, France and its ally Britain have been on high alert, awaiting the inevitable moment when the Nazi power turns its attention westward. Both sides have declared war on one another. The next logical step is to fight.

Yet, until this morning, absolutely nothing has happened.

In the meantime, Paris has been transformed by preparations for combat: sandbags line bridges, buildings, and monuments such as the Eiffel Tower; the city is blacked out from dusk to dawn; stained glass windows have been removed from cathedrals as a precaution against aerial bombing; and great trenches have been dug in public parks as air-raid shelters.

Posters in cafés remind patrons that German spies might be eavesdropping on their conversations. Yet these placards, like the trenches and sandbags, are so commonplace and have hung on the walls so many months that they are all but ignored.

Even today's air-raid sirens fail to instill fear. The Germans may be invading Belgium, Holland, and Luxembourg, but to the people of Paris they are hardly an immediate threat. The Boche, as the French derisively call the Germans, are hundreds of miles away, soon to be beaten back by the vaunted French army.*

---

* Boche is derived from caboche—meaning head or cabbage, and refers to the French view that the Germans are thickheaded.

At 7:30 p.m., Ludovic-Oscar Frossard, the French minister of propaganda, makes it official: "The *real* war has begun," he announces.

But Monsieur Frossard's pronouncement, delivered over the radio in the measured cadence of a career bureaucrat, comes so late as to be laughable. The people of Paris have already seen and heard the cacophony of this "real war" for themselves.

And they are unconcerned. The real war may have begun, but Paris is safe.

Let the weekend begin.

TAKING PARIS

1

General Erwin Rommel has had a very busy weekend.

The Meuse River rages fast and cold. The loyal admirer of Adolf Hitler paddles a small rubber assault raft toward the west shore. Locals blew the bridges one day ago. This exposed crossing is the only way. Rommel and the young Wehrmacht soldiers spilling over the sides of the cramped black inflatable are not alone. All around them, German troops dig their paddles into the green current, desperate to reach the far shore, where heavily fortified French troops lay down thick rounds of fire.

"On the steep west bank . . . the enemy had numerous carefully placed machine-gun and anti-tank nests as well as observation points, each one of which would have to be taken on in the fight," Rommel will report. "They also had both light and heavy artillery, accurate and mobile."

Some French defenders are hidden in concrete bunkers on the high rocky bluffs, while others aim their M29 machine guns out the

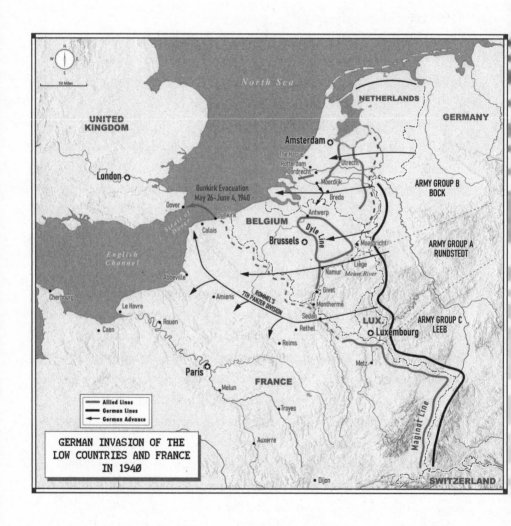

GERMAN INVASION OF THE
LOW COUNTRIES AND FRANCE
IN 1940

windows of abandoned homes on the water's edge. Still other French fighters launch heavy artillery from the ruins of the Crèvecoeur Castle, near a mighty bend in the river where spotters have a clear view of the German attackers.

For the first time in days, at a time when he needs it most, the wiry, forty-eight-year-old Rommel enjoys little air support. The only covering fire for the general and this band of young infantry soldiers from the 7th Rifle Regiment—almost all less than half his age—comes from the shore behind them, as tanks from his 7th Panzer Division unleash lethal rounds at French positions.

Yet the Meuse must be crossed.

Wehrmacht troops have been practicing this moment for months on the Mosel River in the secrecy of Germany's Black Forest, with Rommel in particular driving his men hard to perfect their crossing tactics. This is his first tank command after a highly decorated infantry career and he is desperate to succeed. The time has now come to put that training to use.

One hundred yards wide at the Leffe crossing point, and fast enough that any man or vehicle attempting to ford its waters will be swept away, the meandering Meuse is a daunting geographical blockade between the rugged Ardennes Forest and open countryside leading straight into France's heart and soul: the capital city of Paris.

The two-thousand-year-old city on the banks of the Seine River is the most sublime and resplendent city in Europe. The City of Lights, as Paris is known, is famous for its architecture and museums, thinkers and writers, ideals and poetry, cuisine and history. As King Francis I, former ruler of France, once stated: "Paris is not a city; it is a world."

Such is the allure that Germany's despotic supreme leader, Adolf Hitler, once an aspiring painter of watercolors, has a long-standing fascination with Paris's beauty. Hitler has never set foot in the City of Lights, but despite his admiration he still seethes about the punitive terms of surrender France imposed on Germany at the end of World War I. The Führer is determined to conquer Paris and humiliate its citizens with a display of total Nazi power.

"When at last," Hitler wrote in his manifesto, *Mein Kampf*, "the will-to-live of the German nation, instead of continuing to be wasted away in purely passive defence, can be summoned together for a final, active showdown with France, and thrown into this last decisive battle with the very highest objective for Germany; then, and only then, will it be possible to bring to a close the perpetual and so fruitless struggle between ourselves and France."

Hitler dreams of oversized German flags bearing the swastika, symbol of his National Socialist—"Nazi"—Party, flying from the Eiffel Tower. In this fantasy, museums like the great Louvre will be looted and priceless works of art shipped to his own capital city of Berlin, which will be redesigned and reconstructed, completing his goal of humbling the French even further by ensuring that Berlin's wonders far outstrip those of Paris.

Adolf Hitler is very close to realizing that dream.

. . .

THE BATTLE FOR FRANCE began on May 10, just three days ago. More than a million German soldiers poured across their border, determined to crush the French army and its British ally, which has sent nearly a half million troops to aid in the defense. Utilizing a technique known as blitzkrieg—"lightning war"—combining fast-moving divisions of Germany's ten panzer tank divisions accompanied by fighter planes and dive-bombers in the skies above, Hitler's unstoppable forces are attacking with a speed never before seen in warfare. It is the panzers at the forefront, punching through enemy defenses and using speed to expand the fluid battle lines. They do not wait for the infantry, as is the tactic of French tanks. Wehrmacht foot soldiers simply do their best to keep up.

The German forces are split into tactical armies, with German

Army Group B spearheading the attack in the north. Their mission is to slice through Luxembourg, Belgium, and the Netherlands, not only capturing those nations but also luring British and French troops into battle. Unbeknownst to the Allies, this is a fatal trap.

Meanwhile, German Army Group A silently approaches from the east, using the dense Ardennes Forest to conceal what will become known as one of history's greatest surprise attacks. Their job is to dash all the way from the German border to the English Channel, then link up with Army Group B to completely surround and annihilate the Allied forces. Known as a "double envelopment," this tactic is among the oldest in military history, used by Hannibal to defeat the Romans at Cannae in 216 BC. On paper, it looks like two sides of a vise pressing together, squeezing the conquered army in between. If successful, Hitler will accept the French surrender in due course, then have Paris and all of France to call his own.

But the bold plan will fail if German Army Group A cannot cross the impregnable Meuse. Flowing 575 miles from northeast France all the way to the North Sea, this serpentine river twists through valleys lined with high cliffs. "Mosa," its Latin name, roughly translates as "maze," for the many abrupt bends and U-turns on the waterway's journey to the sea.

And it is not just the Meuse that serves as a natural barrier between Germany and France but also the mountainous terrain on both banks, making for impregnable natural defensive positions.

France's top military leader, the intellectual General Maurice-Gustave Gamelin, has every confidence the Meuse will stop the German invasion. He is the architect of "stand-and-take-it warfare," as some in the press label his strategic mindset.* The white haired Parisian calls the river "Europe's best tank obstacle" and has planned his battle strategy accordingly. *La Meuse est infranchissable*—"The

---

* *Time* magazine, June 10, 1940.

Meuse cannot be crossed"—the general is fond of stating. In 1939, *Time* magazine named Gamelin "the world's foremost soldier," almost ensuring that those words are treated as gospel.

But just ten days before Germany attacked, a French military attaché in Switzerland passed along intelligence to General Gamelin in Paris stating that the Germans would invade through the Ardennes Forest, then attempt to cross the Meuse. The attaché was ignored. Gamelin's belief in the invulnerability of the Ardennes is so profound that he also rejected a 1938 study by his own commanders stating that not only will an attack through the forest succeed but German troops will race to the Meuse River within sixty hours.

In fact, Rommel's panzers need just fifty-seven.*

---

* The word "Panzer" in German means tank. The French preferred the more specific term *chars Allemands*—"German tanks"—to describe these invading machines.

2

General Erwin Rommel is determined to prove Monsieur Gamelin a fool.

Rommel's woolen battle uniform is drenched in sweat and river water as he digs his paddle into the current. His knee-high black leather riding boots are soaked. The general is exhausted, having slept little since the invasion began. Yet he ignores the near misses of gunfire and geysers of artillery rounds landing in the water all around him. Instead, Rommel shouts encouragement to the brave boys paddling alongside him.

"I now took over personal command of 2nd Battalion of 7th Rifle Regiment and for some time directed operations by myself," the general will report of his temporary return to infantry command. "I crossed the Meuse in one of the first boats and at once joined the company."

The assault raft reaches the shore near a ruined waterfront château. Rommel orders the riflemen into position, shouting for them to keep their heads low. French artillery zeroes in, launching a withering series of rounds. Nevertheless, the general commands a handful of young soldiers to paddle the assault rafts back to load infantry still waiting to cross.

Rommel desperately needs artillery of his own to pin down the French. But the big guns are stuck in traffic somewhere on the narrow roads of the Ardennes, materials for constructing pontoon bridges having been deemed more important.

The general is hoarse from shouting orders. There are still five hours before sunset. The air sings with small-arms fire. Rommel's men take heavy casualties. Death comes as a surprise, whether from a machine-gun bullet hundreds of yards away or a shell fired from a mile distant; few of these teenagers catch a glimpse of the man who pulls the trigger and have even less chance to shoot back. After months of training, four exhausting days on the move, and the adrenaline surge of advancing on an enemy position in broad daylight, these young warriors perish. More than eighty German soldiers are killed, while still others are turned into mist by direct artillery hits, forever to be listed as "missing" in the official casualty report.

Yet Erwin Rommel defies death. He does not wear a helmet, preferring a high-peaked officer's cap, which not only alerts French sharpshooters to his commanding rank but also leaves him vulnerable to the slightest high-velocity metal shell fragment. Despite the heavy fire, he strides back and forth along the waterfront, finally spotting a location where his combat engineers can build a ferry. Work begins immediately. Rommel orders local houses set on fire to provide a smoke screen protecting his engineers from snipers. When construction bogs down, the general personally leaps into water up to his hips to assist.

The ferry is built within hours. As French artillery runs out of ammunition and ceases firing, Rommel's personal panzer command tank becomes the first armored vehicle floated across. By morning, thirty more panzers will be over the Meuse.

But one laborious crossing at a time is too slow.

The general hastens the German advance by ordering the construction of a pontoon bridge at a crossing between Leffe and Bouvignes. Thirty miles to the south, near the city of Sedan, fellow panzer generals Heinz Guderian and Georg-Hans Reinhardt have also successfully fought their way over the Meuse and are constructing their own temporary bridges.

By May 14, just four days after the invasion of France, the myth of the uncrossable Meuse is no more. French officers desert their commands. Those caught in the act by their superiors are executed with a shot to the head. This reminder to stand fast does little good. Lacking leadership and facing certain death in the path of the unrelenting German advance, entire French units raise the white flag of surrender. One major is captured attempting to escape dressed like a woman, uniform pants beneath the dress giving him away. So many French give up that the Germans do not have time to imprison the defeated men, simply ordering them to throw down their weapons and march east into Germany, their rifles then hurled under tank treads and crushed. Amazingly, most French do as they are told. When a lone lieutenant colonel indignantly refuses three direct orders to surrender, Rommel orders him shot.

Yet there is no celebration for General Erwin Rommel. Not yet. The general and his fellow panzer commanders know the blitzkrieg must roll on. His men are exhausted and coated in dust, still fueled by adrenaline and now euphoria. One by one, the seven tank divisions fan out over a twenty-mile front and advance west across France. The air vibrates with the rumble of panzers. Rather than wait for supplies to catch up, tanks refuel at abandoned roadside gas stations. The roads are clogged with refugees and still more French soldiers eager to throw down their arms. There is little resistance.

French throats choke from terror at the sight of the German onslaught, but Erwin Rommel is stirred: "In a light morning mist, with the rising sun behind us, the tank column rolled on towards the west," he will confidently write.

Paris is just 150 miles in the distance.

And nothing now stands in the way of Adolf Hitler's army.

It's all happening so fast.

3

MAY 16, 1940
PARIS, FRANCE
5:30 P.M.

W inston Churchill has come to save France.

It is six days since the German onslaught. Two days ago, as General Erwin Rommel was crossing the Meuse, the Netherlands harbor city of Rotterdam was leveled by the Luftwaffe. Nearly nine hundred civilians were killed and eighty thousand made homeless. The German officer accepting the Dutch surrender, a small, corpulent Prussian named Dietrich von Choltitz, was unrepentant about the devastation. Knowing the German mindset toward such all-out war, Churchill shudders to think that a similar fate awaits Paris.

Britain's newly elected prime minister strides into the French foreign minister's office here at number 37 Quai d'Orsay, followed closely by three of his top military commanders. The bonfires of burning government documents remain lit, smoky sweet smell of burning paper wafting in through the open windows. An oversized battlefield map balances on an easel. The mood among the assembled French dignitaries is grim.

Yesterday morning, Churchill awoke to a frantic phone call from his French counterpart, Paul Reynaud. "He spoke in English, and evidently under stress: 'We have been defeated,'" Churchill will later quote Reynaud. "As I did not immediately respond he said again: 'We are beaten; we have lost the battle.' I said: 'Surely, it can't have happened so soon?' But he replied: 'The front is broken near Sedan: they are pouring through in great numbers with tanks and armored cars.'"

So it is that Winston Churchill has flown to Paris to meet with the Anglo-French Supreme War Council. He wears a bow tie and waistcoat. His breath is Romeo y Julieta cigar and luncheon champagne, wreathed in Penhaligon's Blenheim Bouquet aftershave.

Churchill's ambition is to find ways Britain can help stop the German advance. He is upbeat, certain there is a way to reverse France's stunning battlefield fiascos. The sixty-five-year-old prime minister remains standing as the French commander in chief, General Maurice-Gustave Gamelin, steps forward to brief the group on the war status.

"At no time did we sit around a table," Churchill will recall. "Utter dejection was written on every face. In front of Gamelin, on a student's easel was a map, about two yards square, purporting to show the Allied front. In this line was drawn a small but sinister bulge at Sedan.

"The General talked perhaps five minutes without anyone saying a word."

General Gamelin is a polished intellectual, able to speak freely on painting and philosophy. The portly Churchill is just five feet six inches but fairly towers over the diminutive general with the white bristle mustache and pale raccoon rings around his eyes.

During World War I, Gamelin helped plan the counterattack that led to victory at the pivotal First Battle of the Marne. This success and many others during the war propelled him up the career military ladder. Yet many who know Gamelin comment about his "soft" hand-shake and reclusive behavior more befitting an academic than a soldier. Prime Minister Reynaud, known for his strong opinions, openly considers his top general "gutless."

But this enigmatic persona is no longer an issue, for General Gamelin's days as a figurehead are all but over. At sixty-seven, the mortifying defeat at the Meuse ensures that this is his last command. No one in the room knows that the general suffers from an advanced form of syphilis, which affects the brain, causing lapses in judgment, memory, and concentration, yet they have seen clear evidence of that behavior in the last five days. Brief completed, there is nothing for Gamelin to do but stand next to his battle map and answer questions.

In addition to Winston Churchill, British generals Sir John Dill and Hastings "Pug" Ismay, as well as Air Chief Marshal Sir Philip Joubert de la Ferté, are in attendance.*

The downhearted French contingent consists of Gamelin, Prime Minister Reynaud, and French defense minister Édouard Daladier. These seven men are the Allies' most influential military minds. The fate of France—and likely England—rests upon decisions that must be made in this room tonight. Now is the time to speak up.

Yet, "there was a considerable silence," Churchill will recall.

As awkward as this moment might be, General Gamelin's humiliation will soon run far deeper.

The heavy stillness continues as Churchill leans forward to study the battle map. He is a former cavalry officer and graduate of Sandhurst,

---

* In particular, Pug Ismay led a fascinating life. Born to a British legislator in India in 1887, he was educated at Charterhouse School in Britain. He did so poorly on his examinations that he was ineligible to pursue university studies at Cambridge, so he reluctantly attended Sandhurst. He went on to serve in the Indian Army, followed by Camel Corps in British Somaliland in lieu of the cavalry posting for which he had always longed. This was the circuitous path that led to Churchill selecting Ismay as his chief military assistant in May 1940.

Britain's military academy. Twice in his lifetime, he has served as First Lord of the Admiralty, sending men and ships into combat. He also knows what it is like to fail horribly, ordering thousands of men to their deaths, as during his unsuccessful Gallipoli operation in World War I, a horrific debacle that saw Churchill banished from power for twenty long years.

So battle maps are nothing new to Winston Churchill.

The prime minister scrutinizes the ominous red line denoting the Nazi advance. Most troubling is the fact that the lead German elements are now outside Laon, less than a hundred miles north. Paris could fall in a day—perhaps even tonight. Nazi Germany controls Poland, Czechoslovakia, Austria, Norway, Luxembourg, and Denmark. Conquering France and the Low Countries will place all of western Europe in the hands of Adolf Hitler. Should that occur, England stands alone, the certain target of Hitler's next invasion.*

Yet Churchill seizes upon one glimmer of hope. The battle can still be won—but only if the reserve troops held back to defend Paris rush immediately to the front. General Gamelin, of all people, knows this. Such a stand by the Ninth Army won the pivotal First Battle of the Marne in September 1914. French legend holds that six thousand reserve infantry troops traveled from Paris to the battlefield in a convoy of six hundred taxicabs, then launched the counterattack designed by Gamelin himself. As recently as a week ago, the French reserve consisted of their Seventh Army, a collection of divisions under the

---

* Spain, Portugal, Ireland, Sweden, and Switzerland—all located in western Europe—will remain neutral throughout World War II. Spanish dictator Francisco Franco, who rose to power with the help of Adolf Hitler and the German army during the Spanish Civil War, stationed armies in the Pyrenees Mountains to prevent any attempt at invasion of the Iberian Peninsula. The Swiss also zealously defended their mountainous borders, often shooting down both Allied and Axis aircraft violating their airspace.

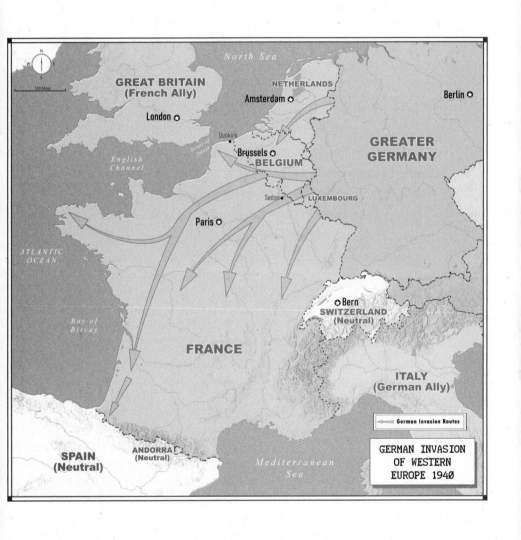

command of the dashing and self-absorbed General Henri Giraud. A force this powerful can surely stop the Germans.

Then Churchill notices a mistake. No one has marked the current location of the soldiers who will make this last desperate stand.

"Where is the strategic reserve?" asks Churchill. He says the words in English, then repeats them tentatively in his poor French, his voice a combination lisp and growl. "*Où est la masse de manœvre?*"

"*Aucune,*" answers Gamelin.

None. There are no reserves. Gamelin has already sent Giraud's Seventh Army to the front.

In disbelief, the prime minister asks how the general plans to launch a counterattack.

General Maurice-Gustave Gamelin can only shrug.

4

I was dumbfounded," Winston Churchill will write of General Game-lin's incompetence. "It was one of the greatest surprises of my life."

Optimism dashed, the prime minister turns his back on the map. Churchill has a most difficult decision to make. There will be no discussion of what happens next. The verdict is his alone.

Churchill walks to an open bay window. Bonfires rage on the lawn below. This is the last desperate act of a government eager to flee its capital. Rather than waste time walking up and down steps with armloads of paper, civil servants open windows and hurl official government documents onto the green grass below. Foreign Ministry bureaucrats pick up the errant forms and reports and pitch them into the fires. Others tip wheelbarrows full of files into the inferno. Bits of paper escape the flames and whirl dervish-like into the sky.

As Winston Churchill can see for himself, the sight of France's official secrets being publicly burned should be a clear signal of dark days to come.

Yet Paris remains calm.

The façade of the Quai d'Orsay, as the French Foreign Ministry Building is more commonly known, faces the Seine. The Treaty of Versailles, that oppressive and brutal document bringing Germany to its knees at the end of World War I, was drafted within these walls.*

Far beyond the flames, on the other side of the river, Churchill sees sycamore trees lining the broad boulevards of the Champs-Élysées. The Luxor Obelisk sprouts seventy feet above the Place de la Concorde roundabout, its base packed in sandbags.

To Churchill's left, but out of his line of sight, the thousand-foot-tall Eiffel Tower stands as a symbol of all that is great about France. A lone flagpole at the very top flies the national flag, an enormous red, white, and blue tricolor.

To Churchill's far right, the six-hundred-year-old Cathédrale Notre-Dame de Paris looms over the Seine, its legendary towers home to Emmanuel, the fourteen-ton bell that has tolled over Paris since the seventeenth century.† Its melancholy peal is synonymous with state funerals and times of national sadness, when the people of Paris line

---

* The Treaty of Versailles placed the blame for World War I on Germany. Staggering reparations were levied, leading to the economic devastation that gave rise to Adolf Hitler's National Socialist Party. Germany was also ordered to demilitarize, adding further friction between herself and her neighbors.

† The Cathédrale Notre-Dame de Paris has a total of ten bells, each of which is tuned to a different musical note. Emmanuel, considered the Grand Bell, is in the key of F sharp. Known as the bourdon, it is the heaviest bell and has the lowest tone. The true weight is 14.6 tons (13.2 tons in metric weight). Emmanuel has rung for French royal coronations and funerals, Christmas, Easter, papal visits, the ends of the world wars, and moments of mourning such as the September 11, 2001, terrorist attacks on New York City. Notably, when many other bells from Notre-Dame were melted into cannonballs during the French Revolution, Emmanuel was spared. It's worth noting that the other bells are named Marie, Gabriel, Anne-Geneviève, Denis, Marcel, Étienne, Benedict-Joseph, Maurice, and Jean-Marie. All survived the harrowing cathedral fire of April 15, 2019.

the streets dressed in black, crepe paper of the same color tied to streetlamps, which have been lit during daylight as a sign of mourning.

Much closer in the same direction stands the Louvre, undoubtedly the world's most revered museum. Its curators did not wait for a German invasion to begin protecting its thousands of treasures, sending them into hiding nine months ago. To conceal their departure, the Louvre closed for three days. The public was told the reason was repairs. Instead, more than 3,000 priceless works of art were spirited from the museum and hidden in châteaus throughout France. The public was stunned to find the Louvre nearly empty when it reopened. If nothing else, this moment of foreshadowing began to mentally prepare Parisians for a potential German occupation.*

It is inconceivable to Winston Churchill that Paris might soon be under the thumb of Nazi Germany. The origin of the title la Ville Lumière—the City of Lights—came about when lighting was installed along city streets centuries ago in an effort to decrease the crime rate. But that term took on a whole new meaning when Paris became a beacon of philosophy, science, cuisine, the arts, and those interested in the freedom of a life well lived. This period is known as the Enlightenment.

Winston Churchill believes Adolf Hitler will extinguish that light. The Führer's tyrannical rule silences free speech and imprisons those suspected of speaking against him. He believes in the superiority of the Germanic people and a hierarchy of races: white, blue-eyed, blond-haired Germans stand on top.

Already, forces under Hitler's command are conducting ethnic cleansing in conquered nations. During the invasion of Poland in September 1939, a German task force known as the *Einsatzgruppen*

---

* Pieces at the Louvre considered "valuable" were placed in a crate with a yellow circle painted on the exterior; major works were marked with a green circle; and world treasures were marked with a red circle. Leonardo da Vinci's *Mona Lisa*, perhaps the most famous work of art of all, was placed in a crate with three prominent red circles.

assembled mass firing squads to shoot more than 10,000 Jews and members of the Polish elite.

Since 1933, special prisons in Germany known as concentration camps have housed homosexuals, attorneys, priests, Communists, Jehovah's Witnesses, Roma, Blacks, and, of course, the Jews who are seen as a threat to the security of Nazi Germany. Inmates are subjected to torture, malnutrition, and execution. The first of these, a camp named Dachau just outside Munich, was opened just five weeks after Hitler was named chancellor. One year later, in 1934, Hitler increased his total power over the German people, uniting the chancellorship and presidency of Germany into a single, all-powerful title: Führer—"supreme leader." Just one month ago, in April 1940, a new German camp named Auschwitz opened in Poland. Under ideal conditions, it is less than a day by train from Paris.

There are approximately 150,000 French citizens of Jewish extraction now living in the City of Lights, all of whom would come under Adolf Hitler's policies of racial persecution. Thousands of Jews who fled prewar Germany and the fighting in Poland have taken refuge in France, and are now joined by thousands more running from the fighting in Belgium and the Netherlands. In addition, Paris is home to a significant population of African Americans who have fled racial persecution in America. Among them is singer Josephine Baker, who recently concluded a successful run at the Casino de Paris, performing a song and dance revue with white French singer Maurice Chevalier.

Whether or not these Jews and Blacks live or die; whether or not Paris remains free; whether or not France turns the tide against the Nazi invasion—these outcomes now rest on the sloping shoulders of Winston Leonard Spencer Churchill. A decision to send more troops might rescue his ally. Refusing to do so, even at the risk of imperiling Great Britain, will certainly damn France.

Yet Winston Churchill is a gambler. "You must put your head into the lion's mouth if the performance is to be a success," he believes.

Churchill is equally sure France is doomed. "The French are evidently cracking, and the situation is awful," Churchill announces to his war cabinet upon returning to London. The prime minister commands his chiefs of staff to draw up a plan for waging war without their faltering ally. The document will be given a blunt and pessimistic title: "A Certain Eventuality."

Yet the prime minister sends more military aid anyway.

Because, for now, Paris remains free—and calm. Restaurants and cafés are doing robust business. There is no rationing of food or gasoline. Booksellers in the stalls on the Left Bank of the Seine do uninterrupted sales.

"It is hard to explain this air of confidence which seems to have filled Paris in this dark hour," the *New York Times* will observe. "The people, perhaps, are thinking of the Marne and other miracles that have in the past saved France. But above all is the obstinate confidence in the French Armies."

But as the people of Paris will soon realize, that confidence is misplaced.

Deeply misplaced.

5

Colonel Charles de Gaulle is a patriot.

One hundred miles east of Paris, the tall, proud French officer orders his 4th Armored Division to attack. The dawn smells of exhaust and strong brown tobacco smoke. His two makeshift tank battalions rumble to life and begin their slow advance toward the crossroads town of Montcornet as first morning light limns the horizon. If successful, the French will take control of the roads leading north and east, blocking the crucial German supply column from delivering ammunition and food to the hungry panzer divisions racing across northern France.

In a last gambit before being fired, General Maurice-Gustave Gamelin has pulled troops away from the Maginot Line to cut off the German advance. Colonel de Gaulle's tank division is part of that reconfigured Sixth Army, as this desperate measure has been christened.

In typical fashion, de Gaulle had no problem questioning his supe-

22

riors about their tactics. "Why not, even now, mass all our armor in one strike force and smash the Nazis to pieces?" he badgers General Alphonse Joseph Georges upon being given command. As a longtime advocate for armored combat, de Gaulle has dreamed of sending tanks into battle utilizing rapid attack and constant movement. And while it is the Germans who made this strategy famous as blitzkrieg, it is a philosophy de Gaulle espoused as early as 1934 in his book, *The Army of the Future.**

Georges's response was at once fatalistic and encouraging. "The 1st Division was annihilated in Belgium. The 2nd Division was destroyed while in transport on the River Oise. The 3rd Division fought gloriously in bits and pieces but was overwhelmed. Yours is all that is left. There it is, de Gaulle. You have long held the idea that the enemy is putting into practice. Now is your chance to act."

.   .   .

A LIT GITANE DANGLES from de Gaulle's lips. The fingertips on his right hand are stained nicotine yellow. He wears his helmet buckled tightly under his chin and a long leather coat over his uniform jacket. If the colonel is nervous, he does not show it, lost in cigarettes and solitude. Long before this war began, he dedicated himself to preparing for a tank assault just like this. To be here, in this moment, the attack finally about to begin, has the feel of destiny for this man who strongly believes such a thing exists. There is no place for nerves.

"His tall figure is silhouetted against the sky like, in the distance, the twin gothic towers of Laon cathedral," one correspondent will write of the colonel's regal presence. "He smokes one cigarette after another and his binoculars never leave his eyes."

Charles de Gaulle's towering six-foot-five-inch height and prominent Gallic nose earned him the nickname "the great asparagus"

---

* In his memoirs, de Gaulle will claim that Adolf Hitler personally read and enjoyed *The Army of the Future.*

during his education at Saint-Cyr, the French military academy. But that physical appearance and haughty demeanor conceals a man of great complexity. De Gaulle is an avid reader, writer, historian, and conservative Catholic. He wears his wedding ring on his right hand due to a World War I bullet wound to his left. De Gaulle and his wife, Yvonne, have three children, among them twelve-year-old Anne, the youngest, born with Down syndrome. De Gaulle is normally reserved in his displays of physical affection, except with Anne, upon whom he dotes.

"Called upon yesterday in extreme urgency to form a new division," the colonel writes Yvonne in the lead-up to battle. She is still at their home in Colombey, near the German border. The military historian in de Gaulle takes pride in the fact that the house is near the site of the Battle of Catalaunian Plains, where Attila the Hun was defeated by a coalition of Romans and Visigoths in 451.

"We will see what happens," de Gaulle cautions Yvonne. "The events are very *serious.*"

In closing, de Gaulle reminds Yvonne to prepare for the worst possible outcome. She should be ready to flee. "Assure yourself very *discreetly* about an eventual means of transport. But I assure you, *in conscience*, that I don't think things will come to that."

De Gaulle knows his chances of success are slim. This quixotic attack is folly. Yet his orders state that he must slow the German advance. He has no other option. "The war is beginning as badly as it could," de Gaulle has resolved. "Therefore it must go on."

The forty-nine-year-old colonel's courage has few equals. He speaks fluent German and during World War I often crawled across the barbed wire and open space of no-man's-land in the dead of night to enemy trenches, where he gathered valuable intelligence by listening in on conversations. De Gaulle was eventually captured. He spent almost three years in a prisoner-of-war camp. He was brutally punished for each of his five failed escape attempts, and yet he never stopped trying.

That bravery is on display now. De Gaulle's 4th Armored Division existed only on paper when he took charge five days ago. The colonel's journey to his mythical unit was abysmal. While being chauffeured to the front in his black Talbot sedan, he endured roads clogged with "miserable processions of refugees" and "a good many soldiers who had lost their weapons."

De Gaulle sees a fighting force that is unshaven and discourteous, with many French soldiers even believing that the policies of Adolf Hitler are preferable to those of their own government. "Better Hitler than Blum" was a popular rallying cry under the rule of France's former socialist premier—and little has changed. Having so little belief in their own government, many of these men have little interest in defending their own nation. Visions of World War I still haunt many French. The nation lost almost 2 million military and civilian lives, fueling ambivalence toward another conflict.

Yet, in the midst of chaos, de Gaulle created order.

"The spectacle of this frantic population and military disaster," he will write, "filled me with a fury without limits. What a stupid waste . . . whatever I was able to achieve afterwards, it was then that my resolution was made."

De Gaulle finds men who want to fight. The colonel personally culls a motley collection of heavy Char B1, medium-weight Char D2, and obsolete Renault R35 tanks from retreating French units, alternately cowing and inspiring the broken and defeated, a knight errant hinting at glory for any soldier willing to pledge allegiance.

Yet building an army and winning battles are two different achievements.

De Gaulle has long argued with French military leadership about the importance of a modern mechanized force. *Time* calls him "a lanky, pale, mustached military innovator who for twenty years has pounded home one point in conferences, articles, reports: if France was to meet Germany on equal terms she must have the motors of offense—tanks, trucks, motorcycles, airplanes." But his new tank commanders barely know how to drive their vehicles, let alone fire on the move.

And unlike panzers, which are equipped with radios, the French have no way to communicate once hatches are closed for battle. The 4th also lacks air support, possesses little reconnaissance, and lacks an infantry large enough to hold any territory de Gaulle's army might capture. His men do not even have maps to show the way and must rely on roadside signs for direction.

Perhaps worst of all, the thickly armored but plodding B1s have a fuel range of just twelve miles. They will run out of gas halfway to Montcornet and must stop to be refueled again before battle—a process quite the opposite of blitzkrieg.*

None of that matters to de Gaulle. This attack is about honor.

The colonel stands alone as he watches the tanks roll out, his subordinate officers having already learned to stand at least ten feet away to avoid the colonel's harsh criticism.

The column moves forward, splitting in two in an attempt to encircle Montcornet. Charles de Gaulle steps into the Talbot's passenger seat for a ride to the front.

Finally, after a week of retreat, the French army is on the attack.

---

* The French Char B had a top speed of seventeen miles per hour, compared with twenty-five miles an hour for the Panzer III and Panzer IV models. Much of this was due to armor thickness: the Char B, Somua S35, and British Matilda II had frontal armor measuring 2.4, 2.2, and 3.1 inches, respectvely. The Panzer III's front armor measured just 1.2 inches. The Panzer IV's armor matched that of the Matilda.

6

The Nazis are waiting.

In an amazing and unfortunate coincidence, the 1st Panzer Division under General Heinz Guderian charges into Montcornet in the dead of night, just hours before Charles de Gaulle's tanks roll into battle. Adolf Hitler is nervous about the aggressive panzer advance and has ordered a temporary stop. So, rather than occupy an empty market town, as de Gaulle had hoped, his 4th Armored Division drives headlong into perhaps the finest tank command in the world, led by one of the foremost authorities on armored warfare.

The battle begins with the French tanks encircling Montcornet. Their advance is hardly silent, marked by a ground-shaking rumble and creaking treads, but somehow the element of surprise is total. De Gaulle throws away the French tactical manual, ordering his thickly armored Char Bs to fight in the German fashion, firing and then advancing quickly forward into enemy lines. In no time, the French inflict enormous casualties on a German force enjoying its first day of complete rest in a week. Most surprisingly, German shells bounce off the Char Bs, providing a poignant reminder that the French are a true match for the Nazis when given the chance to fight.

But even as the battle unfolds, it is not just French soldiers displaying their mettle; it is also their commander. Charles de Gaulle gets as close to the action as he can, always standing upright, his great height an easy shot for an attentive sniper. After a week of retreat and cowardly leadership, the colonel's natural bravado is an inspiration.

"He leaves his car and chauffeur protected by a hedge or a wood, and heads off, very visible, too visible, but with a complete indifference to any danger, on to a bit of high ground, to study with his binoculars the positions of the enemy and the possibilities of an offensive," one French observer testifies.

A major on de Gaulle's staff is equally amazed. "Everybody admired him," the officer will write. "What did he owe his bravery to? I think to his greatest quality: mastery of himself."

Without realizing it, the 4th Armored Division comes very close to capturing General Guderian and his superior officer, General Paul von Kleist, as the two meet to discuss strategy. This would have been a staggering blow to the German war effort. "A few of his tanks," Guderian will later admit of de Gaulle's advance, "succeeded in penetrating to within a mile of my advanced headquarters."

Then the Stukas show up.

The Luftwaffe JU 87 attacks by diving almost vertically on a target, releasing bombs from an extremely low angle. Special "Jericho-Trompete" wailing sirens are either mounted on the wing's leading edge or the front of the fixed main gear fairing, emitting a high-pitched whine meant to install terror in those on the ground as it plunges toward earth. The Stuka has been in service just five years, but its slow airspeed, short range, and fixed landing gear mean it is already outdated. A British Hawker Hurricane fighter plane has no problem against the Stuka in an aerial dogfight.

However, on this day in Montcornet, unhindered in the slightest by a single French aircraft—and certainly not by a Hurricane—the Stuka pilots of the Eighth Air Corps patiently, methodically, and eagerly deposit bomb after bomb on French positions. And when their meager payload of just three explosive shells runs out, MG 17 machine guns in each wing strafe any man caught in the open.

Throughout this pummeling, de Gaulle remains unfazed. Neither Stuka dive-bombers nor artillery shells trouble the colonel, who scolds any of his officers showing fear or attempting to take cover with a simple shouted command: "Behave."

So the French do not quit easily. It is 9:00 p.m. when Colonel de Gaulle finally orders a retreat. The sun set thirty minutes ago. Yet the Stukas are relentless, chasing the French column back to Laon by moonlight. The country road is lined by marsh and farmland, offering no place to hide almost seventy armored vehicles and hundreds of men. The tanks are protected from strafing by their thick armor, but the infantry commuted into combat in simple passenger buses whose thin metal skins cannot stop a 57mm Mauser machine-gun cartridge.

Finally, the 4th Armored Division turns off the road and blends into the darkness of the Samoussy Forest. They are still seven long miles from Laon, but thick stands of oak and beech offer total concealment. Exhausted, the men sleep where they can. Others gather to relive the day, reclining against motionless tank wheels, smoking, passing a bottle, guarding the light of their cigarettes with cupped palms. Twenty-three tanks have been lost. More than one hundred Frenchmen are dead. But these exhausted men live to fight another day.

Meanwhile, in Laon, a wide-awake Colonel Charles de Gaulle sits alone, rehashing the action. Cigarette butts fill his command post ashtray. He broods, listing the reasons how he could have won today's battle. In the end, he decides, the loss was due to inexperience. "We were lost children," he will lament of the confusion engulfing his force when the Stukas started dropping bombs.

29

The colonel finds pencil and paper. He writes to his superiors at French Sixth Army headquarters, located an hour away in Moussy, desperately requesting reinforcements. A courier is dispatched.

The reply comes at midnight.

General Robert Touchon promises nothing. Colonel de Gaulle and the 4th Armored Division are on their own.

Yet there is hope: word about today's attack has reached scattered French units looking to make a stand. Throughout the sleepless night, motorized infantry, armored cars, motorcycles, and forty new D2 medium tanks pour into Laon. The rumble and din cuts through the darkness of the blacked-out town. De Gaulle can see that the troops are raw and inexperienced. The fresh-faced young tank commanders poking their heads out of the turrets are still boys, only recently graduated from Saint-Cyr. But in the end they are all soldiers. These raw recruits have come to fight.

The colonel leaves no doubt who is in charge. Order replaces fear. "He exercised a command that was independent, exclusive, authoritarian and egocentric, based on his conviction that his judgement was, in every case, the best," staff officer Captain Paul Huard will write of de Gaulle's leadership.

Thus reinforced, Colonel de Gaulle retreats to his command post.

"I do not know where the events are leading," he writes Yvonne. The colonel's attitude has changed. Instead of advising her to stay in Colombey, he gently lets his beloved wife know it is almost time to abandon their home. "Be ready to leave if necessary."

As for himself, the colonel has no intention of running.

"If I live, I will fight," de Gaulle fervently believes. "Wherever I must, as long as I must."

And so the colonel's war continues.

7

There is no war in Paris.

A two-hour drive west from Colonel Charles de Gaulle's headquarters in Laon, the French capital is "a strange mixed picture of emptiness and normal gaiety," in the words of one newspaper correspondent.

Paris is in its nightly state of blackout. The air is warm, not yet the thick heat of summer. Waiters in black jackets and long white aprons serve champagne by the light of a full moon as sidewalk cafés do brisk business: wicker chairs, laughter, cigarette smoke, espresso spoons clinking porcelain saucers, a rattle of loose change to pay *l'addition*. Inside, where it is brightly lit, string quartets perform up-tempo ditties, the music wafting out over the outdoor revelers, musicians hidden from those patrons by blacked-out windows.

The French government has prohibited newspapers from publishing stories of the recent defeats, but the people of Paris know the Germans are coming. It is impossible to believe otherwise, and the pretense of normalcy is growing thin. The city is absent young men, all off to fight in the war. Grand boulevards like the Champs-Élysées are completely empty. Taxis are impossible to find, for reasons no one can explain. Bus service was recently suspended.

As midnight approaches, the revelers are treated to the odd sight of automobiles packed with families, luggage, and pets driving past the bistros. The cars form a slow line, some headed south to the Rive Gauche, others west to the Porte d'Auteuil. Many have a mattress tied to the roof. All are clearly abandoning Paris. It is the well-off from the 8th and 16th arrondissements who have the means to leave behind their jobs, homes, and daily routine. Their despair is overcome by the relief of being safe.*

This is the first sign that Parisians are fleeing, just like the Belgian and Dutch refugees who traveled south into the city. The first wave of refugees from the Low Countries was wealthiest, arriving by car. The second group were able to afford a ticket on "trains packed so tight with humanity, baggage, dogs, and pets that no single other soul could be accommodated," in the words of the *New York Times*.

A third wave—the poorest—still walk toward Paris.

"A boot had scattered an ant-hill and the ants were on the march," French pilot Antoine de Saint-Exupéry will write, viewing the migration from the air. "Laboriously. Without panic. Without hope."

This shell-shocked mass of humanity fights for space with Allied troops marching into battle from the opposite direction. *New York Times* correspondent Drew Middleton will later write of a "road filled with refugees. Some afoot, others in farm carts laden with household goods. Down on this march of the helpless swept the Luftwaffe.

"Two ME-109's with machine guns blazing set about the refugees

---

* An arrondissement is an administrative district within a city. The city of Paris numbers its twenty arrondissements in an outward-spiraling sequence that begins with the 1st near the Louvre in the city center. The 8th contains the Arc de Triomphe and the affluent 16th is adjacent, on the right bank of the Seine River.

as though they had been a column of tanks. We could hear the screams from our road."

After the fighter planes zoom into the distance, Middleton and his driver offer help. But there is nothing they can do. "A youngish woman who'd been pushing her baby in a perambulator was dead. So was her child. Four people on a farm cart had also perished; one of the horses was dead, the other screaming in pain. Calls for help and mercy rose along the length of the column."

Yet the refugees press on, trickling into the capital after their long journey, desperate to board a train for somewhere very far away. At the Gare de Lyon, Austerlitz, and Montparnasse—all of which provide departures to the safety of southern and western France—hordes of Belgian refugees mingle with desperate Parisians. Babies cry. Elbows create space. The stale air is thick with dried sweat, unchanged diapers, bodies gone a week without bathing.

There is no room for personal luggage in the passenger cars, so policemen in steel helmets collect it all, then push great barrows full of refugee suitcases to the baggage car. Red Cross nurses and doctors squeeze in, tending to women and children. Many refugees have been waiting on their feet since nightfall for departure and will remain standing until, hopefully, arriving in the South of France at dawn.

· · ·

THE GERMANS ARE TURNING NORTHEAST, wheeling toward the English Channel and temporarily leaving Paris alone. The feint toward the city was yet another ruse to fool the Allies. Meanwhile, two hundred miles north of Paris, elements of the French, British, and Belgian armies are completely cut off. Pressed on three sides by Nazi forces, they fight by day and retreat toward the sea by night, desperate to avoid annihilation.

But there is no escaping the German onslaught. Men arrive at the English Channel to find beachfront roads cratered from air raids. The normally pleasant ocean scent of seaweed and salty breeze is replaced by the stench of mutilated corpses and rotting flesh. There is no food and most fresh water is contaminated. As the number of Allied troops grows to an astonishing 250,000 British and 110,000 French, thirst and empty bellies only add to the desperation.

Even worse, the long miles of sand offer no protection from German artillery or dive-bombers. One beach, in particular, best illustrates the Allied plight. "At Dunkirk, the spectacle was prodigious, appalling . . . Day and night the sea air was filled with screaming gulls and bats of death," *Time* magazine will describe the Stuka attacks.

"When the soldiers reached the sea they hid . . . 'like rabbits among the dunes,'" *Time* adds. "They were in smoke-grimed rags and tatters, many shoeless, some still lugging packs and rifles, others empty-handed in their underclothes after swimming canals. They were too din-deafened and inured to horror to be fully sensible of the incredible cataclysm that still raged over them. Some clutched souvenirs—a blood soaked doll for a small daughter; a machine gun snatched from a crashed German plane with which one squad of men kept on shooting at new attackers and got two. Ambulatory wounded joined the rest in staggering into the oil-scummed waves."

The port cities of Calais and Boulogne are filled with Allied soldiers praying in vain for evacuation; both garrisons are being slaughtered as they fight to the last man. Dunkirk is the last line of defense. From the seaside holiday town, where troops might have lolled on the sand as civilians before the war, England is clearly visible on the other side of the Channel. The distance is just twenty-one miles. The alluring sight, so close and yet so far away, nurtures the slimmest of hopes that the Royal Navy will find a way to get them home.

"I had time to reflect on things. I thought of the carnage," one British engineer will remember of his long hours in Dunkirk. "The piled up dead of civilians and British soldiers, the wrecked buildings and the terrible smell of roasting bodies. I thought of the stream of refugees who had been made homeless by Hitler's savage onslaught and I wondered how it was all going to end. My thoughts were of home too. I wondered if I would ever see my family and friends again. I thought of the girl I was to marry and wondered if I ever would. My mind would still not accept the fact that we were defeated. I had been bred with the idea of English invincibility, our glorious past and the battles which our soldiers had fought and won against massive odds."

The Allied forces can retreat no further. Soldiers of the British Expeditionary Force and the French army huddle in the sand, German Stuka dive-bombers and Messerschmitt fighters doing battle with Royal Air Force Spitfires and Hurricanes, but not a rescue ship in sight.

All they can do is wait—and hope.

. . .

A RUMOR TRAVELS through the revelers at the sidewalk cafés in Paris, fueled by an official government announcement, passed in whispers and Gallic shrugs: "Arras has fallen." General Erwin Rommel's 7th Panzer Division has raced all the way across northern France, only to be surprised by a British attack at that vital crossroads. The Allies stunned Rommel by taking control of the battlefield early on, awaiting the promised assistance from the French. But that help never came. Once again, lack of communication is an issue. Seventh Panzer regrouped and pushed the British back.

The battle ended at dusk, little more than two hours ago. The news is already flashing around Paris.

Amiens, another vital choke point, is also under German control. In just eleven days the Germans have taken 2 million French soldiers prisoner, killed another 100,000, and dashed from one side of France to the other without losing a single battle.

Yet, the sidewalk revelers remind themselves, the night is young. There are no Germans in Paris. Arras and Amiens are both one hundred miles north of these grand boulevards. There is little shortage of food and wine, and certainly no reason to end tonight's party.

Even as the orchestras keep playing on this night under a full moon in Paris, some drinkers put down their champagne coupes and walk home to pack a bag. The Métro is still running and provides quick transport to the main train *gares*.

But for those who remain at the sidewalk cafés, just blocks from the tumult of the train stations, the wine still flows. Waiters hover from a distance, watching for the raised index finger requesting another pour. Patrons ignore the rumors about German soldiers raping women and disfiguring children in territories they conquer, and of intellectuals being taken away, never to return. During the German conquest of Poland, the capital of Warsaw was heavily bombed and mass executions were conducted by firing squad, an average of two hundred per day. Adolf Hitler explicitly ordered his troops to "kill without pity or mercy all men, women and children of Polish descent or language."

There is no reason to believe the Nazis will treat Paris any differently. If anything, given Adolf Hitler's public disdain for all things French, the streets could run red with the blood of the butchered.

Yet the party continues. Each man and woman sitting at these tables is aware they must soon choose whether they will remain in Paris if the Germans capture the city or flee beforehand.

Until then, all they can do is wait—and party.

8

The Americans are playing war games.

And Colonel George S. Patton has waited twenty years for this night.

More than 4,500 miles from Paris, the outspoken, white-haired Patton meets with a select group of America's top generals. As a fluent French speaker who has spent considerable time in France, he takes no joy in the rapid German advance. *"De l'audace, encore de l'audace, toujours de l'audace"*—"Audacity, audacity, always audacity"—is a personal motto he quotes frequently, borrowing a line from Parisian and key French Revolution figure Georges Danton. Patton cares deeply about many things, but there is often no telling what those might be.

Such as the reasons Paris might soon fall. Lessons about waging war have been learned during the German dash across France—lessons vitally important to a man in love with tank warfare.

It is an education that may save Patton's career.

The meeting location is Bolton High School, an architectural marvel built of Indiana limestone. The enormous front doors are bronze, the auditorium is lit by designer chandeliers, the waxed hardwood floors are heart pine, and classroom lighting fixtures are designed by Tiffany & Co. of New York City.

But tonight's top secret summit does not take place amid that luxury. The conversation is far too explosive. Instead, the officers have descended into the school basement, where they smoke and debate in private among cleaning supplies and textbooks.

Tonight's topic is armor—tanks in particular. The men in this room practiced their own version of blitzkrieg during just-concluded war games and are energized by the experience. Though reluctant to apply such a volatile pro-German term to their strategy, these officers have seen firsthand what happens when armored columns are unleashed to attack. They hope to not only duplicate blitzkrieg but to find a way to do it better.

Colonel Patton is well aware that the Nazis did not invent blitzkrieg but in fact leaned heavily on the writings of British military theorist Basil Henry Liddell Hart and a French colonel named Charles de Gaulle, whose book about armored warfare, *The Army of the Future*, was translated into German in 1935.

Lieutenant General Frank M. Andrews, a pilot with absolutely no experience in armored warfare, requested the impromptu gathering. Going around the room, General Adna Chaffee Jr. is deliberate in his opinions. Son of a famous general, the lined and drawn face of the natural-born leader provides no hint that he will be dead from cancer in a year. Chaffee and Patton met for the first time here in Louisiana, forming a close bond discussing the future of armored warfare.

Equally vocal is Brigadier General Bruce Magruder, an infantry officer with a longtime passion for armored tactics. Magruder joined the Army as private in 1904 and became one of the few enlisted men in Army history to rise all the way up the ranks to general. His seniority in the room is eclipsed only by three-star general Stanley D.

Embick, old enough to have graduated West Point in 1899. Embick commands the U.S. Third Army.

And then there is Patton: six feet two inches tall, tailored uniform, Cuban cigar, flair for profanity, and a long laundry list of opinions and eccentricities.

The fifty-five-year-old George Patton was America's top tank expert two long decades ago. He was a colonel then and he is a colonel now. West Point graduate, Olympian, swordsman, equestrian, and decorated World War I hero, the once-mighty Patton was set adrift when Congress defunded the Tank Corps in 1920. Armor was no longer independent from other branches of the Army and became the property of infantry divisions. Patton transferred to the cavalry in the slim hope of reviving his career. His good friend and fellow tank commander, a young captain named Dwight Eisenhower, also saw the writing on the wall and transferred to a desk job as a staff officer. The two men are diametric opposites in personality, but both share the West Point education that has formed the bedrock of their military knowledge. Patton graduated in 1909 and Eisenhower in 1915.

Despite that pedigree, lesser men were promoted above them. Patton and Eisenhower hang on, waiting for the stroke of luck that will once again place their careers on the upswing. It has been twenty years of disparate postings and playing politics, all the while trying not to appear desperate while praying for that elusive general's star.

Colonel George S. Patton, a devout Episcopalian with a penchant for profanity and belief in reincarnation, knows that prayer all too well.

Tonight might see it answered.

· · ·

EVERY OFFICER IN THE BASEMENT was ordered to Louisiana for three weeks of mock warfare. More than 66,000 soldiers took part, trudging through swamps and farmland. General Embick laid out the plans. Chaffee and Magruder commanded mock battles. Patton traveled from his post in Maryland to choose the winner.

The U.S. Army is the seventeenth largest in the world, right behind tiny Romania. Its manpower is 450,000 soldiers, compared with 3,180,000 for Nazi Germany. Cavalry horses far outnumber tanks in the American arsenal. Chief of staff General George C. Marshall organized these war games to heighten America's readiness for war and adopt new fighting strategies. Due to a shortage of armored fighting vehicles, trucks have been used as a substitute, with "TANK" painted in white letters on the sides. A shortage of machine guns meant that many soldiers were armed with a broom handle instead.

Those war games ended this afternoon. A critique in the high school auditorium follows. But as he looks on, Brigadier General Frank Andrews gets the feeling that many conclusions lack total candor. So he summons this group to the basement.

In time, tonight will become legendary. Patton and these general officers will forever be known as the "Basement Conspirators." The great General Adna Chaffee will be christened "Father of the Armored Force." But right now, in this dank room, there is no sense of the heroic. This discussion threatens U.S. military doctrine. The mere act of being present risks each man's career.

General Andrews pushes for answers anyway. He well knows the fate of those who buck power. Andrews is an outspoken advocate for creating a separate branch of the Army dedicated to flight. The U.S. Army has squadrons of fighters and bombers, all subordinate to infantry command. Andrews's proposed "Army Air Corps" would be independent, the pilots free to experiment with new tactics and rules of engagement. In 1939, after describing the United States as a "sixth-rate air power" in a passionate public speech advocating a larger air corps, Andrews was reduced in rank to colonel in an attempt to force his retirement. Only General Marshall's intervention saved Andrews's career.

Time and again here in Louisiana, tanks spearheading drives into "enemy" territory have produced astounding results. Though technically impartial, Patton even tried to help a friend of his in the cavalry gain an edge by suggesting that he jam tank radio frequencies, but even that bit of inside information could not prevent armor from winning the mock battles. In one instance, combining tanks and motorized infantry saw seventy-five miles of forward progress in a single day—a pace far beyond anything the average foot soldier can accomplish. "The makeshift force worked smoothly and inspired the leading officers to take thought of the future organization of such a unit," notes one official Army history of the war games.*

But powerful generals within the U.S. Army still believe in waging war just like the French, using tanks as infantry protection. Their tactics are no different from those utilized during the trench warfare of 1918. "The development of mechanization," the official Army history will note, "had followed lines which were too conservative for rearming America. Mechanization needed preferential treatment in equipment and personnel, and it was being given a back seat and forced to play second fiddle to the horse and foot corps under the Chiefs of Infantry and Cavalry."

The U.S. cavalry leadership, in particular, has such disdain for mechanized combat that they refuse to even speak the word *tank*.

None of those generals have been invited down to the basement.

As General Marshall's assistant chief of staff for operations, General Andrews has the overwhelming task of making sure the entire Army is ready for war. So he listens closely as the Basement Conspirators plead for an independent armored division, labeling it the "Alexandria Recommendation."

There is no transcript of what is said in the basement of Bolton High School tonight—no note of which passionate argument leads General Frank Andrews to give the Alexandria Recommendation

---

* Army Ground Forces Study No. 27, "The Armored Force Command and Center," 1946.

his complete backing.* Absolutely no evidence will be found as to whether Colonel Patton contributes greatly to the conversation or has the political sense to speak only when asked, letting General Chaffee share their ideas.

It does not matter.

War is coming. In time, Charles de Gaulle and the people of Paris will benefit mightily from this night in a high school basement.

As for Colonel George S. Patton, his prayer is about to be answered.

---

* The Army Air Corps became a separate branch of the U.S. Army on June 20, 1941. On September 18, 1947, the name was changed to the United States Air Force, which became its own branch of the U.S. armed forces. General Frank Andrews was killed in 1943 when the B-24 bomber *Hot Stuff* flew into a mountainside in Iceland. Andrews Air Force Base in Maryland (now Joint Base Andrews), home to Air Force One, the aircraft which transports the president of the United States, was named in his honor. General Andrews is buried in Arlington National Cemetery.

9

Charles de Gaulle is already a general.

It is Tuesday. The introverted loner and his armored division are halfway between Paris and Dunkirk. A long cigarette dangles from the corner of his mouth. He is now the youngest general in the French army, but the euphoria of being promoted five days ago has passed. It is once again time to fight. De Gaulle stands outside a village cemetery where granite tombstones are etched with the names of World War I British dead reposing with Doudelainville's ancestors. The scene is anything but restful.

The 4th Armored Division numbers more than one hundred tanks of all sizes and speeds, but it is the thirty-three thickly armored Char B1 *bis* tanks now lining the narrow country road in single file that form the backbone of his tank corps.*

---

* The B1 *bis* is the second version of the Char B1, thus the addition of *bis*, meaning encore.

Each weighs thirty-three tons and carries three powerful guns: a 47mm SA 35 anti-tank weapon on the rotating turret, a Reibel machine gun, and a forward-facing 75mm howitzer poking from the main body. The exterior is painted camouflage. The interior is six feet by six feet wide, four feet high, and painted mustard yellow. The crews number four men: commander, driver, loader, and Morse code operator. There are no seats except that of the driver; the commander stands in his narrow hatch while the rest crouch on the steel floor. Each tank carries 50 rounds of ammunition for the commander's 47mm, 250 for the machine gun, and 74 rounds for the 75mm. In case of engine trouble, a mechanic also squeezes into the crew compartment. And while there is an escape hatch in the floor of the engine room, every man will perish simultaneously if an enemy round pierces the hull.

This horrible, fiery death befell dozens of Allied soldiers at a battle near here yesterday. The road ahead is a cemetery unto itself, lined with the charred turrets and twisted cannon barrels of those mangled British tanks. The metallic fatty-pork stink of burning flesh lingers in the air.

De Gaulle's armored division, which existed only on paper two weeks ago, has traveled from one side of France to the other in six days. Atlantic Ocean has replaced pastoral farmland. Now the 4th Armored Division prepares to destroy the bridges over the river Somme at Abbeville. Ninety-seven miles north of that port city lies Dunkirk, where the German army is giving all its attention to strafing and bombing the trapped British Expeditionary Force. Once the BEF is annihilated, the Nazis will turn south for Paris. De Gaulle's orders are to blow the bridges and stop them.

The 4th Armored Division will roll out at five o'clock sharp. The men prepare for battle, shouting to be heard above the din of engines and a friendly artillery barrage dropping rounds on the village of Huppy, just two miles up the road.

Other tankers relieve themselves behind cemetery walls. This is a necessity before spending an unknowable number of hours confined with three other men in a bumping, grinding, steel-bottomed berth the width of two coffins with absolutely no knowledge of when that side panel alongside the treads will once again open to allow relief. The piss bottle has remained a constant in the short history of tank warfare, but no man likes to foul the cabin with the stench of excrement lowered into whatever container he can find as his brethren look on.*

Loaders arm weapons. Commanders study maps of the route that will guide the attackers through Huppy, which must be taken by force, then through the crossroads at Les Croisettes before moving on to Abbeville. The weather is cool here near the coast. Open turret hatches bring sorely needed fresh afternoon air into each hull but cannot displace the pungent aromas of oil, gunpowder, and stale sweat that have worked their way into every crevice. The mood is eager, pensive, anxious, professional.

General de Gaulle takes in each detail. "You saw him everywhere—that leather jacket, his casque, and the inevitable cigarette," one French journalist will write. "Tough, ruthless, inhuman, letting nothing and nobody count except the battle."

It has been a week of crushing heat and de Gaulle is exhausted from the long days and nights of travel. He is gruff and sarcastic when he deigns to speak at all. The general continues to eat and sleep little, preferring to spend nights smoking Gitanes, sipping coffee, and obsessing about battle maps. By personal preference, he is almost always alone. The men do not love him but respect his aloof behavior. "All those who have done something worthwhile and lasting have been solitary and silent," de Gaulle reminds the division chaplain when questioned about his arrogance.

---

* This inconvenient aspect of armored warfare remains true to this day. There is no room for a toilet within the cramped confines of a tank.

De Gaulle's initial brush with the Germans at Montcornet, as well as a secondary attack two days later, earned him a modest level of fame in France. The general gave a radio interview on May 21 that was broadcast around the nation, in which he proclaimed: "The leader who speaks to you has the honour to command a French armored division. This division has had a hard fight, and we can say very directly, very seriously—without any bragging—that we have dominated the battlefield from the first to the last hour of battle."

So popular was this statement of triumph, the first the French people had heard after ten days of defeat, that de Gaulle was quickly promoted to brigadier general. He also became a symbol of hope—so much so that during the push westward from Laon, with his tanks lacking radios to establish their proper location, worried Paris newspapers reported him missing in action. Throughout his life, the general's great height and haughty demeanor have made him accustomed to being recognized, so this minor celebrity is nothing new. Nonetheless, de Gaulle is pleased, thinking this respect his proper due.

Tomorrow will certainly put the general's new reputation to the test. The battle for Abbeville will be completely different than Montcornet. The French 4th Armored Division will not enjoy the element of surprise. Instead, they will be expected. The 88mm cannon the enemy hides in the hills above Abbeville can punch a hole through three inches of steel from a mile away. The 37mm Pak 36 anti-tank guns lining the road between here and there are no less lethal. Whether the Germans destroy the 4th Armored Division in the same devastating fashion they eviscerated the British 10th Hussars yesterday depends upon the tactical leadership of General de Gaulle.

Yet, win or lose, bridges demolished or left intact, Abbeville may be de Gaulle's last battle.

In Paris, General Maxime Weygand, the seventy-three-year-old World War I veteran now in charge of the French military, secretly wishes to launch one last great attack against the Germans to restore battered French dignity.

After that, having no faith whatsoever in General de Gaulle's chances of triumph, Weygand plans to surrender Paris to Adolf Hitler.

De Gaulle suspects the end is near. In his heart, the general is beginning to believe France "virtually lost." He once again writes Yvonne, gently demanding her to flee if she hasn't already, and reminding her to bring the good silver lest it fall into the hands of looters.

Yet as the general's popularity grows, so do expectations. And unlike men who find such pressure crushing, de Gaulle believes challenge to be one and the same as destiny.

At 5:00 p.m., General Charles de Gaulle gives the order to attack. As his Char B1s roll forth, each tank commander pokes his head out of the turret hatch, touching a brow in salute as the procession passes the tall figure standing on the side of the road.

On to Abbeville.

But first Huppy.

10

The French tanks are too far apart.

Twenty-nine Char B1 *bis* rumble into this small village, lined up like ducks. They are alone, General de Gaulle preferring to hold back the infantry for now.

Under normal conditions, the entirety of the small village of Huppy is a five-minute stroll from southern entrance to northern exit. One main road splits the town, houses set back from the narrow lane. The air smells of pine forest and cow farms. Somewhere within this very narrow stretch of land are hidden soldiers of the 57th Bavarian Infantry Division. They are new to the war, just arrived today from Remagen, Germany, and eager to make their mark. The practice of replacing battle-weary troops with fresh reinforcements has already been shown to give the Germans an advantage over the exhausted French. And while they have no armor to speak of, the Nazis are fortified with anti-tank guns more than capable of winning the day.

The French 4th Armored Division knows that General de Gaulle has sent them to draw fire—thus the lack of infantry. But too great a separation leaves a tank vulnerable, allowing enemy gunners to focus their arsenal on one armored vehicle at a time. So as the Char B1s funnel into Huppy, those that have fallen behind struggle to catch up.

But their timing is inconsistent, closing the separation too quickly, now making it almost impossible for enemy gunners to miss, leaving not just one tank but the entire group vulnerable. "The tanks were slow in coming together," one worried French officer will lament, "and then it seemed to me they were too close together. The enemy had a great many very well placed anti-tank weapons."

The Nazis open fire without warning. The Char B1s rock violently as enemy rounds meet French steel. The sound of enemy machine-gun bullets and anti-tank shells colliding with each thick hull is that of a thousand staccato sledgehammers. Inside each tank, it is the same: teeth rattle, adrenaline spikes, panic.

And then, amazingly, relief. Just a little, but enough.

To the amazement of German and French alike, nothing penetrates the Char B1s' dense construction. Pak 36 and 75mm rounds ricochet off the sloping exterior, spinning wildly into the evening air. The danger is no less real to the crews inside each tank, but mortality is not so close anymore.

Now it is the French who take aim.

General de Gaulle has given strict orders that his tanks maintain forward movement at all costs, searching for enemy guns while firing on the move. Even as the incoming fire continues, drivers in the forward left portion of the hull scan the battlefield through viewing slits—one at the very front of the B1, one immediately to the driver's left.

Behind the driver, at the rear of the crew compartment, tank commanders stand atop a small ladderlike step just above the floor, searching for targets. The three-foot-long 47mm gun pokes straight forward, loaded and primed, soon to deliver an armor-piercing round into enemy position at seven hundred meters per second. The extent of the commander's exterior vision is whatever can be seen through a gunsight no wider than the mouth of a Chablis glass. There is no right or left. His eye and the barrel of the big gun are synced. What he sees is what soon will die.

The commander's right hand holds the sight steady while his left reaches for the electrical turret rotation switch. Rounds continue to rock the B1's hull. A half minute is required for the complete turret revolution needed to scan the entire battlefield. But that is unnecessary. With each anti-tank round they fire, the 57th Bavarian clearly reveals their positions.

The tank commander moves his right hand to the 47mm firing mechanism. His left takes hold of the gunsight.

The turret is no place for fat men. Six inches is all that separates the breech of the 47mm gun from the commander's torso. A shock wave washes over him as he pushes the firing mechanism, pressing his eyebrows flat. The shell explodes forward, traveling down the barrel of the gun and rocketing toward whichever teenage German whose muzzle flash has given him away, destroying the young man's hopes and dreams in the time required to take a final breath.

Quickly the commander swings open the breech guard, hinged on the left, removes the spent shell, then reaches down and to his right for the fresh round being lifted up to him by the loader. Slamming the foot-long projectile into the chamber, the commander bangs shut the breech guard and instantly places an eye to the gunsight to find a new target.

The men inside the Char B1s barely knew what the crew compartment of a tank looked like eleven days ago in Montcornet. Now they are surgical in their movements and sure of their roles. They do not yet swagger into battle like the finest panzer crews, but their confidence grows with every engagement.

One by one, German gun positions are destroyed. The road ahead is clear.

De Gaulle's infantry arrives to ensure the streets are free of snipers. A British unit, the vaunted 51st Highland Division, provides additional infantry support. A seventeenth-century castle in a forest of old beech trees remains standing. Despite being well within range of the German artillery, the general commandeers the stately building for a command post and field hospital. An ancient prison cell in the north tower is ideal for prisoners. A captured Nazi swastika flag is laid out as a tablecloth. Throughout the evening, the general keeps track of the battle by venturing out in a lightweight tank, as always refusing to show fear.

De Gaulle, in the words of the 4th Armored Division's official history, was "always in the front line, often among the advance reconnaissance units, with his headquarters exposed to enemy fire . . . although he had no air support and his tanks were subject to constant attacks by Stukas, he always stood with the hatch of his own tank open and, if on his feet, refused to notice bombs and thundered at anyone who threw themselves on the ground."

Emboldened, French tank commanders press on toward Abbeville.

"By the evening we had taken Huppy and there we were at Mont-de-Limeux, from which the Germans had fled in disorder before leaving their supper in their traveling kitchens," one commander will exult. "We took 400 prisoners!"

As the French tanks push closer and closer to the bridges, the Germans fall back. Victory seems assured. This marks the first time any French unit has forced a Nazi retreat. Yet communications once again become an issue. De Gaulle cannot be everywhere at once and loses track of the battle. He is unaware that his advance units are nearing the Somme.

The general knows only that the Char B1s remain under enemy attack as they press on. Lack of gasoline and ammunition are becoming an issue, yet the tanks rumble forward, often crushing enemy anti-tank guns under their heavy treads rather than waste a round by opening fire. The Germans continue to flee in panic, terrified of the suddenly unstoppable French armor.

"An atmosphere of victory hung over the field," de Gaulle will remember. "The wounded were smiling. The guns fired gaily. Before us, in a pitched battle, the Germans had retired."

But as dusk settles at 9:00 p.m., bridges over the Somme in sight, de Gaulle gives the order to pull back. He has no idea how close he has come to total victory.

The French attack again at 4:00 a.m., but the advantage is lost. As de Gaulle's army rested, refueled, and reloaded during a short night of sleep, the Germans filed back into their old positions, renewed in their desire to beat back the French. The big German 88s, which many consider the most lethal artillery piece on either side of the war, seal the French fate with precision delivery of armor-piercing rounds that decimate the otherwise indomitable Char B1s.

"The division," one French officer will lament, "had reached the limit of its powers."

. . .

CHARLES DE GAULLE'S DEFEAT is applauded as a moral victory. Even the general sees it that way, writing to Yvonne of his "great success."

Yet the bridges over the Somme still stand. De Gaulle is relieved of command.

But this is not the end for Charles de Gaulle, nor has his love for France diminished. For all de Gaulle's brooding and silence, the general is a man of deep passion about the true nature of his country and what it stands for.

"All my life I have had a certain idea of France," he will write. "This is inspired by sentiment as much as by reason. The emotional side of me tends to imagine France, like the princess in the fairy stories or the Madonna in the frescoes, as dedicated to an exalted and exceptional destiny. Instinctively I have the feeling that Providence has created her neither for complete successes or for exemplary fortunes.

If, in spite of this, mediocrity shows in her acts and deeds, it strikes me as an absurd anomaly, to be imputed to the faults of Frenchmen, not to the genius of the land. But the positive side of my mind also assures me that France is not really herself unless in the front rank . . . our country, as it is, surrounded by others, as they are, must aim high and hold itself straight, on pain of mortal danger. In short, to my mind, France cannot be France without greatness."

So it is that the general will not back down "until the enemy is defeated and the national stain washed clean."

And as General de Gaulle will soon learn, that enemy is everywhere. And the stain is still spreading.

11

MAY 28, 1940
LONDON, ENGLAND
3:00 P.M.

Winston Churchill takes the floor.

One hundred and seventy miles across the English Channel from Abbeville, and at almost precisely the same time General de Gaulle orders his 4th Armored Division to attack, the prime minister is formally recognized by the longtime Speaker of the House of Commons, Edward FitzRoy.

Churchill rises slowly from his front-row seat. The chamber is full to the backbenches. Cirrus clouds of tobacco smoke layer over the room. The exhausted prime minister dramatically dons round-framed glasses while removing his notes from a jacket pocket. Churchill normally inserts stage directions into written speeches, reminding himself when to expect laughter or a round of applause. But this is not that sort of speech. This, in fact, is news of the worst kind.

So Churchill is startled as a cheer rises before he speaks a single word. He begins his preamble, then launches into the meat of his dire oratory:

"The situation of the British and French Armies now engaged in a most severe battle and beset on three sides and from the air, is evidently extremely grave," Churchill tells Parliament, his voice dark. "The House should prepare itself for hard and heavy tidings."

In the months to come, as life grows more desperate in England, Tuesdays will mark Churchill's weekly lunch with King George VI at Buckingham Palace. No staff will be allowed in the room and the men will serve themselves from a side table. The king will chain-smoke British-made Wills cigarettes and ask questions. Churchill will brief the sovereign on the wretched state of the war in the most candid and honest way he knows how. George VI was initially opposed to the selection of Churchill as prime minister. In time, lunch by lunch, they will become friends—even allies.*

Yet there was no such lunch with the sovereign today, and Winston Churchill is quite sure he has no allies. Churchill is just hours away from losing the title of prime minister, if his enemies get their way. After less than three weeks on the job, there are questions about his leadership, sobriety, and, above all, ability to save the nation.

Churchill has spent the past few days—and more than an hour this morning—squabbling with Britain's foreign secretary about peace with Germany. The prime minister is determined to fight like a true Briton as on distant battlefields like Khartoum and the Crimea, never bowing to a foreign conqueror in the face of desperate odds. Yet the tall, patrician Lord Halifax is equally adamant that Churchill seek peace with Adolf Hitler and Germany despite knowing all too well that this armistice will be dictated on the Führer's terms.

Royal luncheon or not, Churchill has still enjoyed his daily ration

---

* These luncheons—"Tuesdays" to Churchill—will begin on June 10, 1940. Churchill's favorite Pol Roger vintages at the time are 1928 and 1934. It has been estimated that he drank 42,000 bottles of this champagne in his lifetime. This is a remarkable amount under any circumstances and made all the more prodigious by the fact that Churchill did not discover Pol Roger until he was thirty-four.

of Pol Roger with lunch, a habit he has enjoyed since 1908. "I could not live without champagne," Churchill often says, paraphrasing Napoleon. "In victory I deserve it. In defeat I need it."

Today is not a victory, and it is not yet a defeat. But as every man here in the House of Commons knows, and as the people of London learned while reading their morning newspaper, Belgium has officially surrendered to Germany. If France is the next domino to fall, Adolf Hitler's Third Reich will own complete control of western Europe. There is no longer any army on the continent capable of rising up to defeat Germany. The likelihood of this conquest of the continent remaining in place for decades is very real. Europe is about to become a fortress, a prison, and a tomb, completely sealed off from the world—the residents of all nations within destined to live out their lives in the iron grip of Nazi tyranny without any hope of rescue or escape.

This is not just an ideological theory or even fatalist thinking, as Churchill was accused of believing before the Phony War ended on the morning of May 10. It is fact. And while the pressing matter of Great Britain's future weighs heavily upon Churchill, he is more immediately consumed by the staggering reality that more than a quarter million British soldiers are stranded on the beach at Dunkirk, soon to be forever confined within Hitler's Fortress Europe.

The British troops are faced with four choices: fight to the death; find a way to punch a hole through the Nazi lines and escape; remain in Dunkirk and hope for rescue; or fly the white flag of surrender.

Winston Churchill adds a fifth option: victory.

"I have only to add," he tells the House of Commons, "that nothing which may happen in this battle can in any way relieve us of our duty to defend the world cause to which we have vowed ourselves; nor should it destroy our confidence in our power to make our way, as on former occasions in our history, through disaster and through grief to the ultimate defeat of our enemies."

. . .

"HARD AND HEAVY TIDINGS" have already begun. Unbeknownst to the prime minister, just yesterday nearly one hundred soldiers of the Royal Artillery's Cheshire Regiment were captured while retreating to Dunkirk. They were bravely fighting a rear guard action to cover the retreat of other units, putting their own lives in jeopardy so that others might reach safety, when the men ran out of ammunition and were forced to surrender. The British soldiers, along with a handful of French stragglers, lay down their arms and put up their hands.

The German soldiers accepting their surrender are not common troops of the Wehrmacht, as the regular German army is known. These young men are elite members of the brutal 1st Panzer Division of the Waffen-SS, the Nazi Party's military branch, men who do not recognize such legalities as codes of the Geneva Convention that guarantee a prisoner humane treatment.

By tragic coincidence, as Prime Minister Churchill speaks in London, and as General Charles de Gaulle's B1 *bis* tank commanders open fire on the Germans at Huppy, the Cheshire Regiment is being ordered at gunpoint to strip off their uniforms and boots. Their pant pockets and rucksacks are searched. Personal letters and photographs are destroyed so the bodies will never be identified. Naked but still maintaining their composure, every man refrains from panic as they are herded into a small milking shed near the French village of Wormhoudt. There is barely enough room for the entire group.

The SS throw grenades into the barn, but two British soldiers hurl their bodies atop the explosives to stifle the blasts, giving their own lives to save those of their comrades. Enraged, the callow SS soldiers then fire into the barn with semiautomatic weapons. When that is done, the Nazis walk slowly past the bodies, searching the pile of corpses for survivors. A single shot is fired into the back of the head of any British soldier who moans or cries out when kicked. In this way, eighty British and one French soldier are murdered. Fifteen more survive by hiding for hours under the corpses of their friends.

. . .

"THE TROOPS ARE IN GOOD HEART, and are fighting with the utmost discipline and tenacity," Churchill tells Parliament. He cannot possibly know the sacrifice now being made by the men of the Cheshire Regiment, but his words invoke the spirit of their selflessness—indeed, that of the entire British Expeditionary Force, huddled on the sands of Dunkirk, prepared to give their lives in the pursuit of freedom.*

Then Churchill adds, somewhat mysteriously, that a plan is already in motion to save those British lives. "I shall, of course, abstain from giving any particulars on what, with the powerful assistance of the Royal Navy and the Royal Air Force, they are doing or hope to do."

Operation Dynamo has begun.

The British are coming home.

---

* Wilhelm Mohnke, a Hauptsturmführer (the SS equivalent of captain), a founding member of Adolf Hitler's SS bodyguard, and a close confidant of the Führer, ordered the executions. Mohnke survived the war but was never prosecuted for the massacre.

12

M r. Ambassador sips sherry as bombs fall on Paris.

William Christian Bullitt Jr., American envoy to France, steps onto the balcony as air-raid sirens howl. The legendary Paris sky is a blue postcard darkened by German bombers droning like Napoleon's bees. Bullitt and the small cast of generals and diplomats now joining him to watch the action were about to enjoy a Monday lunch hosted by Minister of the Air Laurent Eynac.

"Since it seemed wholly improbable that the Germans would bombard the center of the city of Paris," Bullitt will write in a telegram to his superiors at the U.S. Department of State, "instead of seeking the air raid shelter, we went out on the balcony to see the planes."

Today should be a triumph for the dark-eyed, impeccably dressed Eynac. British intelligence has broken Nazi codes, informing the French in advance of this afternoon's "Operation Paula" attack on Paris. Just one hour ago the code to scramble all French fighter aircraft was messaged to local squadrons via the powerful radio transmitter atop the

Eiffel Tower, ensuring that the Germans would receive a blistering welcome. Scheduling a lunch to demonstrate that the Armée de l'Air is every bit the equal of the Luftwaffe sends the strong message that French airpower can save the nation.

But the Germans, for the first time in the war, are most definitely bombing the heart of Paris, and a communications breakdown means that precious few French aircraft have taken flight to greet them. Waves of Heinkel bombers, twenty-five planes in each, fly over at an untouchable 30,000 feet—a height too great for bombing accuracy, but a clear indicator that everyplace and everyone in the city is a target.

Bullitt and the other guests sip their drinks as they witness the destruction. "The discipline of social poise has its advantages in warfare: nobody so much as dropped his glass," observer Eric Sevareid of CBS news will recall.

On the streets below the balcony, school children march to the underground, patriotically singing "La Marseillaise." Jagged heaps of broken glass litter the sidewalks. Office workers returning from lunch join the rush. A seven-story apartment house crumbles from a direct hit. Fires burn around the Eiffel Tower, sending up shafts of black smoke. Streetlamps bend in two. Shell holes pock the pavement.

French antiaircraft batteries fire back, rattling Minister Eynac's salon and giving the balcony a precarious feel. White puffs of smoke dot the high altitudes as shells explode.

Suddenly a large German bomb explodes in a field just one hundred yards away. Bullitt is showered by flying glass as every window shatters. The balcony threatens to detach from the building.

Then comes the deafening whine of a second bomb dropping directly on top of Bullitt and the other guests. The groan of bending metal and splintering of wood bursts forth in an instant as the roof, then floor after floor, is penetrated by the falling ordnance. There is no time to flee or press flat to the floor. A single German bomb is soon to kill a handful of the most powerful men in Paris. There is no chance of survival.

The bomb stops falling.

The nose cone of the ordnance is ten feet away from Ambassador Bullitt, protruding from the ceiling of the salon. An open wine bottle remains upright on the sideboard.

But there is no explosion.

Sherry glass clutched firmly in hand, Bullitt walks back into the devastated room to study the bomb.

Ambassador Bullitt is forty-nine and complicated, a lanky, French-speaking, Yale-educated intellectual once married to a prominent Bolshevik sympathizer. Prematurely bald and fond of wearing a carnation in his lapel, he was America's first ambassador to the Soviet Union before accepting the Paris posting. Bullitt once coauthored a biography of President Woodrow Wilson with psychiatrist Sigmund Freud, and his lone work of fiction outsold books by fellow American writer Ernest Hemingway, who described the ambassador as "Bill Bullet or Bull Billet, a big Jew from Yale and fellow novel writer" in a 1927 letter to writer F. Scott Fitzgerald. Hemingway and Bullitt have become friends since then, often shooting skeet at Bullitt's country residence when the writer finds his way back to France.

Bullitt knows enough about German weaponry to recognize that this bomb may not be a dud, but in fact an explosive device weighing several hundred pounds equipped with a time-delayed fuse capable of detonating at any minute.

William Bullitt and Minister Eynac agree to postpone lunch. "Heavy bombs fell on all sides of the building, and we went down to the air raid shelter amid flying glass and plaster. We were obliged to remain in the shelter for a period of one hour," Bullitt will write.

A second wave of German bombers strikes at 1:50 p.m. A total of 1,060 bombs fall on Paris today. Ninety-seven buildings are leveled. Sixty-one fires continue to burn after the all clear sounds at 2:18.

Forty-eight French civilians are dead.

"Two cars of guests at the luncheon were struck and burned up in the courtyard at entrance of the building," Bullitt will elaborate in his telegram. "My car was untouched and I was entirely uninjured."

"God must be with me."

.   .   .

IT IS THE PEOPLE OF PARIS who feel abandoned. A city that showed compassion for Belgian refugees—but largely refused to join them on the road—now struggles with the decision to flee.

"Paris knew, now. Paris knew what the northern cities knew," American journalist Eric Sevareid will write of June 1940. "Thousands of Paris cars emerged from their courtyards and garages, with mattresses tied to their tops; and the families of Paris swelled to a river, the stream of human particles flowing to the south."

The Paris exodus is beginning.

13

The British exodus is nearly complete.

For the second time in a week, Prime Minister Winston Churchill rises to speak. Commons quiets. An undisciplined white pocket square sprouts from his breast pocket like a wild radish. The design of his bow tie is lightly speckled. His pocket watch, like that of Washington, Napoleon, and Wellington, is a Breguet, hanging from his waistcoat by a gold chain. Churchill dons black-framed glasses and opens his speech. Eighteen foreign diplomats look down from the gallery, a stark reminder that the war in France has increasingly global consequences.

Six days ago in this chamber, Churchill alluded to activities being undertaken by the Royal Navy and the Royal Air Force. These concluded at 2:23 p.m. today. Now comes the time to share the details of Operation Dynamo. The British Expeditionary Force has fled France, leaving behind their "luggage," as Churchill likes to call the tanks, vehicles, howitzers, and armament too cumbersome to transport.

These will have to be replaced, at considerable cost to a financially strapped British government.*

. . .

"FROM THE MOMENT that the French defenses at Sedan and on the Meuse were broken at the end of the second week of May, only a rapid retreat to Amiens and the south could have saved the British and French Armies."

The prime minister speaks slowly, teasing out words for emphasis.

"However, the German eruption swept like a sharp scythe around the right and rear of the Armies of the north. Eight or nine armored divisions, each of about four hundred armored vehicles of different kinds, but carefully assorted to be complementary and divisible into small self-contained units, cut off all communications between us and the main French Armies.

"It severed our own communications for food and ammunition, which ran first to Amiens and afterwards through Abbeville . . . Behind this armored and mechanized onslaught came a number of German divisions in lorries, and behind them again there plodded comparatively slowly the dull brute mass of the ordinary German Army and German people, always so ready to be led to the trampling down in other lands of liberties and comforts which they have never known in their own . . . This armored scythe-stroke almost reached Dunkirk.

"Almost. But not quite."

---

* The genius behind Operation Dynamo was Vice Admiral Bertram Home Ramsay, who had previously retired in disgrace after clashing with a superior officer. Recalled due to war, Ramsay was charged with planning the evacuation. From his office in a cave eighty-five feet below Dover Castle, Ramsay masterminded the planning and operations. The ports of Calais, Boulogne, and Dunkirk were all originally part of the plan, but the first two fell to the Germans. Operation Dynamo began on May 26. Ramsay was knighted for his success but did not survive the war. On January 2, 1945, Ramsay was involved in a plane crash over France. He is buried at the Saint-Germain-en-Laye New Communal Cemetery just outside Paris. Bertram Home Ramsay was sixty-one.

. . .

THIS AFTERNOON'S SPEECH was written over several days, first dictated slowly to a shorthand stenographer, then revised over and over as Churchill shared it with advisers. The final draft was completed yesterday, typed onto pages in short paragraphs the prime minister likens to that of the Psalms, and once again revised by Churchill until just moments ago.

Members of Churchill's Conservative Party are mixed in their response. Some Labour members cry. Other members of Parliament are depressed by the military's failure in France and how it reflects on their political future. Conservatives withhold applause on the opposite side of the aisle. The prime minister's beloved wife, Clementine, is equally unimpressed.

But Churchill is not speaking to them. His words are directed at those who would make peace with Adolf Hitler. American president Franklin Roosevelt—indeed, all the American public, so strongly influenced by pro-Hitler acolytes like aviator Charles Lindbergh of the soon-to-be-formed America First Movement and U.S. ambassador to the United Kingdom Joseph Kennedy—must know the reality of the situation. More than ever, Britain needs American military and financial help. But Churchill cannot grovel. Britain is nobody's weak sister.

. . .

"WHEN A WEEK AGO TODAY, I asked the House to pick this afternoon as the occasion for a statement, I feared it would be my hard lot to announce the greatest military disaster in our long history."

It has been twelve minutes. Churchill continues:

"The enemy attacked on all sides with great strength and fierceness, and their main power, the power of their far more numerous Air Force, was thrown into the battle or else concentrated upon Dunkirk and the beaches. Pressing in upon the narrow exit, both from the east and from the west, the enemy began to fire with cannon upon the beaches by which alone the shipping could approach or depart. They sowed magnetic mines in the channels and seas; they sent repeated waves of hostile aircraft, sometimes more than a hundred strong in one formation, to cast their bombs upon the single pier that remained, and upon the sand dunes upon which the troops had their eyes for shelter. Their U-boats, one of which was sunk, and their motor launches took their toll of the vast traffic which now began. For four or five days an intense struggle reigned. All their armored divisions—or what was left of them—together with great masses of infantry and artillery, hurled themselves in vain upon the ever-narrowing, ever-contracting appendix within which the British and French Armies fought.

"Meanwhile, the Royal Navy, with the willing help of countless merchant seamen, strained every nerve to embark the British and Allied troops; 220 light warships and 650 other vessels were engaged. They had to operate upon the difficult coast, often in adverse weather, under an almost ceaseless hail of bombs and an increasing concentration of artillery fire.

"Nor were the seas, as I have said, themselves free from mines and torpedoes. It was in conditions such as these that our men carried on, with little or no rest, for days and nights on end, making trip after trip across the dangerous waters, bringing with them always men whom they had rescued. The numbers they have brought back are the measure of their devotion and their courage. The hospital ships, which brought off many thousands of British and French wounded, being so plainly marked were a special target for Nazi bombs; but the men and women on board them never faltered in their duty."

. . .

Now CHURCHILL SWITCHES HIS FOCUS, directing his comments to the British public. Parts of the speech will be broadcast on the radio tonight, though read by a news presenter, so the prime minister must leave no room for interpretation. The fear of German troops making a dash of their own across the Channel is very real. Churchill is honest about this threat without sowing panic.

"I would observe that there has never been a period in all these long centuries of which we boast, when an absolute guarantee against invasion, still less against serious raids, could have been given to our people. In the days of Napoleon the same wind which would have carried his transports across the Channel might have driven away the blockading fleet. There was always the chance, and it is *that* chance which has excited and befooled the imaginations of many Continental tyrants. Many are the tales that are told. We are assured that novel methods will be adopted, and when we see the originality of malice, the ingenuity of aggression, which our enemy displays, we may certainly prepare ourselves for every kind of novel stratagem and every kind of brutal and treacherous maneuver."

. . .

AMERICAN JOURNALIST Edward R. Murrow listens to Churchill's speech with a newfound appreciation for the British prime minister. The thirty-two-year-old Murrow, quickly becoming one of the most famous voices in broadcast journalism, has a passion for the spoken word. He hears a man with a full grasp of the formidable task before him—and a clear vision of how to prevail.

"I have heard Mr. Churchill in the House of Commons at intervals over the last ten years," Murrow will tell his American radio audience. "Today, he was different. There was little oratory. He wasn't interested in being a showman. He spoke the language of Shakespeare with a direct urgency as I have never before heard in that House. There were no frills and no tricks. Winston Churchill's speeches have been prophetic. He has talked and written of the German danger for years. He has gone into the political wilderness in defense of his ideas. Today, as Prime Minister, he gave the House of Commons a report remarkable for its honesty, inspiration and gravity."

. . .

IT IS PAST FOUR. The assembled politicians will soon go home for dinner, disperse to private clubs, or perhaps just walk three minutes across Bridge Street to St Stephen's Tavern, where the division bell will ring if they are called back to the House. But no matter where they debate the success or failure of the prime minister's speech today, the defiance of Churchill's closing remarks will long be on their minds.

For Winston Churchill now speaks directly to Adolf Hitler.

. . .

"WE SHALL NOT FLAG OR FAIL," Churchill promises, his jaw set and voice charged. "We shall go on to the end.

"We shall fight in France," the prime minister emphasizes, acknowledging that 140,000 British soldiers remain on French soil, to the south and east of Dunkirk, determined to stop the Nazi advance on Paris.

"We shall fight on the seas and oceans. We shall fight with growing confidence and growing strength in the air. We shall defend our island, whatever the cost may be. We shall fight on the beaches. We shall fight on the landing grounds. We shall fight in the fields and in the streets. We shall fight in the hills.

"We shall never surrender."

14

Erwin Rommel delights in the shocking British defeat.

The victorious general beams as he surveys this Norman fishing village. Sun just broke through the morning fog. Rommel's newly awarded Knight's Cross rests snug against his throat, layered over his Pour le Mérite medal.* The general stands alone and unarmed, shoulders back, chin upraised, visor casting shadow over his eyes, surrounded on all sides by British soldiers who would give anything to shoot him dead.

---

* Rommel was awarded the distinctive Iron Cross First Class and Second Class in World War I. This silver-framed, cast-iron, cross-shaped medal was first established by Prussian king Friedrich Wilhelm III in 1813 as a symbol of courage during the Napoleonic Wars. The Knight's Cross, Nazi Germany's highest military award, is similar in appearance but has a swastika in the center of the cross. This award only came into being by order of Adolf Hitler on September 1, 1939. The distinguished Pour le Mérite, first awarded in 1740 by King Frederick II of Prussia, was given to civilians and members of the military to denote extraordinary personal achievement.

Rommel is at peace. There is no rush to assemble his men and launch another blitzkrieg. It is over. It is done. For the first time in a month of fighting, Erwin Rommel takes time to bask in his enormous success.

If not for Rommel's 7th Panzer Division, these British would be safely home. An armada of 67 merchant ships and 140 other small vessels assembled off the French coast two days ago, ready to swoop in for a Dunkirk-like rescue. But thick fog, German artillery, a lack of radio communication between ships, and the wiles of Erwin Rommel scuttled that dream.

Rommel pays no attention to the man on his left, Major General Victor Fortune of the 51st Highland Infantry Division. The 51st fought at Abbeville alongside General Charles de Gaulle, impressing the French commander with their courage. The Highlanders are renowned for their toughness, with the *Washington Post* referring to them as a "most famous outfit of fighting men" in a January 1938 front-page story.

As the Germans turned south after capturing Dunkirk, the Highlanders fell back from the Somme River along with the French Ninth Army, staying barely ahead of Rommel's panzers on their dash to the English Channel. But Rommel was relentless, ordered by Adolf Hitler to prevent another Dunkirk at all costs. Winston Churchill's "never surrender" speech nettled the Führer. Hitler promises "total destruction" of the Allies, and Rommel is just the man to see it done.

The 51st might have escaped farther south to the large British-occupied port at Le Havre, where the Royal Navy would have easily rescued them. But in Paris the French government is now publicly accusing Great Britain of desertion. To stave off such criticism, Winston Churchill assured French prime minister Reynaud that Britain "would never abandon her ally in her hour of need." It was a tactical comment on Churchill's part, intended to ensure that France would continue fighting.

But those words spelled tragedy for the Highlanders. General Fortune is under orders of the highest level to not only remain with the French Ninth but also to suborn his command to that of their generals. So the mechanized British remain loyal, hunkering down to fight alongside an ally that still rides into battle on horseback.

For this reason, the 51st will forever remember the fight for St. Valery as the moment Winston Churchill and the British government abandoned them.*

The battle was fruitless, a holding action to buy time for rescue vessels to approach the beach. But Admiral Sir William James, commander in chief of naval operations in the English harbor at Portsmouth, learned too late that the smaller civilian craft lacked radios to communicate with the larger military ships. This lapse, combined with thick fog and precision German artillery, doomed what was known as Operation Cycle. Now, Admiral James can only write in his official report that the withdrawal will never occur.†

The French surrender first, laying down their weapons at 8:00 a.m. this morning.

Low on rations and almost out of ammunition, Major General Fortune continues following orders from London, even as duty to the French yoke is lifted. He finally makes the difficult choice of radioing his superiors for permission to spare the lives of his men.

To the surprise of absolutely no one, the Fascist nation of Italy joined the war on the side of Germany on June 10. There, it is tradition

---

* The 51st Highland Infantry is a Scottish unit, leading many to still believe eighty years later that they were disposable and easily abandoned. In part, lyrics of the song "The Beaches of St. Valery" read: "We never believed high command would just leave us. / So we fought every inch of the way . . . An' with no ammo or food we had done all we could, / so we surrendered at St. Valery . . . Just a deep sense of shame as though we were to blame, / Though I knew in my heart we were not."

† The ruddy James, a highly decorated lifelong naval officer, was the subject of several paintings by his grandfather while still a young boy. One of these featured James staring at a soap bubble and was used in an advertisement for Pears soap. For this reason, James still went by the nickname "Bubbles."

in some armies for a general to be handed a bottle of brandy and a loaded pistol if he surrenders. But when the proud and caring Fortune orders his elite unit to lay down their arms at 10:00 a.m., he is not allowed this abrupt exit. Instead, the general is forced to endure the shame washing over proud Scots whose lineage has not been conquered for six hundred years. Almost to a man, the 51st prefer a fight to the death.

At first, many Highlanders think the order is a joke. Others burst into tears. A handful escape into the French countryside and make for British-held Gibraltar, 1,000 miles south.

Many of them make it.

The rest of the 51st are Rommel's prisoners, and now just moments from beginning a grueling march into Germany. These thousands of defeated soldiers sit on the quay in stunned confusion, easily policed by their armed German captors. They will spend the war as slaves in the salt mines of Thuringia alongside inmates of Nazi concentration camps, but their fate is no longer a concern to the general with the broad smile sending them into hell.

.   .   .

GENERAL ERWIN ROMMEL is a romantic, fond of writing love letters to his wife, Lucia. So, he is aware that St. Valery would be immensely charming any other day of the year. The village rests in the cleft between spectacular three-hundred-foot cliffs rising abruptly from the shoreline. Seagulls wheel in the sky now that the guns have stopped firing. The salty seafront air has also returned, replacing the acrid aroma of gunpowder. On any other day, as Rommel well knows, the English Channel might present a calming vista rather than an uncrossable moat between France and Mother England.

But Erwin Rommel has unleashed total war on this hamlet. The view is no longer idyllic, now marred by the sights and smells of wounded and dead on both sides. Equally jarring is the wanton destruction, such as that of the wrecked French armored cargo vessel *Cerons*, decimated while attempting a rescue at ebb tide. The *Cerons* rests in shallow water, a tangle of steel with a single undamaged smokestack, her unmanned 100mm guns pointing aimlessly into the leaden sky.*

Far more gruesome is the scene at the base of the chalk cliffs outside town. Unable to make their way into St. Valery but still hoping for rescue by sea, soldiers from the British perimeter defenses tied together blankets and rifle slings on which to descend. Those makeshift "ropes" often broke or proved too short. The incoming tide laps at broken bodies and frayed blankets littering the black-pebble beach.

This destruction is of Rommel's architecture. Not content to merely surround the British forces, the general placed his artillery and machine guns on the high ground west of St. Valery and dropped rounds onto the Highlanders' positions. And as the *Cerons*'s crew—now also Nazi prisoners of war—can attest, Rommel was just as brutal toward any ship daring to come within range. Using the high cliffs and the ocean to his tactical advantage, the general created a de facto wall along the Norman coast that prevented invasion by sea and penned the hapless 51st Highland Division inside the tiny harbor with no way out.

For genius such as this, Erwin Rommel has become one of Adolf Hitler's favorite generals. The two met a week ago at Army Group A headquarters near the Belgian border. Rommel is galvanized by this association, enjoying his rising star. Rather than be weary of combat, Rommel grows more audacious with every fight. The general is not only undefeated and has taken thousands of prisoners with minimal loss of German lives; his force is now legendary. The French have nicknamed the 7th Panzer: "la Division Fantome"—the Ghost Division—for their ability to attack from out of nowhere.

---

* The *Cerons* remains there to this day. She is still visible off the coast at low tide. Her 100mm guns were removed from the ship in 1995 and are now the site of a memorial atop the cliffs overlooking the harbor.

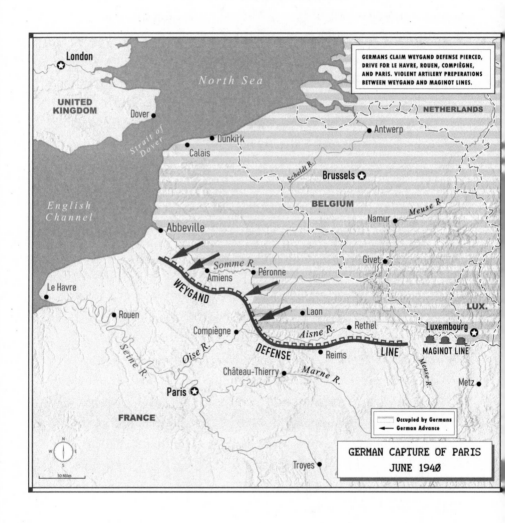

GERMANS CLAIM WEYGAND DEFENSE PIERCED, DRIVE FOR LE HAVRE, ROUEN, COMPIÈGNE, AND PARIS. VIOLENT ARTILERY PREPERATIONS BETWEEN WEYGAND AND MAGINOT LINES.

London

North Sea

UNITED KINGDOM

Dover

NETHERLANDS

Strait of Dover

Dunkirk

Antwerp

Calais

Scheldt R.

Brussels

English Channel

BELGIUM

Namur

Meuse R.

Abbeville

Givet

Somme R.

Amiens

Péronne

WEYGAND

Le Havre

Rouen

LUX.

Laon

Luxembourg

Compiègne

Aisne R.

Rethel

DEFENSE

Reims

LINE

MAGINOT LINE

Oise R.

Seine R.

Château-Thierry

Marne R.

Meuse R.

Metz

Paris

FRANCE

Troyes

N
W   E
S

50 Miles

Occupied by Germans
German Advance

GERMAN CAPTURE OF PARIS
JUNE 1940

Yet, for all Rommel has accomplished, today's victory is perhaps the most significant. The matter is still in doubt, but the surrender of the 51st Highland Division will soon be seen as the end of Allied resistance. Hundreds of thousands of French and British troops are scattered throughout France, and the Royal Air Force relentlessly attacks German troop columns, but St. Valery marks an irreversible turning point in this conflict.

Finally, as Erwin Rommel well knows, it is time to take Paris.

The people of Paris know too.

15

The City of Lights is empty.

The dawn is quiet enough to hear expensive shoes echoing on cobblestones. But there are no footfalls. Paris's grand boulevards are without pedestrians, bicycles, motorcycles, taxis, drunks, soldiers, or even *les putains*. Shops are covered with iron shutters. There is no morning aroma of coffee and fresh croissants, no scrape of waiters setting up chairs and tables on sidewalks. Trains don't leave Paris. There are no newspapers. Children do not skip to the Métro singing "La Marseillaise."

The people are gone.

Prime Minister Paul Reynaud and his government have left, too, fled to the city of Tours, taking with him the propaganda machine that prevented the people of Paris from knowing the truth about Nazi Germany's winning streak. Among those who accompanied Reynaud is the new French undersecretary of state for national defense, General Charles de Gaulle. Reynaud and de Gaulle are eager to move the

French military to the North African nation of Morocco to continue the war. Commander in Chief Maxime Weygand is just as eager to surrender. The three met with Winston Churchill in Tours last night to find a solution. Left unsaid is that the Anglo-French alliance is in tatters.

But as the politicians haggle, and de Gaulle prepares to fly to London to continue negotiations with Churchill, the unthinkable is occurring.

Paris, to use a military term, is now an open city. The French will not defend it. Hitler's army is free to enter. Rather than fight for Paris and see its beauty leveled, Reynaud is surrendering his capital without firing a single shot. After the savage fighting across northern Europe, the complete destruction of Rotterdam, the barbaric cruelty of the German SS, and the tens of thousands of lives lost and bodies maimed in battles big and small, the biggest prize of all will not be contested. The French love Paris so much they would rather see it in German hands than reduced to rubble.

The Nazis know this.

And they still plan to destroy Paris.

The Eiffel Tower, Louvre, the Arc de Triomphe, Les Invalides, Notre-Dame, the Tuileries Garden, the Jardin du Luxembourg, the Moulin Rouge, and on and on, treasure after countless treasure, built over centuries by peasants and kings—all will cease to exist this morning at 8:00 a.m. French antiaircraft guns have all been disassembled, so there will be no way to defend the city. Bomb after German bomb will level Paris.

The city's residents, fearing rape, torture, and precisely the sort of massive destruction the Germans visited on Warsaw and Rotterdam, have run away in terror. The narrow winding roads of the French countryside are choked with these refugees. The citizens of Paris now sleep in pastures and fight one another for simple amenities like bread and gasoline. Industrious farmers sell glasses of water to parched travelers. Cars are abandoned when their fuel tanks run empty. A heartbreaking 90,000 children will become separated from their parents, many never to be reunited.

"All day long streams of cars and trucks, loaded down until the springs gave way, poured out of the city," the *International Herald Tribune* reports of Paris being emptied. "I do not know exactly when they began to realize that their city and perhaps their lives were in danger, when they made up their minds that they would have to run."

Homes are locked. Bed frames, bathing suits, tennis racquets, dinner plates, family portraits, and the many trinkets that make up daily life are left behind. Pets are killed rather than let them starve. Stuffed cardboard suitcases are bound tight with twine. Children agonize over which toy makes the trip and which becomes a memory. Women wear fur coats in June. Bicycle stores and cigarette vendors sell out.

Not everyone is gone. The elderly and infirm are left behind. Police, firefighters, and garbage men are still at their posts. The Métro is empty but running. A handful of cafés will soon open to serve the occupiers. Paris's legendary brothels—among them Le Chabanais, Le Sphinx, La Fleur blanche—have no plans to close, confident their services are just as popular with Germans as they have been with the French.

In all, 2 million citizens of Paris ran away. The last fled at midnight, whereupon the Prefecture of Police ordered the city gates closed. It is decreed that in order to prevent unnecessary conflict with the occupiers, no more Parisians will be allowed to leave when the gates reopen. Sixteen citizens, unable to escape, will kill themselves today.

"Americans joined the rush, most of them business men who had waited until the last minute," the *International Herald Tribune* will add. "But the American Embassy was open for business and staying open for business. Ambassador William C. Bullitt and most of his staff will be at work at their offices at 2 Avenue Gabriel, no matter what happens."

. . .

THE CLOCK IS TICKING.

By a strange twist of fate, Ambassador Bullitt is also now the mayor of Paris. The departure of the French government has thrust this position upon him until power is transferred to Germany. Bullitt is a firm believer in the French cause and has strongly petitioned President Franklin Roosevelt for assistance. "The evacuation of Paris has added a million to the number of men, women, and children . . . whose lives can be saved only by American aid."

Bullitt's pleas have gone unanswered, the White House maintaining a strong animus toward the French cause. But the ambassador has not given up. The United States embassy has worked relentlessly to get Jewish refugees to America, often bending French and American immigration laws in the process. "The Ambassador . . . was very much in favor with what we were doing," diplomat William C. Trimble will remember. "We really twisted regulations and we got an awful lot of people out."*

Bill Bullitt's most urgent mission is saving Paris. He has no intention of leaving, a position he has made clear by posting signs in English, French, and German in front of the embassy: "This building is under the protection of the United States of America."

Not taking any chances, Bullitt has armed the embassy staff with Thompson submachine guns and burned his secret codes. Previous American ambassadors remained in Paris during the French Revolution, the Napoleonic Wars, and the War of 1870. Bullitt has no intention of being the first to break that tradition. "Since the age of four,"

---

* Among the loopholes used by the Americans was falsely designating a refugee as a skilled agriculturalist or a university professor, professions that were given preferential treatment for their expertise. One recipient of such a passport was famous war photographer Robert Capa, who posed as a farming expert hoping to improve the agriculture of Chile.

he writes to President Roosevelt, "I have never run away from anything however painful or dangerous when I thought it was my duty to take a stand."

However, knowing the dangers, he also dashes off a personal note to Roosevelt: "In case I should get blown up before I see you again, I want you to know it has been marvelous to work for you."

For the gregarious ambassador, the diplomacy required to coax the Germans into leaving the city intact is second nature. Working through the night before the occupation, Bullitt arranges a sunrise parley between French army officials and the incoming Germans.

By 6:00 a.m. it is agreed: Paris will be spared.

Now all that remains is for the Nazis to formally enter the city.

Ambassador Bullitt hears the distant creak of tank treads as columns of panzers rumble toward the heart of Paris. A lone soldier on a motorcycle was perhaps the first Nazi to arrive, somehow finding his way inside long before sunrise to buzz the 11th arrondissement. Now the rest of the army follows. German spies in Paris planned the route weeks ago. The conquerors advance through the suburbs of Argenteuil and Neuilly-sur-Seine. Their armored vehicles travel in single file, snaking into the city in a line that seems to go on forever. Many soldiers have taken the time to bathe in the Canal de l'Ourcq this morning, then afterward shaving, polishing helmets, and pressing their uniforms. After the invasion of Poland, some of these same men murdered and raped. In Paris, the Wehrmacht is determined to impress.

"Behind the tanks rolled anti-tank units, still dusty and laden with evidence of the furious fighting in which they had taken part to the north," reports the *New York Times*.

"As the long shadows of morning retreated, more and more Nazi contingents streamed into the capital . . .

"Motorized infantry, riding in steel-shielded trucks mounting machine guns to command the broad streets, converge from the Seine bridges to the Place de l'Etoile."

"The Star," as l'Étoile translates into English, is the hub of Paris. Twelve boulevards spoke outward. At the very center rises the Arc de Triomphe, France's most sacred military site. The structure is 164 feet high, its walls inscribed with the names of great French victories and brave soldiers. The Tomb of the Unknown Soldier rests beneath its arch near an Eternal Flame.

The soldiers do not travel beneath the shade of the arch as they prepare to parade down the Champs-Élysées. The historic honor of being the first Nazi to profane this sacred site is reserved for Adolf Hitler.

Paris is anything but quiet right now. The sound of hobnailed Nazi jackboots on the cobblestones of the Champs-Élysées echoes loud and clear. Endless long gray lines of soldiers goose-step smartly toward the Place de la Concorde. German troops march three abreast, again giving the appearance of a column with no end. One excited group of Nazi soldiers breaks off to climb the Eiffel Tower, where they hoist an enormous swastika flag over Paris.

"They were well-fed and husky, tough-looking and able," American embassy staffer William C. Trimble observes, watching the German arrival from his small bedroom overlooking the Place de la Concorde. "They poured in all that day. And then afterward came the reserve groups . . . and they were rather older men who composed a military garrison. But they were also able and almost as well disciplined. We also saw many of the fifth column collaborators who had been paid by the Germans . . . there was no question about that. It was awful."

As a final reminder that Paris is now a German playground, Generalmajor Walter Warlimont makes a triumphal entrance by ordering his personal pilot to land his Fieseler Fi 156 Storch aircraft on the Place de la Concorde.

At 3:30 p.m., American ambassador William Bullitt authorizes the transfer of power to General Bogislav von Studnitz. Bullitt does not personally take part, preferring to send an envoy because he finds the Nazis repulsive. Nonetheless, Paris now belongs to Nazi Germany.

Adolf Hitler's thick, dark curtain is descending on Paris. Free speech is abolished. Paris radio stations broadcast German music. The Germans strip the Paris police of all rifles and pistols. The ideals of the French national motto—*Liberté, Égalité, Fraternité*—are gone.

Perhaps forever.

"This is the shell of Paris," the *New York Times* will lament the following day. There is no byline. "The shell witnesses the obscene triumph of a man and an idea that have invaded not only a city but a century, out of the murk of past time. But it is only the lovely shell that Hitler has captured. He has not captured the true Paris. Never can he, his tanks, his robot battalions penetrate the walls of that magic city. For all their violence it remains inviolate, forever.

"Paris of Voltaire, Rousseau, Victor Hugo, Balzac, Anatole France, Montaigne; Paris of Madame Roland, Lafayette, Danton, Zola, Chateaubriand; Paris of Racine, Moliere, Corneille; Paris of Gautier, Daudet and Rabelais; Paris where democracy had its modern rebirth; Paris that taught the world to paint and build; Paris that laughed, Paris that used words for rapiers, Paris that turned the troops out to march with muffled drums in the funeral trains of poets; Paris where the creative imagination of modern man burned at its fiercest and brightest; Paris of museums, libraries, universities in which the mind could range at will; Paris the spiritual, Paris the city of love, Paris the city of light, Paris that quickened the pulse of youth and ministered to the serenity of age; Paris the volatile and profound:

"This is not Hitler's Paris, not today, not ever."

A thin crowd of French citizens lines the Champs-Élysées, witnessing a massive conquering force assembled in the city's main plaza. It is a tragic moment, and they are right to be devastated.

But as horrible as this might be, life in Paris is about to get worse. Much worse.

Their only hope is a tall, arrogant man who smokes too much.

16

General Charles de Gaulle has fled the country.

"France," says the general, speaking the single word with deliberation. An engineer watches de Gaulle's sound check through a small rectangular window.

The weather outside is warm without rain. De Gaulle spent an hour this afternoon with Winston Churchill before the prime minister left to deliver a speech in the House of Commons. De Gaulle then resumed work on what some will call the most important address in the history of his nation.*

De Gaulle now sits at attention in a swivel chair upholstered in silver-gray Bedford cord, facing a curved Art Deco desk made of Australian

---

* In an extraordinary historical coincidence, the speech Churchill delivered is commonly remembered as "This was their finest hour," which is considered one of the great speeches in British history. That de Gaulle and Churchill could not only deliver such major addresses to their respective nations within hours of one another but to also have spent time together on the same day is unprecedented.

walnut veneer. A large black microphone, small lectern, and two turntables occupy the desktop. The general's hair is slicked back tight against his head. He dresses for movie cameras instead of radio—leggings, polished boots, crisp tunic cinched tightly around his narrow waist with a wide belt—as if this moment is being filmed for posterity.

"Ex-general" Charles de Gaulle, as the officer is now known in France, has Churchill's blessing to address the French people from the British Broadcasting Corporation headquarters here on Portland Place. Studio 4B is the smallest in the building, more often used to read the news or play music. By design, the acoustics are dead, reinforcing the sensation that de Gaulle is completely alone, his words absorbed into the fabric walls of silk and hemp, bouncing off nothing and no one as they launch into the ether.

The past week has been one upheaval after another. This may explain why, for once, the general looks nervous.

The broadcasting light goes on.

.   .   .

"THE LEADERS WHO, for many years past, have been at the head of the French armed forces, have set up a government.

"Alleging the defeat of our armies, this government has entered into negotiations with the enemy with a view to bringing about a cessation of hostilities. It is quite true that we were, and still are, overwhelmed by enemy mechanized forces, both on the ground and in the air. It was the tanks, the planes, and the tactics of the Germans, far more than the fact that we were outnumbered, that forced our armies to retreat. It was the German tanks, planes, and tactics that provided the element of surprise, which brought our leaders to their present plight.

"But has the last word been said? Must we abandon all hope? Is our defeat final and irredeemable? To those questions I answer—No!

"Speaking in full knowledge of the facts, I ask you to believe me when I say that the cause of France is not lost. The very factors that brought about our defeat may one day lead us to victory.

"For, remember this, France does not stand alone. She is not isolated. Behind her is a vast Empire, and she can make common cause with the British Empire, which commands the seas and is continuing the struggle. Like England, she can draw unreservedly on the immense industrial resources of the United States.

"This war is not limited to our unfortunate country. The outcome of the struggle has not been decided by the Battle of France. This is a world war. Mistakes have been made, there have been delays and untold suffering, but the fact remains that there still exists in the world everything we need to crush our enemies some day. Today we are crushed by the sheer weight of mechanized force hurled against us, but we can still look to a future in which even greater mechanized force will bring us victory. The destiny of the world is at stake.

"I, General de Gaulle, now in London, call on all French officers and men who are at present on British soil, or may be in the future, with or without their arms; I call on all engineers and skilled workmen from the armaments factories who are at present on British soil, or may be in the future, to get in touch with me.

"Whatever happens, the flame of French resistance must not and shall not die."

．　．　．

In Lisbon, American writer A. J. Liebling hears de Gaulle's speech on the radio in the lobby of the Grande Hotel do Monte Estoril. Like many who fled Paris, Liebling has traveled to neutral Portugal to find a ship or plane to take him away from Fortress Europe. Liebling will remember de Gaulle's speech: "The voice spoke of resistance and hope; it was strong and manly. The half-dozen Frenchwomen huddled around the radio cabinet where they had been listening to the bulletins of defeat and surrender ceased for a moment in their sobbing.

Someone had spoken for France; Pétain always seemed to speak *against* her, reproachful with the cruelty of the impotent."

. . .

DE GAULLE'S SPEECH lasts four minutes. In that time, he has gone from a general to leader of a nation known as Free France that exists in his febrile imagination. Finished with what will become known as the Appeal of 18 June, the general walks across Portland Place to dine at the iconic Langham Hotel.

Everything about Charles de Gaulle's life has changed in just one week. Determined to carry on the fight against Germany, most likely from North Africa, de Gaulle appealed to Winston Churchill for help. In an extraordinary bit of statesmanship, the two men agreed to form a brand-new nation twining the two countries. France and Britain would be one. Prime Minister Churchill's cabinet agreed to this radical realignment.

But Prime Minister Reynaud's cabinet said no. Instead, a majority argued that the time had come for French soldiers to investigate terms of surrender. After a 13–6 cabinet vote in favor of opening negotiations with Nazi Germany, Paul Reynaud knew he had lost control. He saw no other choice but to resign as prime minister of France.*

His replacement is the eighty-four-year-old World War I hero, Marshal Philippe Pétain, who immediately asked Germany for their terms. The French army ceased firing shortly after noon on Monday, June 17.

"In Berlin, traffic stopped at mid-street," *Time* magazine will report. "Women kissed and cried. Strangers embraced. Radios played 'Deutschland Uber Alles' over and over, and over and over, and re-

---

* Reynaud and his mistress, Hélène de Portes, will leave the new government headquarters in Bordeaux by car. Outside Montpelier, he hits a tree. A suitcase in the back seat flies forward, almost completely decapitating de Portes. Reynaud will later be arrested by the Pétain government for his opposition to their policies, then handed over to Germany. Reynaud will spend the remainder of the war in German custody.

peated the news that Adolf Hitler had received, through Spain's Francisco Franco, Marshal Pétain's offer to surrender."

But Charles de Gaulle has no intention of giving up.

In the eyes of Marshal Pétain, this makes de Gaulle a threat to national security. De Gaulle is stripped of his rank. Facing arrest and imprisonment, the general fled to Britain in a cramped de Havilland Dragon Rapide biplane provided by Winston Churchill. His hastily packed suitcase contains four shirts, one pair of pants, and a single photograph of Yvonne and the children, whose current whereabouts he does not know. Even as the general tries to rally the people of France to his cause of resistance, he frets that his family will be captured and held hostage unless he returns to face charges. Left unsaid is that de Gaulle places the future of France above the fate of his family. He will not return until he saves the nation. Charles de Gaulle stands alone. He has no plan, no army, and absolutely no right to proclaim himself leader and supreme commander of the construct known as Free France. But with tonight's radio address he has done just that.

"I appeared to myself, alone and deprived of everything, like the man on the edge of an ocean he was hoping to swim across," the general will write. "I felt that a life was ending, a life that I had lived in the framework of a solid France and an indivisible army. At the age of forty-nine I was entering into an adventure."

So with that adventurous spirit in mind, it is appropriate that de Gaulle dines at the Langham tonight. The world-renowned British explorer Henry Morton Stanley kept a room there between African expeditions. But de Gaulle's adventure is far different than Stanley's African journeys. The better comparison is with Napoleon Bonaparte, trounced at Waterloo exactly 125 years ago today. It is almost certain de Gaulle will also suffer overwhelming defeat in his vainglorious, idealistic, quixotic, downright absurd attempt to single-handedly defeat Adolf Hitler.

De Gaulle knows this. Yet there is no going back. He does not feel comfortable in Britain, thinking the coffee too watery, the blond tobacco of Craven "A" cigarettes no match for Gitanes, and the English language currently escapes him. But the call to resist has been issued. The fight is publicly announced. And no matter what Marshal Pétain might say, Charles de Gaulle is still very much a general.

In the morning comes good news: Yvonne and the children are in England. They endured the crossing crammed into the cabin of a small Flemish vessel. They were at sea as de Gaulle recorded his radio address. Like the general, they escaped France with very little. The good silver has been left behind.

But that is not important.

What matters is that Charles de Gaulle is now reunited with his wife and children.

The general may not have an army, but he is no longer alone.

17

Adolf Hitler takes ownership of Paris.

Spring is now summer. Sunday dawns cool and clear. The Nazi swastika flies over the Arc de Triomphe as Hitler's chauffeured Mercedes sedan purrs down the Champs-Élyées. Street signs in German point the way. The Führer is dressed in uniform. Paris policemen snap to attention and salute.

Yesterday, in the Compiègne Forest north of Paris, inside the same railway car in which German officials signed the articles of surrender ending World War I—sitting in the same seat once occupied by Supreme Allied commander and French general Ferdinand Foch—Adolf Hitler laughed and mugged for newsreel cameras as the situation was reversed. France's new prime minister, Marshal Philippe Pétain, put his signature on the document formalizing an armistice between France and Germany. The war is over. Nazi Germany is the winner.

Only now, with that moment of triumph still a close memory, does Adolf Hitler tour Paris as its conqueror. Like any first-time visitor, the failed watercolor painter eagerly takes in the most famous sights: l'Opéra, Napoleon's Tomb, Sacré-Coeur, and the Champs-Elysées. "That was the greatest and finest moment of my life," he gushed to an aide after visiting Napoleon. In a burst of inspiration, Hitler orders that the remains of the emperor's son be exhumed in Vienna and transported here to lie alongside his father.

The Führer poses for a photograph in front of the Eiffel Tower, an instantly iconic image that will soon flash around the world, enraging world leaders suddenly fearful of Nazi Germany's predations. He also orders that two World War I memorials be destroyed because he finds them insulting to the German people.*

Three hours after his arrival, just before 9:00 a.m., Adolf Hitler leaves Paris. He will never return, although he is so entranced that he will order that all German soldiers be given the privilege of spending at least one leave from the battlefield in the City of Lights.†

"Wasn't Paris beautiful?" Hitler asks Albert Speer, his favorite architect, as they drive to Le Bourget Airfield. "But Berlin must be far more beautiful.

"When we are finished in Berlin, Paris will only be a shadow."

. . .

ON JUNE 30, 1940, Führer Hitler decrees that all works of art in Paris be "safeguarded" by Nazi Germany. The process of scouring bank

---

* The first of these memorials was a massive monument on the Place Denys Cochin to Charles Mangin, a general known for his *la guerre à outrance* ("all-out war") and leadership of colonial troops from Africa. He later oversaw France's occupation of the Rhineland after World War I, infuriating Hitler and other Germans by forcing the local women to serve in a brothel for his Senegalese soldiers. The detonated Mangin memorial was replaced in 1957 by a much smaller statue on the Avenue de Breteuil. The head of the original statue can be found within the Musée de l'Armée in the Hôtel des Invalides. The other memorial was for British nurse Edith Cavell, shot by German troops for assisting in the escape of Allied soldiers. It's worth noting that Cavell still has a prominent memorial in London near Trafalgar Square.

† The formal name of this edict is *Jeder einmal in Paris*—"Everyone once in Paris."

vaults, homes left empty by refugees, and the city's many museums for treasure begins. The best pieces will be marked on the back of the canvases with a small black swastika and made available to Hitler and his top generals. Among those works Hitler has long coveted for his personal collection is *The Astronomer* by Vermeer, not so much because the subject celebrates German scientific brilliance, but because he enjoys taking things that belong to Jews.*

On the same morning, Ambassador William Bullitt breaks centuries of tradition and drives away from Paris in a chauffeured limousine, the first American ambassador to France to abandon his post. His efforts to save the city have been misunderstood. Instead of heroic, superiors in Washington believe Bullitt abandoned the French. The people of France view the ambassador as a Nazi collaborator. Just as substantially, Bullitt's determination to remain at his post has angered President Roosevelt, who is eager to steer clear of war in an election year and no longer sees the need for an envoy in a Paris without a French government.

So Bullitt makes for the French border with Spain, then on to Lisbon. The U.S. embassy is now in the capable hands of its caretaking staff, which are under strict orders not to allow the Nazis to occupy that piece of American soil.

As long as Ambassador Bullitt remained in residence, the American embassy in Paris was the last vestige of freedom, an island of democracy in regular contact with the outside world, a witness holding Nazi Germany accountable for whatever brutality and outrage they may perpetrate here in the City of Lights.

---

* *The Astronomer* was stolen from property belonging to Jewish financier Édouard de Rothschild, who had already fled to America. The twenty-inch-tall painting was packed into case H13—the H standing for Hitler—and shipped to Germany on February 3, 1941. It now hangs in the Louvre Museum in room 837, on the second floor of the Richelieu wing.

But now tall, bald, outrageous, independently wealthy Bill Bullitt is gone.

As Charles de Gaulle has already announced over BBC radio from London, this is no longer just a European war but a second world war. America can no longer remain silent.

Until Paris is once again free, this conflict will never be over. Liberty, equality, and fraternity—ideals the free world idealizes as the finest way to spend mankind's short time on earth—will not return until that day. For Paris is not just a city but a symbol of hope, requiring brave men and women to find some way to step outside their normal selves and daily lives to do the impossible: bring down Adolf Hitler and his armies.

On this warm June morning, those men and women have no idea when and where they will be called. Most have no idea they will be called at all, considering themselves too ordinary to take on such a monumental task.

But they will hear this call, just as clear as clarion. Not today, perhaps, but in time. Fortress Europe is now closed off from the world. No nation on earth is strong enough to defeat Adolf Hitler. Nazi Germany possesses the might, manpower, and tactical advantage to throw any invader back into the sea. But as Paul wrote to the Romans, suffering produces perseverance; perseverance produces character; and character produces hope.

Thus, possessing just a single kernel of hope, the resistance begins to grow.

THE RESISTANCE

18

Winston Churchill wants to fight dirty.

Tonight is a working meal at 10 Downing Street. The relentless Churchill rose from his daily nap two hours ago, refreshed and ready to labor well into the night. He is dressed in pink silk underwear, workaday coat, and bow tie rather than a dinner jacket, and sips Pol Roger as colleagues arrive. The stress of being a wartime leader does not show on his pale round face. If anything, friends have noted, Churchill looks and behaves ten years younger. Cigar in one hand, silver champagne tankard in the other, he now thinks of a provocative letter that came his way recently, soon to be the primary topic of tonight's agenda.

The evening's first course, a clear broth, will be served shortly after nine. Head cook Georgina Landemare well knows that Churchill detests creamy soups. Red and white wine will be offered with the main course, although the prime minister will maintain a bottle of champagne for personal consumption, positioning the ice bucket near his chair so he need not wait for a servant to offer a refill. Ice cream with chocolate sauce is Churchill's preferred dessert, followed by a plate of Stilton cheese. Brandy, cigars, and conversation will conclude the meal.*

Dinner routine is the one constant in Churchill's life right now. It is two tumultuous months since he rose to prime minister. The world has been turned upside down. Churchill and Great Britain are now synonymous, his every decision and sentence scrutinized.

Two days ago, in a radio address to the British people, Churchill raised the stakes in his personal war against "that man," as he refers to Adolf Hitler, vowing that Britain would not bend a knee.

And London will never be an open city.

"Be the ordeal sharp or long—or both—we shall seek no terms, we shall tolerate no parley, we may show mercy—we shall ask for none," Churchill promised.

"We would rather see London laid in ruins and ashes than it should be tamely and abjectly enslaved."

Hitler gets the message. The Führer issued Directive No. 16 today, officially authorizing the invasion of Britain. The *New York Times* is reporting from Berlin that "Germany tonight raised the threat of a shattering bombardment of London in a sharp answer to British Prime Minister Winston Churchill's promise of a street-by-street defense of the metropolis."

Operation Sea Lion, as the attack is known, will begin by launching waves of German bombers against England. Landings will then be executed up and down the British coast—Lyme Regis, Portsmouth, Brighton, Dover, Ramsgate—all followed by the inexorable and inevitable conquest of London.

---

* The British-born Landemare began her career at age fifteen as a Kensington Palace scullery maid. In 1909 she married French chef Paul Landemare, who trained her to cook classical French fare. She worked for the Churchills on a permanent basis from 1940 to 1954. She died in 1978 at the age of ninety-six.

Winston Churchill is not cowed.

The prime minister lacks the resources to invade Europe in a tradi-tional sense. But he nonetheless believes this is the perfect time to at-tack. "Existence is never so sweet," Churchill has written, "as when it is at hazard."

Among the guests now enjoying pre-dinner libations are Churchill's thirty-nine-year-old parliamentary private secretary, Brendan Bracken, and his eccentric scientific adviser, Frederick Lindemann, known by one and all as the "Prof." Both men are regular guests at Churchill's banquet.

As a young man, Winston Churchill served as a newspaper corre-spondent covering the war between Britain and a group of Dutch set-tlers known as Boers in South Africa. These guerrilla fighters did not wear uniforms or practice conventional tactics. And yet they frustrated and often defeated a much larger and more professional British Army. Ever since, Churchill has harbored a romantic fascination with the Boer fighting force known as "commandos." As recently as Dunkirk, Churchill has encouraged his generals to use commando-style tactics of all-out war, even ordering them to "prepare hunter troops for a butcher-and-bolt reign of terror."

Now the dinner conversation turns to making commandos a regu-lar part of British strategy. For the past two weeks Churchill has pon-dered a suggestion to form a new covert fighting force. He foresees a group of undercover killers with no rules or ethics, working behind enemy lines to disrupt and kill by any means possible. The men would be vagabonds, cutthroats, and ruffians, perhaps even hardened crim-inals comfortable operating without structure or direction. They must be volunteers. Some might even be women. Death will be all but certain.

This is the subject of the letter that weighs so heavily on the prime minister's mind. It was written in the form of a proposal by Churchill's glowering, outspoken minister of economic warfare, Hugh Dalton.

The prime minister does not like this prickly Socialist. In fact, Dalton even sits across the aisle from Churchill as a member of the Labour Party, making him a direct rival.

But it is Hugh Dalton whose words speak to Churchill's fascination for unconventional warfare. Written several weeks ago, then passed upward to the prime minister's desk through political channels, Dalton's manifesto offers a partial solution to Britain's few military options: "We have got to organize movements in enemy-occupied territory comparable to the Sinn Fein movement in Ireland, to the Chinese guerillas now operating against Japan," noted the fifty-two-year-old Etonian. "This 'democratic international' must use many different methods, including industrial and military sabotage, labour agitation and strikes, continuous propaganda, terrorist acts against traitors and German leaders, boycotts, and riots."

Dalton also suggests that he be given the chance to lead this band of marauders. "Not a military job at all. It concerns Trade Unionists, Socialists, etc., the making of chaos and revolution—no more suitable for soldiers than fouling at football . . . surely, the War Office have enough on their plate at the present."

A typical Churchill dinner can go to midnight and beyond, but this evening's meal is done by 11:15. The prime minister retires to the Cabinet Room and summons Dalton. A formal document has been prepared, creating a commando force known as the Special Operations Executive. The organization will be top secret for security purposes, operating with minimal oversight. Hugh Dalton will be in charge.

All that remains is Churchill's signature.

"The letter to be signed by him was on the table," Dalton will record in his journal. "I ask whether he is really sure that he wants me to do a little more."

"Yes," Churchill replies. "Certainly."

In time, nicknames like "Churchill's Secret Army" and "Ministry of Ungentlemanly Warfare" will be applied to this new unit. But right now there is no tongue-in-cheek romance, only practicality. Hugh Dalton and the SOE represent Churchill's slim hope of defeating Adolf Hitler. Even bomber aircraft missions into Nazi Germany have had little effect. Aggressive missions by the SOE, no matter how brutal they might be, are an antidote to the impotence Hitler imposes upon Churchill and Britain.

On Monday, July 22, the war cabinet formally agrees to Dalton's new role.

Dalton records Churchill's marching orders in his journal:

"'And now,' said the P.M., 'go and set Europe ablaze.'"

19

Paris is as dark as a deep depression.

After a weekend of revelry, twenty-eight-year-old Jacques Bonsergent steps off a train at the Gare Saint-Lazare. He strides happily from the platform into cold autumn night. The city is almost black. Streetlights along Rue du Havre remain unlit. The German army just canceled 10,000 automobile permits, ending civilian headlights. Windows of apartments and private homes are shuttered, residents walking room to room by flashlight and candles.

Today is Sunday. Bonsergent spent the weekend at a country wedding. He traveled with good friends, who walk at his side now. This happiness is a memory they will long remember. With the exception of Marcelle Dogimont's bride, all are men: happy, tipsy, walking carefully. Stories about pedestrians blundering into lampposts and falling off curbs in the darkness of Paris curfew are a regular part of life after just four months of occupation.

Bonsergent is an engineer by trade, born on the Breton coast, an ex-soldier educated at a Paris technical school in the 13th arrondissement.

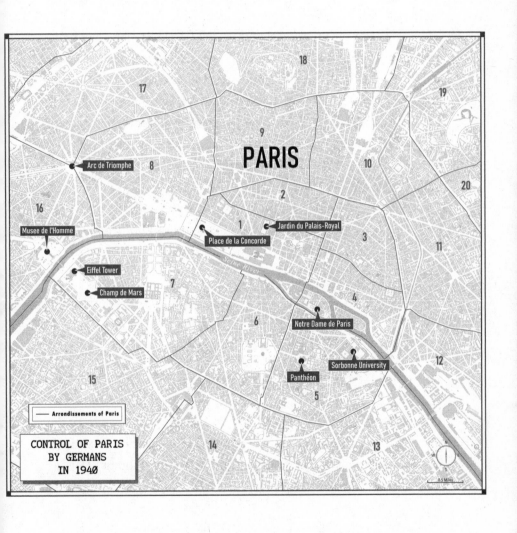

18

17

19

9

PARIS

Arc de Triomphe   8   10

20

2

16

1   Jardin du Palais-Royal

Musee de l'Homme   Place de la Concorde   3

11

Eiffel Tower

7

Champ de Mars

4

6   Notre Dame de Paris

Sorbonne University   12

Panthéon

15   5

13

14

— Arrondissements of Paris

CONTROL OF PARIS
BY GERMANS
IN 1940

0.5 Miles

His hair is beginning to thin, he has an easy smile, and his ears are almost too large. So far, life under occupation is an adjustment. Food rationing and the curfew have changed daily habits, yet life remains civil. The Germans are polite but firm. The French appear to have nothing to fear.

The wedding party approaches the café Mollard, at more than half a century one of the oldest brasseries in Paris. Three drunken Germans suddenly block the sidewalk. In the spirit of occupation, in which everything in the City of Lights now belongs to Nazi Germany, one soldier grabs lustily at the bride. The Frenchmen—in particular, groom Dogimont—take exception. Words are passed. A heated scuffle. Jacques Bonsergent is a sensible sort and chooses not throw a punch.

But someone hits a Nazi.

As the soldiers momentarily forget about the wedding party and help their fallen friend, a quick-thinking Bonsergent orders his companions to disappear. He will solve this before it gets out of hand.

Too late.

The enraged Germans grab him. The innocent man is dragged into a nearby hotel for questioning.

· · ·

JACQUES BONSERGENT HAS PICKED an extremely bad night to be a Good Samaritan. Tomorrow is November 11, the anniversary of the World War I armistice. The date has been a French national holiday since 1922. A moment of silence is held at 11:00 a.m. to mark the moment the war ended. In Paris, le Jour du Souvenir is a time of celebration and rallies. Tomorrow in particular, students will use "Remembrance Day" as an excuse to protest in the streets.*

---

* The treaty to end World War I was signed at 5:00 a.m. To allow time for news of the cease-fire to spread along the front lines, Allied commander Ferdinand Foch stipulated that the war would officially end six hours later, at 11:00 a.m. There is also evidence that Foch enjoyed the symbolic notion that the war would end at the eleventh hour on the eleventh day of the eleventh month. In that span of six hours,

But, to the Germans, November 11 marks a day of humiliating defeat. In an effort to suppress French festivities and as a reminder that Nazi Germany is now the victor, all commemorative celebrations and public assemblies are banned. Protest is out of the question.

So the German soldiers are already on edge as Jacques Bonsergent is questioned. The Gestapo have a standardized means of breaking down a witness known as *verschärfte Vernehmung*—"enhanced interrogation." The process begins with simple rations of bread and water, a hard bed, and sleep deprivation. Exercise to exhaustion is next. Twenty "blows with a stick" are the maximum number allowed, and the head is never beaten, ensuring that a prisoner does not arrive for trial with bruises on the face. More severe brutality like pulling out toenails, stress positions, ice-cold showers in air-conditioned rooms, and running a hot iron up and down the bare spine are also allowed. But interrogation can be as simple as making a prisoner stand in one place for hours while asking question after question.

But that is all to come. For now, on this dark Sunday night, it is enough that Jacques Bonsergent refuses to give the names of his colleagues. He is formally taken into custody. The jail cell is one mile away, in the notorious Cherche-Midi prison, a century-old fortress where every inmate is held in solitary confinement.

Bonsergent's festive weekend of singing, dancing, and celebration with good friends concludes with the dull thud of a wooden cell door slamming shut.

His jailer turns the lock.

"The cell was 10 ft. x 5 ft. with a small window high up on the wall, the door had a small peephole . . ." fellow inmate Walter Bird will write. Bird was imprisoned at Cherche-Midi two days before Jacques

---

nearly 3,000 men were killed. In America, the celebration of November 11 was at first celebrated as Armistice Day. President Dwight Eisenhower formally changed the title to Veterans Day in 1954 in an effort to honor all who served.

Bonsergent. "No exercise apart from emptying our bucket down in the courtyard."

The last two months of 1940 will be among the coldest ever recorded. In this dank world of near starvation, unheated cell, and complete isolation, Bonsergent passes a night. Then another. He sleeps on an old mattress of broken springs stuffed with straw under two horse blankets. The walls were once whitewashed.

Jacques Bonsergent does not witness the Remembrance Day riots, in which Paris students hold the first illegal demonstration against Nazi rule.

It will also be the last.

Inspired by Charles de Gaulle and his impassioned BBC radio pleas for a Free France, 3,000 young people gather at the Arc de Triomphe, resting place of France's unknown soldier. The Cross of Lorraine, de Gaulle's symbol of opposition, has already been defiantly stenciled on streetlamps, above urinals, and on flat surfaces throughout the city.* As the gathering swells, the outlawed "La Marseillaise" is sung with full-throated passion.

The students are disgusted by the "Vichy" government of Marshal Pétain, who signed the armistice with Hitler and now rules southern France in Nazi servitude. The doddering Pétain has sentenced de Gaulle to death in absentia, a further reminder that his allegiance is to Hitler, not France.

"A handful of defeatist politicians surrendered to Germany in the belief that Britain was doomed. They assured Frenchmen everywhere

---

* The Cross of Lorraine has the lowercase t appearance of a traditional cross but with a second horizontal bar. De Gaulle was formerly commander of the 507th Regiment of the Chars de Combat, an armored unit whose members come from the city of Metz, in the Lorraine region. The cross, inscribed with the motto "Honneur et Patrie" ("Home and Country"), was their symbol. Its use as an emblem for Free France was suggested by Georges Thierry d'Argenlieu, a Carmelite priest and one of de Gaulle's officers in London.

this was the case, and most Frenchmen believed them," *Time* magazine describes the situation. "General De Gaulle went to England to rally the French Empire to the cause of fighting on."

But the students flee when the Nazis and Paris police finally step in to break up the mob. Many protesters are shot or beaten. One hundred are arrested. These students are eventually placed on trains bound for Germany and Poland, destined to spend the war at hard labor in concentration camps.

In the Cherche-Midi prison, night after freezing night passes. A lonely Jacques Bonsergent languishes in his cell. On December 5, 1940, almost one month after his incarceration, the engineer appears before a German tribunal.

Knowing full well that he might be shipped to a concentration camp, the engineer still refuses to name the friend who punched the Nazi. Instead, Bonsergent addresses the court fearlessly: he wishes the people of Paris to know the precise nature of the German character. Having had a month to think about the words the Nazi court will hear next, Jacques Bonsergent takes full responsibility for punching the drunken barbarian occupier.

There is no transcript of the Nazi proceedings, all of which are directly ordered by Adolf Hitler. The Germans want no record of moments like this. No tentative stenographer transcribes the furious Germanic oaths launched at this arrogant Frenchman or the exasperation of men who would have preferred to spare Bonsergent's life, if only he would give a name.

The verdict is as quick as the repudiation: Bonsergent is sentenced to death.

The engineer requests clemency. Denied. In the wake of the student protests, Adolf Hitler is accusing the military commander of France, General Otto von Stülpnagel, of being too soft on the people of France.

An example must be made.

Even if the condemned is innocent.

20

The call to resist is being distributed.

Furtive as sewer rats, the intellectual provocateurs spread out through Paris. The newspapers in their hands could get them arrested. Brutal cold chaps their faces and takes away their breath. Moving quickly and quietly, each man and woman drops an illegal document near public kiosks, knowing the people of Paris will find them in the morning. They are scared but fearless.

This is what it feels like to start a revolution.

Their cell will earn the name Groupe du Musée de l'Homme, because that's where they work: Paris's stereotype-shattering Museum of Man. Most Parisians passively accept the occupation, but for the past six months these idealists have banded together to fight back. Tonight, for the first time, their *cause* has a title: *Résistance.**

Among the men are Pierre Walter, Léon Maurice Nordmann,

---

* Groupe member Germaine Tillion will give the network its title.

Georges Ithier, Jules Andrieu, René Sénéchal, Boris Vildé, and Anatole Lewitsky. Their occupations are unusual for urban guerrillas: ethnologist, Africanist, anthropologist, and so on. Agnès Humbert is an art historian. Yvonne Oddon, Lewitsky's lover, was awarded one of France's first-ever degrees in library science. With the blessing of their employer, this band wrote the stories and printed their homemade newspaper on a mimeograph machine in the museum basement.

When it came time to give the newspaper a name, it was Oddon who remembered that eighteenth-century Huguenot women imprisoned for their faith often carved the words *Resister* into the walls of their cell. So it is, that the first edition of *Résistance* now lands on Paris's doorstep. The subtitle reads: *The Official Bulletin of the National Committee of Public Safety*, harkening back to revolutionary France.*

"Resistance: That's the cry that goes up from your hearts, in your distress at the disaster that has befallen our nation," screams the lead story.

Soon everyone in France who actively opposes the occupation will be known by that single word.

By day the Groupe du Musée de l'Homme are nothing more than mild-mannered museum staff. By night they are the Resistance, born out of the occupation and inspired into action by the broadcast words of Charles de Gaulle. They gather intelligence that might be of use to the British, steal military documents, set up escape routes for downed Allied pilots, and work to build a network of like-minded thinkers throughout France. Thus far, the Groupe du Musée de l'Homme have connected with more than one hundred other intellectuals throughout Occupied and Vichy France to share information and build the cause.

---

* The Committee of Public Safety was founded in April 1793 during the French Revolution to protect France from foreign attack.

"Here we are, most of us on the wrong side of forty, careering along like students all fired up with passion and fervour, in the wake of a leader of whom we know absolutely nothing, of whom none of us has seen a photograph. In the whole course of human history, has there ever been anything quite like it?" Agnès Humbert writes in her journal. In particular, she is offended that books promoting Nazi beliefs about ethnicity are being added to the museum's library.

The group does not have a leader, but the energetic Russian émigré Boris Vildé makes key decisions, among them the strategic choice to expand their public appeals from the simple leaflets they have distributed since September to the four-page *Résistance*. "A marvelous fellow," Humbert says of Vildé. "The man here that I admire the most. His warm handsomeness is matched by his intelligence and his energy. He's a great guy."

In its own way, the establishment known as Musée de l'Homme was resistant even before the war. Museum director Paul Rivet, a balding man who favors wingtip collars and round eyeglass frames, has long preached the equality of man. He is openly against traditional ethnology, which favors measuring each human's head to define their true race. Skeletons and skulls fill the museums displays cases in recognition of this misguided belief, still embraced by the Nazis.

The clandestine work is romantic for some, transcending mere patriotism. The punishments for being found out are severe, with certain imprisonment and likely Gestapo torture. The Nazis have not killed anyone in France for objecting to the occupation, but deportation to a concentration camp is no less a death sentence.

The greatest risk of being the first true resistance group is that German intelligence—the Abwehr—has the luxury of focusing all its attention on Groupe du Musée de l'Homme. From their headquarters in the Hôtel Lutetia in the 6th arrondissement, the Nazis have already contrived to infiltrate their ranks. Unbeknownst to Boris Vildé, Agnès Humbert, or any of the other resistance fighters dropping newspapers

around Paris tonight, Albert Gaveau, who claims to be Vildé's top assistant, reports directly to the SS captain now gathering information
about their group.

Within the museum itself, employees not taking part in the Resistance are growing suspicious, some quietly approaching the police to
launch accusations.

So despite their idealism, energy, passion, and the same love of
country that once fueled the French Revolution, the Groupe du Musée
de l'Homme are already as good as dead.

The brave men and women just don't know it yet.

21

The martyr takes Holy Communion in his cell.

Six miles across Paris from the Musée de l'Homme, Jacques Bonsergent says, "Amen." The Body of Christ is laid upon his tongue. A priest soon concludes the engineer's last Mass.

Then it is time to go.

Bonsergent is driven in the back of a troop transport from the Cherche-Midi prison to a military fort in the Bois de Vincennes. He has eaten his last meal. His mind is clear and resolve unwavering. The innocent man is led to a courtyard. His young body is lashed to a thick pole planted in the ground for purposes of execution. A stone wall rises behind him. Ten paces away, rifles loaded, stands his firing squad. The young Germans have been instructed to aim for the heart.

The Catholic priest has made the journey to the place of execution. He hears Bonsergent's last confession, then steps away. The German commander steps forward to speak with the condemned man. "Tell us a name and I have the order for your release," he says sympathetically.

"I will not say a name," says Bonsergent, to absolutely no one's surprise.

A blindfold is placed over his eyes.

.   .   .

CHRISTMAS EVE 1940 brings more bitter cold.

Parisians awaken. They begin their morning without coffee, a long-disappeared delicacy. Bundled from head to toe, men and women step out into the streets to stand in the morning breadlines. All eyes are drawn to recently posted notices displayed on kiosks throughout the city.

"The engineer Jacques Bonsergent, of Paris, received a death sentence by the German military tribunal for an act of violence against a member of the German Army. He was shot this morning. Paris, 23 December 1940."

Ten mornings ago, Parisians woke up to find *Résistance*.

And now this.

Most citizens have never heard the name Jacques Bonsergent. Yet the news is shattering. Men remove their hats out of respect for the dead. The faithful make the sign of the cross. A new reality is setting in: "These correct people who occupied our country were officially telling us they had executed a Frenchman guilty of not bowing his head to them," author Simone de Beauvoir will write of this morning.

.   .   .

DECEMBER 25, 1940.

Paris is the scene of an amazing Christmas miracle.

The city is transformed for the second morning in a row. In Métro stations, cafés, kiosks, and wherever Bonsergent's death notice is posted, memorials have sprung up overnight. Parisians defied the curfew to pin flowers to the Nazi posters. As an added protest, small French and

British flags also adorn some of the death notices. When the Germans come to remove the flowers and flags, locals replace them almost immediately—though carefully, lest collaborators seeking to curry favor inform the authorities. Paris is a divided city, equal parts supporters of de Gaulle, Pétain, and communism.

It is now six months since Paris fell. Mistrust and fear are part of daily life. The power of Nazi Germany remains unmatched. This occupation could last decades, perhaps centuries. As the handbills make quite clear, life under the Nazi jackboot will never again feel civil. The days of the polite German occupier are gone.

Forever.

22

The restless woman with one leg has a secret.

Three hundred miles northwest of Paris, thirty-four-year-old Virginia Hall of Baltimore, Maryland, limps through the manicured mess of London's exclusive Mayfair district. She has a long chin and a direct gaze to go with her limp. Passing the Connaught Hotel on Carlos Place—sometimes home to Charles de Gaulle—it is clear that Germany's aerial bombardment did not spare these stately Georgian homes. Hip roofs sag. Shattered sash windows and crumbled brick walls let in the February wind. At Grosvenor Square, wooden huts housing the all-female crew of an antiaircraft balloon cover the gardens. It is here, on the east corner, at the Roman temple façade and pillars of Number One, that Hall steps out of the wind into her place of employment: the United States embassy.

But Virginia Hall is not reporting to work today. She is here to quit.

To her coworkers, Virginia Hall is a simple code clerk for military attaché Raymond E. Lee, earning $105 per month. Her job is to decipher incoming missives and encrypt those going out. She is tall and slender and lacks a wedding ring. Hall dresses very fashionably and is fond of wearing trousers for obvious reasons, although they were very much in fashion in Paris before the war. She smokes cigarettes and takes her gin with a splash of vermouth. Hall's spirit can be defined as adventurous with a helping of wanderlust.

This much, Hall's fellow employees know.

And they also know that Hall is a well-traveled veteran of the Foreign Service, having worked in Poland, Turkey, Italy, and Estonia. She not only speaks fluent French but also previously left government work to drive a frontline ambulance during the early days of the war—shifting gears with a standard transmission despite a wooden left leg—then spent two months traveling through Occupied France. Upon arriving in London six months ago, she actually briefed the embassy staff about those exploits. Since then, Hall is known to openly discuss her views about the situation in France and her passionate anti-Nazi leanings.

But Hall is talkative and guarded at once. Other details of her story are familiar to some coworkers but not others:

"Cuthbert" is the name Hall gave her wooden leg.

Cuthbert is hollow.

She speaks very good but imperfect German—the only flaw being a slight American accent.

Despite shooting off her own foot, Hall is normally very handy with a shotgun.

Yet there is one fact about this assertive woman that absolutely nobody at One Grosvenor Square knows:

Virginia Hall is about to become a British spy.

It was back in August, while crossing the border from France into Fascist Spain en route to London, that the American was noticed by one of His Majesty's undercover agents. George Bellows was struck by her beauty and poise, somewhat amazed that a lone woman could travel so easily through hostile territory. Bellows struck up a conversation, pretending to be a salesman. There was something in the way she told her story, so blasé about danger yet specific in her details, that led the spy to hand Hall a telephone number of a "friend" in London. Without telling her why, Bellows suggested Hall give Nicholas Bodington a call. Unemployment is high in Britain. He might be able to help her find a job.

Yet Hall does nothing of the kind. She reaches London on September 1 and lands work at the embassy. She forgets about the phone number, passing autumn and early winter in a mundane job far beneath her level of education and experience. She endures the nightly German bombings like the rest of London, planning all the while to return to America to be with her mother. Life is dull for the woman fond of a risky undertaking. Racing into underground shelters just ahead of falling bombs is her only adrenaline whoosh.

But Hall is being watched. George Bellows has reported back to London about the interesting American. In late January the clerk is surreptitiously approached by the Special Operations Executive about spying for England.

She has no problem saying yes.

Virginia Hall's entire life has pointed to this moment—the travel, the languages, even the hunting accident. She is thrilled to leave embassy life to rejoin the action. The popular notion of a secret agent is a rugged male. And she is certainly not the commando Churchill had in mind when he formed the SOE. Yet no one will ever suspect a woman, particularly one with an artificial leg.

In her own inimitable way, Virginia Hall is the perfect spy.

Thus far, the SOE has been a disaster, unable to infiltrate France or set up an intelligence network. Recruiting someone as inconspicuous as Hall is an attempt to change those fortunes. The SOE currently has nine agents in training. Hill is about to become the tenth. She is the only woman.

In the weeks to come, this American will learn how pick locks, avoid surveillance, shoot weapons ranging from a machine gun to a pistol, and, above all, travel discreetly through Nazi-occupied France while engaging in acts of espionage. She is soon to go by many different names and become a master of disguise whom the German army will pursue as ruthlessly as any soldier, on any front, in this war.

She will also be given a license to kill.

But first Virginia Hall must quit her job. When asked why she is leaving, her only reply is that she is "seeking other employment"—which seems ludicrous on the face of things, given the high unemployment rate and lack of jobs available to American women. Yet no one at the embassy questions her decision: Hall obviously comes from money.

Saying her goodbyes, Hall limps back out into the wan London sunshine, just a few months from setting Europe ablaze in her own inimitable way.

23

The Resistance has a hero.

Far to the east of London and Paris, all the way across the Mediterranean to the Holy Land, General Charles de Gaulle's chauffeured sedan races up the dusty coastal road from Haifa, top down to catch a breeze. Palm trees, olive groves, emerald-blue sea, bright yellow Levant sun beating down with midsummer ferocity. De Gaulle well knows these sights and sensations. Yet the most welcome view of all is the metropolitan skyline of Beirut rising before the general like an elegant jewel. He returns to this ancient city a conqueror, joining a list of victors dating back thirty centuries. To the names of the pharaoh Rameses II, Marcus Aurelius, and Alexander the Great, add that of Charles de Gaulle.

The general was stationed in this "Paris of the Middle East," as cultured Beirut is known, from 1929 to 1931. An apartment on busy Mar Elias Street was home to his entire family. Following World War I and the breakup of the Ottoman Empire, Lebanon became a French colony. It remains so to this day.*

Australian troops camped along the coastal road cheer as the general passes by. Joyful citizens of Beirut line the streets as de Gaulle's motorcade enters the city. Flags and stencils bearing the Cross of Lorraine decorate roadside buildings. The people are not just excited to see de Gaulle in person; they also want to know what he looks like. No one knows. The Vichy government has destroyed all photographs of the general, instead putting out propaganda giving his physical description as heavyset and ugly. So the people are shocked by the individual being driven into their midst.

Seizing the moment, de Gaulle orders his driver to stop the car. The general steps out. Immediately, cautious police surround de Gaulle's vehicle to protect him from his enthusiastic admirers.

But Charles de Gaulle knows what he is doing.

A solitary Lebanese flag flies by the side of the road. De Gaulle brings his considerable height to stiff attention. The Lebanese people see him up close for the first time: small mustache, thin head, immaculate uniform, and the broad hips British wags jokingly compare with those of a woman. This is what France looks like, for in his mind Charles de Gaulle *is* France.

The real France.

The general draws his palm up to the flat black visor of his kepi. His fingertips linger for instant before he tosses off a crisp salute.

"At this gesture," *Time* magazine will report, "the Lebanese went wild, broke the police cordon surrounding the general's car, flocked around De Gaulle cheering."

---

* The Ottoman Empire ruled significant swaths of Europe, Asia, and Africa for six centuries. A small sign now hangs above the front door of de Gaulle's Beirut residence, reminding passersby that he once lived there.

Against all odds, Charles de Gaulle is rallying the world to the French cause.

But "France" actually means many things right now. For it is not Nazi Germany that Free French troops defeated to take control of Beirut. Instead, it is soldiers loyal to Vichy France. Frenchman has killed Frenchman as de Gaulle leads the struggle for his nation's soul.

. . .

THE BATTLE FOR FRANCE is being fought hundreds of miles from Paris.

The fighting has relocated to Africa and the Middle East, and so has Charles de Gaulle's strategic focus. It is little more than a year since he fled France, but the general has miraculously risen from almost total obscurity to become world famous—so celebrated that *Time* has sent a correspondent to Beirut to write a cover article about the Frenchman. The cause of Free France has become synonymous with that of the plucky underdog.

The general's rise began after the June 18 radio broadcast. In truth, few people actually heard the appeal. Citizens of France had little reason to listen to the British Broadcasting Corporation. The BBC also thought so little of the speech that the sound engineer did not bother pushing the "record" button. But three hundred French citizens living in Britain heard the broadcast and were inspired to follow de Gaulle's cause. An additional 7,000 French soldiers who had been rescued at Dunkirk and still remained in England were so filled with hope that they swore allegiance to Free France.*

But the true moment of transformation came when de Gaulle broadcast the speech once again on the night of June 22, 1940. This time the French were listening. The armistice agreement was signed that day. Marshal Pétain had already gone on French radio to tell the nation that

---

* Sadly, thousands of French soldiers rescued at Dunkirk chose to return home from Britain after the armistice. They were promptly arrested and placed in prisoner-of-war camps.

surrender was the best option. Confused and disheartened, the French turned to British radio for a different perspective. De Gaulle continues to broadcast regularly, but the BBC has gone one step further, initiating a regular *Radio Londres* (*Radio London*) show solely for French listeners that does not depend on his presence. "*Ici Londres*," each transmission begins. "*Les Français parlent aux Français!*"—"This is London. The French speaking to the French." The people of France soon defy occupation orders against listening to the BBC. After finally succeeding in placing agents in Europe, Britain's new Special Operations Executive uses the radio show to send coded messages to agents in the field. Not surprisingly, the Germans and Vichy government work mightily to jam the airwaves so the broadcasts cannot be heard.

The effect of the radio cannot be overestimated. Frenchmen risk their lives to join de Gaulle. Two young soldiers brazenly steal a German colonel's personal aircraft in Occupied France and fly it to England. In another instance, a scientist's wife urges him to join the cause. Knowing her husband would never risk the daring journey to England if he knew her one great secret, the woman keeps it to herself. Only when the scientist is halfway across the English Channel does he reach into his pocket and find the note telling him she is newly pregnant.

And when the Vichy government hands the colony of French Indochina over to the Japanese military without a fight, the governor—a five-star general named Georges Catroux who rides into Beirut today at de Gaulle's side—raced to London, dramatically tore three stars off his uniform so he would not outrank the two-star de Gaulle, and pledged his loyalty.

But despite his rank, Charles de Gaulle is no longer a fighting general. He is a visionary, a politician, a true believer, ingeniously taking control of France. His strategy is simple: travel to every French protectorate in Africa to convince them to join his movement. He fails in French West Africa, and Gabon is only taken after a fight, but French Congo, Cameroon, and Chad all abandon their fealty to Vichy and swear allegiance to Free France. De Gaulle sends emissaries to the Pacific outposts of Tahiti, the Gambier and Austral Islands, the Tuamotus, the Marquesas, and New Caledonia for the same purpose. One colony at a time, Charles de Gaulle is now commander of a territorial collection that, if combined, is larger in size than France itself.*

But Morocco eludes the general. The protectorate he once hoped to use as a base to continue the war against Hitler is completely under Vichy control. The major city of Casablanca is the largest Atlantic port in Africa, now teeming with refugees fleeing Hitler, hoping to gain an exit visa from Vichy Morocco for transit to North or South America. Those found to be Jewish are rounded up and placed in internment camps. Not only could de Gaulle stop the injustice if he controlled Morocco, but his army would stand just eight miles from Europe across the Straits of Gibraltar.

Free France has an army of 40,000, an air force of 1,000 planes, and a naval force of seventeen vessels. De Gaulle has enough men and commanders to fight alongside the British as allies once again. And even more men are joining the cause: thousands of the defeated Vichy soldiers here in Beirut are switching their allegiance to Free France.

But the true key to victory remains the United States, which still refuses to enter the war. As the June 18 appeal made clear, de Gaulle believes American might is vital to defeating Hitler's Germany. Despite this unswerving devotion, the general has still not been recognized as the leader of France by the United States. Instead, they have accorded Vichy France full diplomatic recognition and send regular

---

* French West Africa comprised the modern nations of Mauritania, Senegal, Mali (then known as French Sudan), Guinea (then known as French Guinea), Upper Volta, Burkina Faso (known as Upper Volta), the Ivory Coast, Dahomey (Benin), and Niger. The Battle of Gabon was the only significant conflict in Central Africa during World War II. Free French forces waged war against Vichy French from October 27 to November 12, 1940.

relief shipments of food to its starving residents—all of which is con-fiscated by Nazi Germany to feed its soldiers.

Nonetheless, Charles de Gaulle needs the United States. But until America decides to fight, the general urges the Resistance to wage war any way they can.

Even if that means killing just one enemy at a time.

24

The man with ten seconds to live is boarding a train.

Ensign Alfons Moser is thirty, a German naval officer stationed in Paris who could not look more visible and out of place in the working-class Barbès-Rochechouart Métro stop. He wears a spotless pressed white service tunic, white shirt, sharply creased white trousers, shining white shoes, and—because the train station is above ground in the open air—white peaked cap atop his head rather than tucking it under his arm, as regulations require while indoors.

And yet, Ensign Moser feels nothing but safe. Everyone in the station knows it would be suicide to attack a German serviceman. The execution of Jacques Bonsergent is proof. Throughout the fourteen months of occupation, Moser and other Nazis stationed in the City of Lights have grown accustomed to coming and going as they please. Many Germans carry guidebooks to make their way around the city and tote cameras to record the sights, just like regular tourists. They are regulars at local cafés, sunbathe along the Seine in summer wearing just their underwear—and sometimes nothing at all—and make liberal use of the city's prostitutes. There are German-only bars, bistros, brothels, and movie theaters. All clocks in the city are set to Berlin time. The people of Paris must be off the darkened streets by 9:00 p.m., but Nazi noncommissioned soldiers can stay out until midnight. Officers like Alfons Moser have no curfew at all.

But Moser should also know better than to parade his crisp German accent and lightning rod of a uniform so far away from the posh hub of Paris.

Particularly now.

Urged on by the German secret police—an organization known as the Gestapo—Paris gendarmes arrested 6,000 Jews over the past two nights.* Métro stations in some parts of the city have been shut down due to growing unrest. French Communists are also outraged by Nazi Germany's recent invasion of the Soviet Union and are eagerly responding to calls from Soviet dictator Joseph Stalin to take up arms against the Nazis.

As of August 14, the French Communist Party is outlawed. Just yesterday, demonstrations near the Gare Saint-Lazare led to the German pronouncement of the death penalty for such an affiliation. This includes members of General Charles de Gaulle's increasingly popular Free French movement, allegedly aligned with the Communists.

The arriving train slows. Ensign Moser searches for the first-class car reserved for German officers. The platform is thick with commuters. Those millions who fled the city in the great exodus of June 1940 have almost all come back. Some semblance of routine has also returned, but everything from food to gasoline is rationed to fuel the

---

* In German, the Secret State Police is called *Geheime Staatspolizei*, abbreviated as "Gestapo."

Nazi war effort. Citizens have few travel choices beyond a bicycle, bus, or the Métro.*

Most ride the train.

Germans ride the train too. Which is why the French Resistance lies in wait for Alfons Moser.

. . .

HISTORY WILL NOT record why the lieutenant is starting his day so far from the western section of Paris, home to the German occupying force. The Barbès-Rochechouart station lies at the intersection of the 9th, 10th, and 18th arrondissements, where pro-Communist sentiment is high and a German officer in a bright white uniform is certain to be the object of hatred.

Perhaps Moser has chosen a discreet place to spend the night, whether with a woman or man or simply by himself, far from the prying eyes of German navy—*Kriegsmarine*—headquarters at the Hôtel de la Marine on the Place de la Concorde.

Or maybe he is returning from an early-morning errand.

Yet, no matter what brought Ensign Alfons Moser to Barbès-Rochechouart, he is clearly in the wrong place at the wrong time.

. . .

HISTORY WILL ALSO not record the type of pistol twenty-two-year-old Pierre Georges slips from his pocket as he pushes through the crowd. The Germans have ordered the confiscation of every gun in France. The penalty for possessing a firearm is death. The notion of a Frenchman owning a handgun is so absurd that press reports about what happens next will claim the attacker used a knife.

But Pierre Georges—Communist, veteran of the Spanish Civil War, French Resistance leader, soon to adopt the code name "Colonel

---

* It was also not uncommon to see individuals travel by horse and buggy or in cars specially designed to burn coal instead of gasoline. The use of horses eventually disappeared, their starving owners preferring to use the animals as food.

Fabien"—most definitely has a gun. He is married and handsome, a father, with thick, wavy hair and shining brown eyes. Georges's height is on the shorter side. A Polish colleague in the Resistance named Samuel Tyszelman was executed by a German firing squad two days ago. His crime was singing "La Marseillaise" at a public protest and shouting "Down with Hitler!"

Pierre Georges demands revenge. He has waited for a German to come through the station since dawn. Three other Resistance members stand in the crowd. They are not like British SOE operatives, specially trained by a government agency, equipped to accomplish war's hard tasks. They are young men who spontaneously chose to heed the words of Charles de Gaulle and resist. They must be careful whom they trust lest they suffer the fate of other resistance groups like the Groupe du Musée de l'Homme.

Georges is well aware that the Gestapo and Paris police rolled up those brave intellectuals last spring. Their instantly iconic *Résistance* newspaper stopped publication after just five issues, though not before inspiring countless Parisians to join the cause. Museum director Paul Rivet fled the country just in time and is now pursuing his studies of ethnography in South America.

But nineteen other members of Groupe du Musée de l'Homme are not as lucky. They now languish in prison, enduring torture and awaiting trial, their plight a warning to any would-be Resistance fighter to be extremely careful, for a supposed friend may actually be a Gestapo informer.

Pierre Georges trusts the Resistance fighters standing near him on this platform. Like him, they are idealists and patriots, unpaid and self-equipped, learning the skills of rebellion as they go. Details matter: Barbès-Rochechouart has been chosen for its elevated platform, which offers a better chance of escape than a tunnel. Pierre Georges has no personal vendetta against Alfons Moser. The Resistance fighter simply rose from bed in the morning darkness determined to shoot a German officer.

Any officer will do.

The doors open. Moser places one foot inside the train. He is almost away, even though he does not know he is escaping. Bullets slam into his back and skull. The naval officer pitches forward onto the first-class floor. A small entrance wound just above his collar shows trace amounts of brain, blood, bone, and flesh. The exit wound is a gaping cavity. One lung is punctured.

No amount of bleach will clean that uniform.

The ensign lies alone. Strangers cannot help but stare. His heart still beats, stretching those ten seconds far longer than Pierre Georges had planned. If Moser were drunk, passed out in such a position, in the very public space of a commuter train, the scene would be a humiliation, the ultimate sign of weakness and dissipation.

Instead, the dying body of Alfons Moser, the first German officer of this war to be executed by the people of Paris, represents power.

The French are strong enough to fight back.

Adolf Hitler, on the other hand, shows his own ruthless strength by ordering one hundred French prisoners executed to atone for the murder.*

Immediately.

---

* The actual number was later reduced to ten. French leaders wanted the executions carried out in public but the German authorities feared a backlash and conducted the killings in private.

25

The day for atonement has passed.

The night of intolerance is just beginning.

Glass windows buckle and shatter up and down the Rue des Tournelles as the first sticks of dynamite explode. Pavement shakes. Central Paris awakens, instinctively listening for the sound of the aircraft that dropped the bomb, but hearing none. A single detonation makes no sense, yet the curious remain inside, knowing they must wait until morning for an answer. Then comes another astonishing boom a mile distant, followed by more long moments of silence before a third explosion. And then a fourth. A fifth.

And a sixth. All coming from different directions. No pattern or logic, and still no sound of British warplanes.

Only a small handful of Germans and French collaborators know the answer to this mystery. Members of the pro-Nazi Mouvement Social Révolutionnaire are traveling the city with no regard to curfew, completely unafraid of reprisal, in a car loaded with dynamite and

128

blasting caps. The explosives and the car itself have been provided by Helmut Knochen, the venal and deeply anti-Semitic chief commandant of the Nazi occupying security forces.

Knochen's specific order is that the bombers destroy every synagogue in Paris.

In its own way, sowing destruction and confusion is exhausting work, driving all the way across town from the 4th arrondissement to the 16th, then to the 3rd and back to the 4th, before moving on to the 18th and 9th, following a carefully mapped plan to set explosives and be away.

But any fatigue at this extremely late hour is offset by the realization that blowing up a synagogue is surprisingly easy. Even majestic buildings like the temple home of the grand rabbi on the Rue de la Victoire and the Sephardic synagogue on Rue Notre-Dame-de-Nazareth are defenseless. There are no armed sentries. No steel doors. The main entrance is forced, explosive devices are placed inside, timers are set, and the Nazi collaborators pile back into their car, then drive off, listening all the while for the explosion in their wake.

This night was chosen at random by Standartenführer Knochen, who was inspired by the infamous Kristallnacht attacks against Jews throughout Germany in 1938. But in fact the timing is auspicious. Yom Kippur, the Jewish Day of Atonement, was less than forty-eight hours ago. Inside each of Paris's ornate and lovely synagogues, worshippers gathered to celebrate Judaism's holiest day of the year. Many fasted and spent time in prayer repenting for their sins. Within these places of worship, the Jews of Paris enjoyed a rare break from Nazi persecution. They sang. They smiled. They laughed, made small talk, and even complained, confident that German collaborators were not listening to their words.

But when the Jews left their synagogues, the Nazis once again tracked their every movement. Even before occupying Paris, German spies made a list of all Jewish-owned businesses. They compiled addresses of the wealthiest Jews in anticipation of evicting them from their homes, moving in, and appropriating their possessions. Every Jew will soon be required to wear a yellow Star of David affixed to their clothing. It is also mandatory that yellow signs bearing the inscription *"Jüdisches Geschäft"*—"Jewish Business"—must hang in every Jewish shop. More than 150,000 Jewish residents of Paris have visited a police station to officially report their religious affiliation. As of May 20, they are prohibited from working in banking, retail, hotels, and restaurants—all once prominently Jewish occupations. On August 8 it became illegal for a Jew to practice medicine. As of August 13 they can no longer own a radio. And last month, in the 2nd arrondissement, a new anti-Jewish exhibition organized by the Germans opened to the public. Titled *Le Juif et la France* (The Jew and France), its purpose is to show citizens of Paris what Jews look like so there is no chance they can mask their true racial identity.

Yet those slights and extreme inconveniences pale next to the alarming news that the systematic arrest and imprisonment of Jews is now underway. In mid-August, an internment camp was opened in the north Paris suburb of Drancy, utilizing barracks that were once public housing. Guard towers and barbed wire ring the new compound. On August 20, 4,232 Jewish men between the ages of eighteen and fifty were delivered to the camp by Paris police. They are currently being held hostage. Should any German soldier, official, or collaborator be attacked within Paris, Jews will be chosen at random from this group to be executed.

So the ideal of harboring within the walls of the synagogue, finding sanctuary and solace from the outside world, is quite real.

It is also no more.

"Attempts to blow up seven synagogues were made in Paris between the hours of 1 am and 5 am," the *New York Times* will state from Vichy France, no longer able to send reporters into Paris. "In six instances they were successful, and the damage done was considerable, only the external walls of the structures remaining."

So it is that the Jewish residents of Paris no longer have a place to gather.

And no place to hide.

The Jews' only hope for survival is the death of the brutal Nazi regime.

With every passing degradation, it feels more and more like that day may never come.

26

The restless woman with one leg senses trouble.

British secret agent Virginia Hall wakes up knowing she needs to make a decision. She lies in her small room at the Grand Nouvel Hotel, just off the *centre ville*.

Lyon is gray. Plane trees along the Rhône River shed their leaves. It is the season for switching from sweaters to jackets and waiting for the inevitable first snowfall.

Hall has been in France seven weeks. Rather than parachute, like other operatives, she took advantage of her American nationality to travel by ship to Lisbon, then by train into France. The United States is not at war with Germany, so her movements are not heavily restricted. Hall's cover is that of a journalist for the *New York Post*, filing stories from Vichy France. She dresses down to avoid being conspicuous, wearing workingwoman's tweed and heavy-soled shoes, covering her wooden prosthesis with thick stockings. Her official papers—forged back in London—give her name as "Brigitte LeContre."

And she is lonely.

The Special Operation Executive has become successful at landing agents in France. So while a great number of men have been dropped in by parachute, the nature of Hall's work is solitary. She is alone and exposed. Human connection comes when she stops off for a glass of wine at the hotel bar or dinner at a nearby Greek-owned restaurant where the smitten owner feeds her black-market food and refuses to accept her ration coupons. Hall is setting up her own network—code name Heckler—of informants and saboteurs, but that is still a work in progress. Hall even lacks a radio operator to help her communicate with London.

This is the life of a secret agent.

Hall knows this reality and accepts it rather than wallowing in fear or self-pity.

On this particular day, solitude is also a choice. Right now, Virginia Hall could be spending Friday night with a group of SOE agents two hundred miles south in Marseilles. Radio operator Gilbert Turck, code-named Christophe, has invited all agents in southern France to meet at a safe house on the edge of town known as the Villa des Bois—heavy gate, lush garden, the privacy of a suburban location. This is a fine opportunity for Hall to enjoy a smidgeon of companionship in the increasingly volatile world of Fortress Europe.

Tonight is Friday. A weekend by the Mediterranean, particularly under the guise of writing a travel story for the *Post*, would be a great getaway from Lyon, a most dour city in central France now full of starving refugees. At the very least, Hall could feel the sun on her face.

This should be an easy decision, but something is not right.

Christophe is known to have hit the ground hard when he parachuted into France two months ago. Knocked unconscious, he was discovered by Vichy authorities and taken to jail. But for reasons unknown, Christophe was released.

Then, two weeks ago, during another parachute drop, the plane was forced to circle at low altitude for half an hour as the pilot searched for the drop zone. The "Corsican Mission," as the four agents were known, finally managed to jump. Three operatives landed successfully but Lieutenant Daniel Turberville, code-named Diviner, was blown far off course. His head struck a rock upon landing. Once again, the police found an unconscious SOE operative and took him to prison. But as Turberville was taken into custody, his captors found a map leading to a safe house in Marseilles—Villa des Bois.*

Hall does not know about the map, nor that police can pinpoint the villa's location. There's just something strange about inviting every single SOE operative in southern France to the same location at the same time.

Virginia Hall trusts her gut—and something in her gut is telling her not to go to Marseille.

. . .

VICHY POLICE HAVE a name for the Villa des Bois: the "mousetrap."

Feeling just as lonely and exposed as Virginia Hall, SOE agents flock to Marseille. One by one, they pull back the iron gate and knock on the door of Villa des Bois, hoping to see a friend. Maybe someone they knew from training.

Instead, they are grabbed by the waiting police. Each man is arrested. This group constitutes all the "piano players"—wireless operators—in southern France.

Charged with actions contrary to the security of Vichy France, the ten men are shipped to Beleyme Prison, two hundred miles west, in Périgueux. There, torture and questioning leads to more arrests.

---

* Lieutenant Turberville was taken to Beleyme Prison in Périgueux, but while being transferred to a prison in Lyon he escaped on December 2, 1941. The agent was taken in by farmers, who hid him for over a year. Turberville successfully returned to England via Spain in April 1943. Turberville served out the war as an SOE training instructor in England. A plaque in the French town of Beleymas commemorates the Corsican Mission.

The official SOE report calls the arrests a "clean sweep of the British organizers in the occupied zone."

In all of France, just one SOE agent remains. As official documents will note, there is "little left in the field except Miss Virginia Hall."

And, much to London's surprise, that is enough.

27

Winston Churchill needs good news.

The prime minister is in a foul mood. Churchill is spending the weekend at Chequers, his official country retreat. The room is cigars and Christmas, dignitaries and personnel: an ambassador, a bureaucrat, an attaché, a personal secretary. Churchill broods, so lost in worry that not even Pol Roger nor the enormous yule fir in the great hall decorated with ornaments, candles, and baked cookies can lift his mood. It is a long year and a half since Paris fell. The strain of standing alone grows heavier by the day, often bringing forth the "black dog," as Churchill refers to his lowest moments.*

Just this morning, intelligence reports confirmed the presence of Japanese naval vessels in waters near the British protectorate of Singapore. Churchill mulls whether to send a heated warning to Japan's

---

* The expression comes from a term used by Victorian nannies to describe a foul mood. "Black dog on my back" means to get up on the wrong side of the bed. However, Churchill's usage has been used by revisionist historians to suggest that he suffered from bipolar disorder. This has been widely dismissed, although it is clear that he suffered bouts of depression brought on by circumstances of the war.

leadership as a reminder to keep their distance. But that would be a bluff: Britain is going broke. The nation can barely afford to wage war in Africa, let alone open a second front in the Pacific. They are already receiving handouts of food, oil, and raw materials from America through a program known as lend-lease, which carefully skirts American neutrality laws. W. Averell Harriman, the wealthy and polished businessman chosen by President Roosevelt to administer the program, is among Churchill's guests tonight. Left unsaid is that the fifty-year-old Harriman is having an affair with Pamela, the winsome twenty-year-old wife of Randolph Churchill, the prime minister's only son.*

Noting the time, Churchill rises and turns on the radio.

"Here is the news, and this is Alvar Liddell reading it," comes the clipped, articulate voice of the BBC's famous evening reader. Liddell's self-introduction is an assurance to listeners that he is not a Nazi propagandist. When the thirty-three-year-old first began reading the news almost a decade ago, it was BBC policy for Liddell to wear a tuxedo while on the air. That dress code has been relaxed, but Liddell still dons a coat and tie as he broadcasts, his angular face freshly shaven so late in the evening, as if respectfully delivering the information in person.

It was Alvar Liddell whose soothing nightly reports kept England abreast of events throughout the "Battle of Britain" one year ago, when Adolf Hitler's attempted invasion was thwarted by the heroic efforts of the Royal Air Force. The city of London lay in rubble due to nightly German bombings, but Liddell was the upbeat voice of hope, sustaining the nation. On one occasion a bomb landed just outside the BBC's Portland

---

* Chequers has been the official country residence of British prime ministers since 1917. Built in the sixteenth century and renovated throughout the years, the mansion served as a convalescent home for British officers during World War I. Once again a private home after the war, Chequers was donated to Britain by Lord and Lady Lee of Fareham. The name Chequers is thought to derive from the coat of arms of a long-ago owner, which featured the checkerboard pattern associated with the crown's chief financial figure, formally known as the Exchequer. Churchill himself was Chancellor of the Exchequer from 1924 to 1929.

Place studio, causing an explosion clearly audible to listeners. Yet the unflappable Liddell kept calm and carried on as if nothing had happened.

And it was also Alvar Liddell who informed England about the German invasion of the Soviet Union in June of this year. Germany is now waging war in Russia, North Africa, Britain, and in the Mediterranean. This ends the possibility—for now—that Hitler might make another attempt to invade England.

Through it all, Winston Churchill has listened to Alvar Liddell most evenings, just like any normal Briton. So it is not unusual that he turns on the news despite having guests or the fact that radio reception isn't always strong forty miles outside London. Through the intermittent static comes snippets of headlines: "Japanese Navy . . . British ships . . . Dutch East Indies. Japan . . .

". . . *United States.*"

That is extremely odd.

Churchill sits in complete silence, straining to decipher details. His guests are equally confused. The mention of America among the wartime developments is unheard-of.

The butler steps from the kitchen. "The Japanese have attacked the Americans," he announces to the room.

Commander Charles Ralfe "Tommy" Thompson, Churchill's devoted naval envoy, adds a clarification. The Americans, he has deduced from the broadcast, appear to have been attacked at a place called "Pearl River."

This is confusing. The Pearl River is in China. Churchill knows nothing of an American presence in the Far East.

But Alvar Liddell is not done. He once again repeats the information about the attack on American forces, clarifying that it has taken place in Hawaii.

Churchill's foul mood is gone. In its place is a call to action. He announces that he is about to officially declare war on Japan. The attack means America must do the same.

Britain no longer stands alone.

"Good God," says John Gilbert Winant, the new American ambassador to Great Britain. His hair is black and creased on the left. The liberal Republican and former governor of New Hampshire is a private, often shy individual, prone to keeping his own counsel. But he and Churchill have become close friends over the last nine months, sharing the same nonstop work ethic. So Winant has no problem reining him in. "You can't declare war on a radio announcement."

Churchill cedes the point. This is a very dark hour for America. His rambunctious euphoria is replaced by the need to be a statesman. The prime minister turns to John Martin, his senior private secretary.

"Get me the president on the phone—at once."

. . .

IN THE BERKHAMSTED SECTION of Hertfordshire, at a villa known as Rodinghead, Charles de Gaulle entertains a weekend guest. Yvonne sits with the two men, prim in a long skirt, dark hair parted on the right. The family attended Sunday Mass this morning at the Church of the Sacred Heart on nearby Park View Road. The general then enjoyed a private stroll with their visitor, thirty-year-old André Dewavrin, code-named "Colonel Passy." Dewavrin is the general's chief intelligence officer and envoy to the British SOE.

"We came back from a long walk and sat down in armchairs in the drawing room," Dewavrin will write in his memoirs. The air is filled with cigarette smoke and confidential conversation. In just three weeks, a young Resistance leader named Jean Moulin will parachute into the South of France at de Gaulle's behest. Moulin bears a deep scar on his neck, the result of trying to slash his own throat while in Nazi custody last year. Acting on no authority but his own, de Gaulle has named Moulin his delegate of the French National Committee of the unoccupied zone. To convince any skeptics of the veracity of claims Moulin might make in his name, the Resistance will carry a small matchbox concealing a microfilmed document signed by the general. "Mr. Moulin's task is to bring about, within the zone of metropolitan France not directly occupied, unity by all elements resisting the enemy and his collaborators," according to Dewavrin.

Moulin's trademark is a scarf worn at all times to hide the failed suicide. De Gaulle, who considers the dashing, dark-haired Moulin "a great man, great in every way," is in charge of unifying France's many resistance groups so that they might wage war in a coordinated manner.

The importance of Moulin's mission cannot be overstated. This is the general's most significant effort at taking control of the Resistance, just as he controls the Free French Forces in Africa and the Middle East. Even from a remove, commanding a fighting force of Frenchmen within France is a bold step forward.

Meanwhile, as the men talk, the introverted Yvonne remains in the room, no one's idea of a security threat.

Like Winston Churchill, now just fourteen miles away at Chequers, Charles de Gaulle turns on the radio. The news is shocking: *Radio Londres* is announcing the Japanese bombing of Pearl Harbor.

It is too soon to know details about the thousands of American men who lost their lives, the sailors hideously disfigured by fire and shrapnel, nor an exact count of the ships sunk. But de Gaulle is a warrior. He knows exactly what happens to men when bombs explode in their midst and when long machine-gun bullets pierce soft flesh. The general knows precisely how the air smells when a man is burning and the specific octave of the piercing screams let loose by dying boys who will never again chug a cold lager, pray an Our Father, or revel in the carnal heat of entering a woman lying naked below him.

And Charles de Gaulle does not care.

America is joining the fight. Pearl Harbor is an answered prayer.

"The war is now definitely won!" de Gaulle exults.

Yvonne walks alone into the kitchen. Getting down on her knees, she prays that this is so.

28

J ean Moulin sees the light.

And it's green.

The resistant sits on the wooden floor of the twin-engine Royal Air Force Armstrong Whitworth Whitley, wrapped in a blanket as the signal to jump flashes. Coastal German flak rocked the bomber as it crossed into France but the journey has been calm since. Moulin wears his parachute like a backpack, thick straps and buckles riding up over his shoulders and wrapping around his waist and upper legs. He carries a bag of sandwiches. Egress is from a rectangular door just aft of the leg wing.

The fuselage is too cramped for a man to stand upright. Moulin and his two Resistance compatriots crawl to the open hatch. Full moon. A night as cold as charity. Somewhere below is an olive grove and stone farmhouse near the village of Eygalières. Moulin knows the plot of land well: he owns it.

The former prefect spent December in the British Midlands, visiting repeatedly with Charles de Gaulle and also learning to parachute. Now he leaps into the night with his two fellow agents. A fourth canopy follows them to the ground, radio swinging beneath its canopy.

Moulin's cover story is that he is a retired administrator, which is true. His face and that telltale scar on his neck are well known, so there is no sense in trying to hide. More important is his Resistance code name: "Max." It is an alias that will become legendary in the French Resistance.

The Whitley has already turned for England by the time Moulin lands twelve miles off target in a marsh. His shoes are soaked. He can't find the sandwiches. The local mistral wind adds to Moulin's misery, followed by a hard predawn rain.

But Jean Moulin is in France, come to unify the Resistance in the name of Charles de Gaulle. The three resistants find the radio, then set about searching for the farmhouse.

Unification, however, can wait. Jean Moulin has pledged his loyalty to Charles de Gaulle. Yet he is no less enamored of his lover, the fetching Colette Pons. Moulin envisions ten days of skiing in the Alps.

A chalet is the perfect place to rekindle their flame.

29

The chapel is a perfect place for prayer. This small stone building was once a place of worship. Now it is a holding cell.

Monday morning. A wooded hilltop fortress outside Paris. Armed guards outside the thick wooden doors. Two tall stained glass windows letting in pale winter light. Benches without a backrest, once pews, offer a place to sit. The whitewashed walls are dingy and covered in handwriting. Seven members of the Groupe du Musée de l'Homme stand together for the last time in their lives, talking nervous and wondering inside if death will hurt.

It is almost seven weeks since a German court sentenced Pierre Walter, Léon Maurice Nordmann, Georges Ithier, Jules Andrieu, René Sénéchal, Boris Vildé, and Anatole Lewitsky to be shot. The women in their group, including librarian Yvonne Oddon and art historian Agnès Humbert, were also convicted. French law prevents the execution of a woman, so they have been sentenced to five years hard labor in a German concentration camp instead. If it can be considered lucky to be allowed to live behind barbed wire, endure brutal discipline, and live on a starvation diet, then that can be said of these women from Groupe du Musée de l'Homme—the Germans much preferring to transport convicted women to Germany for a quick beheading.

The group was at the forefront of homegrown rebellion until the first arrests were made a year ago in January. *Résistance* lit a fire in the people of Paris that burned far beyond this group of museum employees.

"It is so inspiring to know that there are thousands and thousands of Parisians, anonymous and unknown, working like us—often better than us—to organize a resistance movement that will soon become a liberation struggle," Agnès Humbert journaled just a few days before her own arrest in March.

The group lives on. Germaine Tillion, a thirty-four-year-old ethnographer from the Musée de l'Homme, has taken charge of the Resistance activities. Even as the arrests continued throughout 1941 her identity was never revealed. Tillion originally joined the organization to "do something," not knowing what that might be. She now runs a network numbering several hundred operatives. Tillion has boldly come to the prisoners' aid, sending food when she can, and even wrote a letter to Adolf Hitler requesting clemency for the condemned. Tillion is in touch with Britain's SOE. Not having a radio of her own, she works closely with the one-legged Virginia Hall in Lyon to transmit information back to London.

And yet, despite Tillion's almost miraculous ability to avoid detection, the Nazi investigation of the Groupe du Musée de l'Homme was exceptionally thorough. Information was gathered through torture and paid collaborators, leading to a series of arrests spread out over several months. The men and women were incarcerated first in Cherche-Midi Prison before being transferred to the equally medieval Fresnes penitentiary south of Paris. The Nazis are making Fresnes their preferred choice for captured Resistance and SOE operatives. Once again, however, it is the Groupe du Musée de l'Homme who have had the distinction of going first.

The trial itself was on January 8 of this year. The charge was espionage.

Then came the waiting.

It is forty-six long days since the verdict. Each man in this chapel has been forced to sit and contemplate his impending death. Forty-six days without hope or a future. Ample time to ponder at length the patriotic decision to be resistant and whether that choice will make a lasting difference. They will never know. Written on these walls are the last words of men who went before—condemned who knew precisely how the Groupe du Musée de l'Homme feel right now. Seventy prisoners were shot here on a single day in December. Many scratched farewells into the rock before being led to the post.

It is bitter cold. The chapel is unheated. Execution posts rise from the frozen mud one hundred yards outside. Patches of snow litter the forest where they will be shot. Soldiers wearing ankle-length gray winter coats and black gloves make small talk, bitch about the cold, and tell bad jokes as they wait to do their job. Hell of a way to start the week.

Finally, the Germans come for the condemned.

The chapel doors open. The seven are led out. Unnervingly, they break into song. "The beautiful green hills, French country in full splendor," the men cry, the words of "Vive la France" echoing across the hilltop.

"How beautiful life can be. It feels like a romance. Vive la France. Vive la France."

Long live France.

Shooting seven men requires a massive firing squad. At least sixty armed soldiers face the prisoners as they are lashed to the thick wooden poles, hands tied behind their backs. The executioners stand extremely near—almost close enough to touch. The German teenagers listen for the order to *ziel*—aim.

The view from Mont-Valérien is spectacular, all of Paris spread out beneath the mountain, the Seine a thick artery coursing through a city once revered for its intellectual light and freedom.

A blindfold is placed over the eyes of all seven. They have seen Paris for the last time. Boyish German soldiers find it unnerving to look into the eyes of a man as they kill him, so the courtesy of a blindfold is as much for the firing squad as the men being shot.

No one misses.

Yet the Resistance lives on.

Vive la France.

CASABLANCA

30

Paris is damned.

And Winston Churchill is no longer of a mind to be its savior.

Saturday night has given way to Sunday morning. Churchill speaks animatedly with Harry Hopkins, President Franklin Roosevelt's gaunt and sarcastic special envoy. Brandy. Political seduction. Cigars.

Another American has flown to London to meet with Churchill, but U.S. Army chief of staff George C. Marshall is an early riser. Like Churchill's wife of thirty-four years, Clementine, and most of the prime minister's weekend guests, the general has said his good nights.*

Yet, as Churchill well knows, Harry Hopkins did not fly across the

---

* Marshall's frustration with Churchill's late hours did not go unnoticed. "There was a great charm and dignity about Marshall which could not fail to appeal to one," British general Alan Brooke will write in his journal. "He was evidently not used to being kept out of his bed until the small hours of the morning and not enjoying it much!"

dangerous Atlantic for a good night's sleep. Roosevelt's envoy is the sort of complex man Churchill finds intriguing: well-read, married three times, widowed once, resides in a White House bedroom that once served as Abraham Lincoln's study, dying of stomach cancer. Above all, Hopkins is Roosevelt's right-hand man, ordered around the world, precarious health no matter, convincing foreign leaders that enacting policy in America's interests also serves their own.

Thus, this late-night conversation.

Chequers' household staff waits up, yawning, the breakfast service just hours away. Most servants will not sleep until Churchill calls it a night, yet the prime minister shows no sign of going to bed. Hopkins says a telegram is expected from Washington.

Harry Hopkins keeps talking. He is a pleasant man with a nasal voice and habit of tilting his head to the right as he speaks. The purpose of the London trip is selling the idea of invasion to Churchill. Roosevelt wants a landing in France. Right away. Paris might be liberated by Christmas. The prime minister opposes this preposterous notion for reasons of his own. Churchill is avoidant, preferring to put this matter before his Defence Committee and deflect decision. Hopkins fell ill after his arrival in London four days ago, a delay allowing Churchill time to plot. The meeting will now be held the night of April 14.

President Roosevelt first broached a European landing to Churchill one month ago. "I am becoming more and more interested in the establishment of a new front this summer, certainly for air and raids," Roosevelt glibly wrote on March 9. The arrival of Hopkins and Marshall is a follow-up to the prime minister's underwhelming response: "Even though losses will doubtless be great, such losses will be compensated by at least equal German losses."

Not surprisingly, Hopkins agrees with Roosevelt. He explains to Churchill that public opinion is fickle. Delaying a European invasion will shift the war against Germany to the back burner in the minds of most Americans, moving revenge against Japan to the forefront.

In a strategy drawn up by General Dwight Eisenhower, chief of America's War Plans Division, an assault known as Operation Sledgehammer will land troops on the French coast this autumn to secure a toehold in Europe.

Churchill thinks Sledgehammer is suicide.

But he does not use those words.

Harry Hopkins plies his persuasion, lightly pressing the prime minister to see things America's way—the *Allies'* way.

Even at this late hour, Churchill speaks cautiously, making no promises. He knows how to deal with men like Hopkins, just as Hopkins knows how to deal with men like Winston Churchill..

To Churchill, if the Americans intended to re-create Dunkirk in 1942, they could not have hatched a better plan. The reasons are numerous, starting with vastly superior German manpower. An estimated twenty-five to thirty Wehrmacht divisions—roughly a half million soldiers—stand ready to repel an invasion of France. At most, Britain could land six divisions and the Americans two or three— less than 100,000 troops. Left unsaid is that the British are still scarred from Dunkirk and U.S. troops have never heard a shot fired in anger.

"These were very newly raised," Churchill will write, referring to the freshly drafted American soldiers. "It takes two years and a very strong professional cadre to form first class troops."

Operation Sledgehammer landings would take place at Brest on the Breton coast or at Cherbourg in Normandy. Both are industrial ports located at the tips of long peninsulas. If the landing force is not immediately thrown back into the sea and somehow establishes a beachhead, the Germans would respond by sealing all routes onto the peninsula. Allied forces will be cut off. The Nazis then have the tactical luxury of patiently inflicting endless days and nights of artillery barrages and aerial bombardment. The final act will be the slow encroachment of panzers and foot soldiers.

There would be no escape. And once again Great Britain will suffer most.

"The operations would have to be almost entirely British. The Navy, the air, two-thirds of the troops, and such landing craft as were available must be provided by us," Churchill will write with exasperation.

"Neither we nor our professional advisers," the prime minister adds, referring to his political cadre and military chiefs of staff, "could devise any practical plan for crossing the Channel with a large Anglo-American army and landing in France before the late summer of 1943."

. . .

THE TELEGRAM ARRIVES at 3:00 a.m.

The courier delivers it to Harry Hopkins, who reads it and gingerly hands the delicate message to Winston Churchill. The single scrap of paper is a note from President Roosevelt. His tone is scolding and parental, a blatant attempt to dictate British policy as regards not Europe but their enormous colony of India. Hopkins knows the president has overstepped but can only brace himself for what comes next. Four months after declaring war, America is inserting itself into global matters beyond their immediate concern.

Churchill explodes. Chequers is asleep. He does not care. The prime minister swears blue, an outraged howl echoing off the polished hardwood floors, portraits of predecessors, enormous marble fireplace, polished brass pokers, and towering chandelier dangling from the Great Hall ceiling. Roosevelt's telegram is advice, an idealistic American suggestion. Nothing more. But the prime minister is being squeezed, with Roosevelt using the leverage of altering American manufacturing to provide guns and airplanes as a pretext for a bold attempt to dictate.

Winston Churchill does not like being squeezed.

And he certainly does not like being told what to do.

Harry Hopkins, witnessing the fit of rage, endures. He has been sent on a mission to convince a man with few options to swallow a bitter pill. Now this man shows backbone.

The envoy is a chameleon, a listener, an intuitive. A very good man. So he knows it would now be a miracle if the British accept Operation Sledgehammer, particularly after President Roosevelt just tried to force-feed Indian independence upon a prime minister born of a syphilitic politician father and beloved American mother, a man who has overcome twenty years of political shame and the embarrassment of harassing creditors to hold the highest political office of Britain—something even his self-absorbed father could not attain—only to achieve this honor at a time when Great Britain is not just on the verge of financial ruin but also sucked into the midst of a world war.

And now this: the president of the United States is telling him to break up the British Empire, the only prideful possession Britain and Churchill still enjoys, a century-old collection of colonies and protectorates so vast and global upon which, it can truthfully be said, the sun never sets.

Churchill, as a man and proud citizen of his nation, is in fact in the process of losing absolutely everything. This is not a mild setback, like the time Clementine gave the edict "No more champagne" because debts owed his wine merchant were too high.

Everything: Office. Nation. Empire.

No wonder the prime minister is barking profanity in the dark of night.

Hopkins cannot say so. Not yet. But the special envoy knows he has lost.

Time for bed.

As the two men shuffle to their bedrooms, the prime minister clearly does not want to squander a single British life on a hasty, ill-advised American plan for invading France just to keep U.S. citizens happy. Great Britain has been at war two years, while America has barely dipped a mighty toe in the conflict.

As degrading as occupation might be for citizens of Paris, now is the time for caution.

Not invasion.

31

And besides, Winston Churchill has an invasion plan of his own. The prime minister, believing that wherever he pulls up a chair is the head of the table, sits in the middle of the long, rectangular working space here in the Cabinet Room, his back to the ceiling-high bookshelves, fireplace, and oil painting over the mantel. Seated nearby are Harry Hopkins and General George C. Marshall, nearing the end of their week in London. Also in attendance is Churchill's Defence Committee (Operations) to discuss a final verdict for Operation Sledgehammer.*

Lingering over the meeting is the reality that in some ways it was easier for England to stand alone. Churchill and his war cabinet made unilateral strategies, placing the nation's interests above all. Churchill was Daddy Warbucks to a flailing French government during the

---

* The Defence Committee (Operations) was chaired by Churchill, with membership including the ministers of each branch of the military service and his chiefs of staff.

war in France, providing soldiers and aircraft at Great Britain's convenience—and pulling them off the line when it suited the nation's best interests. The relationship with Charles de Gaulle and the Free French maintains the same needy dynamic, although de Gaulle has lately shown signs of petulance, chafing at any perceived British interference in his own version of this war.

But America is now the strongman. Churchill must tiptoe.

Operation Sledgehammer is being thrust upon Great Britain. Rejecting the plan risks alienating the prime minister's long-overdue ally. Weakly accepting Sledgehammer is a national betrayal. "I had to work by influence and diplomacy in order to secure agreed harmonious action with our cherished ally, without whose aid nothing but ruin faced the world," Churchill will recall.

So Churchill puts on a charm offensive. He speaks to Marshall and Hopkins about "two nations marching shoulder to shoulder in a great brotherhood of arms."

The prime minister writes President Roosevelt, assuring him that any disruption of the relationship between their two nations "would break my heart and surely deeply hurt both our countries at the height of this terrible struggle."

Churchill is justifiably proud that the British Army is reborn since Dunkirk, now numbering more than 2 million men in uniform. This is the greatest fighting force in British history. A large number of these troops have already been sent to protect Britain's colony in Egypt. Winston Churchill is determined not just to *survive* Adolf Hitler—he means to *defeat* the Führer. The formation of the Special Operations Executive was a vital first step. The next is finding a place for his army to pick a fight.

Churchill chooses North Africa.

The decision was made in the summer of 1940. In Churchill's plan, taking control of North Africa is just one step from invading Europe. From west to east along the Mediterranean coast—from the Straits of

Gibraltar to the Suez Canal—this desert land comprises six nations: French Morocco, French Algeria, French Tunisia, Italian-controlled Libya, and Britain's Egypt.

British troops have already pushed a much larger invading Italian army back out of Egypt, then kept advancing, pressing the attack several hundred miles into the desert nation of Libya. Nazi Germany, shoring up their weak Axis ally, joined the fight early in 1941. A newly formed German division known as the Afrika Korps, under the command of a man once referred to by British intelligence as the "obscure German General Rommel," has proven more than capable of defeating the British—having done so time and again over the last thirteen months.

Great Britain's armored divisions currently hold the line at the Libyan port of Tobruk, where they fended off an Afrika Korps siege through the spring and summer of 1941. There is every certainty that Rommel will attack again. In anticipation of a new German offensive against Tobruk, a series of Allied outposts known as the Gazala Line stands ready to repel the Nazis.

Just as Churchill is intrigued by the American Harry Hopkins, a complex ally but not quite a trusted friend now joining him at 10 Downing Street for this late night meeting, so Churchill cannot help but be fascinated by the wiles and cunning of Erwin Rommel, who has shown himself to be a singularly brilliant adversary. This January the prime minister even rose in the House of Commons to take the extraordinary step of praising the Nazi general.

"We have a daring and skillful opponent against us," Churchill stated. "And may I say, across the havoc of war, a great general."

The words are heartfelt. Perhaps jealous. Britain has no such commander.

However much the prime minister might admire him, Rommel must be defeated. Only then can the second step of Churchill's private invasion plan unfold.

And that involves Italy.

Mare Nostrum, as Ancient Romans called the Mediterranean Sea, measures just a few hundred miles from North Africa to the Italian boot. The island of Malta is halfway. The Greeks, Romans, Arabs, and French have all held control of the temperate archipelago through the ages, but it is Britain who has held sway and maintained a naval base there since 1814. America is so far slow to insert itself into the war, but Churchill will wait for them, building his army over time, then use Malta as a jumping-off point to invade "the soft underbelly of Europe," as the prime minister will describe Italy.

Italian troops have shown themselves to be undisciplined and even afraid. The British Army has already fought them and won in North Africa, slaughtering 20,000 Italian soldiers and taking over 130,000 prisoners. In a scene reminiscent of Nero fiddling while Rome burned, one Italian general even sang opera as he was taken into custody.

This is the army Churchill wants to fight.

Much better to invade the Boot and fight Mussolini's army once more than invade France to face Hitler's Nazi steel.

. . .

TONIGHT'S LATE MEETING in the Cabinet Room follows a tight script. Churchill reiterates that British and American troops must wait until 1943 to land in France. Operation Sledgehammer should go away.

Discussion. Talk of a Sledgehammer feasibility study. But in the end America goes along. "We all agreed that there should be a cross channel operation in 1943. It was named, though not by me, 'Round-up,'" the prime minister will write.

Churchill has won.

Yet Churchill's fervor for his preferred battleground has not gone unnoticed.

As George Marshall will later note:

"Churchill was rabid for Africa."

32

An African sunburn can get you court-martialed.

There is nothing to see here. There is nothing to do here. There is only one reason to be here.

So it is that, 2,000 miles south of Paris, a Free French army prepares to *fight*.

Alone.

This unlikely group of castoffs will determine the fate of Winston Churchill's war in Africa. There are no British or Australian or American allies standing shoulder to shoulder out here in the middle of nowhere. Just 3,723 marines, Foreign Legionnaires, and colonial soldiers from Senegal, Madagascar, Central Africa, and Tahiti; two female nurses; and the commanding general's lover and chauffeur—both of whom are the same woman. There are Palestinian Jews and men of color and eastern Europeans who lost their homes to the Germans and joined the Legion's misfits and mercenaries to get revenge.

Here, everyone is a Frenchman.

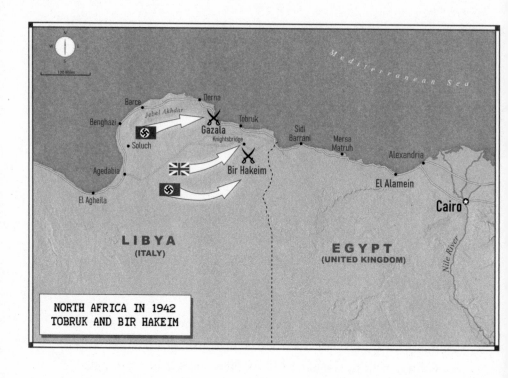

General Charles de Gaulle personally petitioned the British government to arm these units under his authority and incorporate them into the Allied fighting. Now permission has come: France's chance to show its true mettle. The lonely and desolate outpost here at Bir Hakeim marks the first time since the fall of France that Free French soldiers are on their own to fight the Nazis.*

Their commander is General Marie-Pierre Koenig, a veteran warrior who has lived through many a fight. He served as an officer in World War I, fought in the sands of Morocco with the Foreign Legion in the 1930s, and was one of the first French officers to seek out Charles de Gaulle in London to offer his support. Koenig can be terse and distant. He lives the same Spartan lifestyle as his men, indulging in no luxury. In return, his soldiers adore him and bestow upon Koenig the affectionate nickname *le vieux lapin*—the "old rabbit."

As Koenig well knows, there is little worth fighting for at Bir Hakeim, yet absolutely everything is at stake. The ancient stone cisterns giving this old fortress its name, "Old Man's Well," are covered in drifting sand. The fort itself is little more than rundown cement shacks. Since February 14, these soldiers have lived in trenches dug out of limestone and sand, concealing their location and keeping away the sun with tarps, mesh, wooden planks, and even wings of crashed fighter planes. Flies swarm around mouths and nostrils, interfering with any attempt to eat food. Ever-present desert dust combines with beads of sweat to form lines and ridges on each man's face and makes it impossible to comb hair. The sun is so bright that men feel their eyeballs burn as they stare off into the distance day after day, scrutinizing every last detail of

---

* The French Foreign Legion was created by King Louis-Philippe in 1831 as a means of protecting his colonial empire. Membership is open to foreign nationals, but after three years of service a recruit can apply for French citizenship. The Legion is famously known as a place where an individual can take on a new name and identity to start a new life. Following World War II, many German soldiers did just that, fighting as Legionnaires in Vietnam, then known as French Indochina.

the rock-and-sand landscape, searching for the dust cloud of an advancing army.

Soldiers speak of the "cockroach," that maddening buzz in the brain from studying the unchanging horizon too long.

And the heat kills. A soldier cannot control whether or not there is enough water to hydrate properly. But letting the sun bake and blister the skin is a choice. "Considered a self-inflicted wound," one Legionnaire will write, "it was punishable by court martial, but it was very hard not to burn our necks, hands, and any exposed areas of skin. Red, raw, and in pain, the men would sometimes roll sweatily in the sand, in order to obtain some sort of barrier."

This miserable piece of hell offering no shade or creature comforts measures roughly three miles by three miles. The ground is flat sand with a section of mild elevation. Extensive minefields and barbed wire surround Bir Hakeim on all sides. When the convoys bringing water can't get through the fifty contested desert miles between Tobruk and Bir Hakeim, these soldiers lift the hood of a truck, unscrew the radiator cap, and siphon water for a rusty drink. The French have not been assigned to this pathetic desert crossroads so much as banished.

"South of us was nothing but the cruel dunes of the Sahara," notes one Legionnaire. "If Rommel—a hundred kilometers west—wanted to keep mobile and reach Egypt, he'd have to find a way to punch a hole through the formidable Allied defenses further north, or try to round the most southerly point, in which case Bir Hakeim would suddenly become pivotal.

"The French brigade had clear orders to hold our citadel at whatever cost."

The Free French anchor the southernmost point of the Gazala Line. This series of desert outposts represents the British stand against General Erwin Rommel and the Afrika Korps. After this, there is nothing to stop the Germans from taking Cairo if they break through.

The line's fifty-mile spine begins at Gazala, near the crucial port of Tobruk on the Mediterranean, then heads due south to Bir Hakeim—from palm trees and sea breeze to badlands. Garrisons are spaced roughly ten miles apart. Each is controlled by a different nationality: South Africans, British, Indians, French. In all, approximately 90,000 Germans and Italians armed with 560 tanks face off against 110,000 Allied troops with their 840 tanks—though not a single one is allocated to Bir Hakeim.

Yet the French role is to fight a defensive war, not take new ground. Thus, mines instead of tanks. The garrison is well fortified, with concealed supply dumps and anti-tank guns dug deeply into the earth. Trucks and cars are also hidden in deep bunkers, then covered, completely invisible from the air. Every two weeks the men are rewarded with the long drive north to the Mediterranean, there to strip down and splash in the sea for a few hours. In between, the greatest enemy is boredom.

But in all of the world right now, there is no place more important than Bir Hakeim.

And the Free French vow to hold it to the last man.

And woman.

.   .   .

THE FATE OF Bir Hakeim is also in the hands of a small, brilliant Nazi strategist. What General Erwin Rommel will do and won't do is on everyone's mind.

The "Desert Fox," as he is widely known, has become mythic. Legendary. Unstoppable. One does not attack Rommel. That would be stumbling into a trap, even if none is set, for the aggressive general with the Swabian accent seems always three steps ahead.* One simply

---

* Swabian is a German dialect favored by residents of southern Germany. Individuals speaking standard German, such as residents of Berlin to the north, often find it

waits for Rommel to appear out of nowhere, riding with his lead column of panzers, unleashing mayhem. Not a single Allied soldier in North Africa doesn't fear the sudden arrival of his Afrika Korps. Not a single Allied general doesn't wonder if he possesses the cunning and guile necessary to defeat Rommel.

Not one.

Through burning days and subzero nights, the specter of Rommel hangs over the Libyan landscape like one of the sudden vicious sandstorms that blow out of the desert without warning, coating the world in a fine yellow layer of grit, seeping into ears, tears, pores, and straight up the pant legs of the knee-high shorts worn by the Free French into the unseen cracks and folds of a man's groin until all he feels is the chafing that brings withering pain every single time he moves.

Rommel is world-famous and yet a phantom.

He is death.

And he is coming.

The only question is when.

. . .

ROMMEL DOESN'T COME in person for Bir Hakeim. Not at first.

The time is 0930 when three months of waiting comes to an end. A battalion numbering between sixty and eighty tanks, followed by truck-borne infantry and artillery, advance toward the minefield and rolls of barbed wire, "firing indiscriminately as they came, the squeaking of their tracks adding to the fearful cacophony," writes one defender.

The tanks are Italian Carro Armato M13/40s, slow and underpowered, with a too-thin inch of armor forcing the four-man crews to pile sandbags around the turret and across the hull to stop shells and bullets. But the French positions are so well camouflaged that the Italians do not know where to aim. All they see is desert. Unable to target the

---

hard to understand. In Rommel's case, his Swabian accent was most noticeable in times of excitement.

dug-in Legion guns—or any of the camouflaged defenders in their rabbit warren bunkers—the Italians roll forward through the sea of anti-tank and antipersonnel mines on Bir Hakeim's perimeter, sure of victory.

Suddenly the lead tanks are on their own—a tragic mistake in armored warfare. The French 75mm guns have an accurate range of well over a mile. They shell the infantry convoy trailing behind the tanks with deadly accuracy. Troops of the 8th Bersaglieri Regiment are still sitting in their transport trucks when a barrage of heavy fire reduces them to literally nothing. Seeing their comrades' fate, panicked drivers scramble to drive out of range, taking with them the Italian infantry, leaving the M13/40s with no foot soldiers to follow up on their penetration deep into the French minefields.

The proper course of action is to reverse until more infantry arrive. But the 132nd Armored Division—also known as the Ariete Armored Division (*ariete* is Italian for *battering ram*)—mistakenly believe Bir Hakeim is defended by just a handful of men. The armored advance continues, but it is the Ariete who get battered.

The French response is unrelenting.

By 10:00 a.m. it is over. Almost every Italian tank is destroyed. Over one hundred of their soldiers are now prisoners.

The Free French suffer just two casualties.

Then, amazingly, the Italians add to their losses. A column of infantry coming late to the fight advances upon Bir Hakeim and sees the familiar sight of Italian vehicles parked outside the fort. Not knowing these trucks have been abandoned, and thinking the French outpost already conquered, they promptly march straight toward Bir Hakeim, where they are taken prisoner.

Yet even as General Koenig, the driven commander of Bir Hakeim, revels in this minor comedy, he cannot relax.

The Free French did not defeat the German Afrika Korps today. General Rommel thinks so little of Bir Hakeim's defenders that he sent only his Italian allies to take the citadel. In fact, General Koenig will later learn that Rommel promised the Italians it would take "only fifteen minutes" to capture the fort.

Koenig knows something else: General Erwin Rommel is on the move.

And one day Rommel will come to do business with Bir Hakeim.

The Desert Fox has no choice.

33

T he Americans are making a movie.

Seven thousand miles from the Libyan Desert, on the closest patch of sand twenty-one miles away on Santa Monica Beach, the third day of filming a brand-new motion picture about the war in North Africa begins on Soundstage Eight here at Warner Bros. Studios. The action is set against the backdrop of Vichy Morocco. There are guns and death but the pistols fire blanks and no one really dies. Between takes, when hunger pangs and thirst prove too great, the actors can at the very least eat from their brown bag lunches and sip from a water cooler.

The film is called *Casablanca*.

And no one on the set today has knowledge that the Allies are secretly planning a very risky invasion of the real-life version of that African seaport. The plight of France has become a growing international cause célèbre due to the determination of General Charles de Gaulle, but this unlikely blend of romance and fascism will take de

Gaulle's message onto the silver screen for the first time. The world will see the general as the true leader of France, even if President Franklin Roosevelt does not.*

Tall green hills and swaying palm trees border one side of the Warner's lot. The exterior of Soundstage Eight is beige and nondescript like a warehouse, with roll-up cargo doors and a single bright light flashing red when filming is underway. Trucks are parked alongside the building. Painters and carpenters in workingman's clothes build sets. A paved road separates the soundstage from a studio office building.

Nothing special.

The glamour lies inside. Today is the first day filming will take place on the set representing Rick's Café, a mythical nightclub in Casablanca, where real-life refugees now rub shoulders with real-life Nazis and real-life Vichy officials as part of their daily existence—just like in the script.

The massive set is decorated with Moorish arches, small round tables, beaded lamps, padded chairs, and, as its centerpiece, an upright piano on casters. There are women in evening wear laughing gaily while sipping pretend champagne and men costumed to look like Nazi officers smoking real cigarettes. Off-screen, powerful lights hanging from the ceiling by chains cast down bright illumination. Director Michael Curtiz, with his thick Hungarian accent and a résumé that will one day include more than 150 Hollywood films, barks instructions.

Casablanca is based on the play *Everybody Comes to Rick's*, written shortly after the war began. The plot is almost prescient in its setting, predicting North Africa as the war's melting pot. The coauthors, a young teacher named Murray Burnett and writer Joan Allison, unable

---

* Such is the growing worldwide fascination with de Gaulle and his fight for French liberation that in the summer of 1942, Warner Bros. will commission a script entirely based on the general's life. Acclaimed novelist William Faulkner will write more than 1,200 pages of manuscript, but the project is never made.

to find a producer willing to put it on the stage due to undertones of adultery, sold it to Warner Bros. for $20,000.*

Burnett and Allison have not been asked to write the screenplay, which deviates from the play and is not yet complete. Just as with the war itself, the actors do not know how the movie will end. So Curtiz is filming the script sequentially, starting at page one with scenes already written, shooting in the same order they appear in the script. Most of the production will take place right next door on Stage Seven, soon to be known as known as "Lucky Seven" for the string of hit movies filmed there. *Casablanca*'s romantic lead, prickly Humphrey Bogart, a forty-two-year-old Hollywood veteran best known for playing gangsters and getting shot in the last reel, filmed the drama *Dark Victory* on Stage Seven. Director Curtiz just finished filming *Yankee Doodle Dandy* on Stage Seven, a patriotic song-and-dance movie starring James Cagney, another actor more known for portraying gangsters. So there is a comfort level to shooting on Seven.

But the set for Rick's Café is large enough to require a soundstage all its own. Now the statuesque twenty-six-year-old Swedish actress Ingrid Bergman sits next to the saloon piano in a low-cut white dress, sipping a glass of champagne. Bergman is a beautiful woman, blond, with an open face and kind eyes. She is not thrilled to be making *Casablanca*, having hoped to get the part of Maria in *For Whom the Bell Tolls*, based on the book by Ernest Hemingway. Yet here she sits.†

Curtiz is accentuating that beauty by filming Bergman with gauze over the lens to soften her appearance. Special lights catch the sparkle in her eyes. The name of Bergman's character is Ilsa Lund and she has a past. Ilsa is "bad luck," as another character describes her.

---

* More than $350,000 in today's currency. At the time, this was the most money ever paid for an unproduced play.

† That decision would be reversed. Bergman would actually go on to play that role. Filming would begin in July, shortly after completing *Casablanca*.

"Action!" cries Curtiz.

"Playing" the piano is a career musician named Dooley Wilson. A drummer by trade, the fifty-six-year-old Wilson wears a shiny satin tuxedo with thick lapels and a bow tie. He sits with perfect posture on the small piano bench, drapes his fingers over the keyboard just so, and even moves his hands to the right and left as if reaching for a chord—yet Wilson does not actually play a note.*

Wilson's character is Sam. Ilsa knows him well, from a time before the war in Paris. She wants to hear an old favorite song. Like a siren, Ilsa is hoping her former lover will hear their song and come to her.

"Play it, Sam," coos Ilsa in words that will become iconic. "Play . . . 'As Time Goes By.'"

"Oh, I can't remember, Miss Ilsa," protests Sam. "I'm a little rusty on it."

"I'll hum it for you."

Sam plays, but only the melody. Not satisfied, Ilsa asks him to also sing the words. "As Time Goes By" is a powerful statement that love will exist for all time, whether in war or peace. Sam croons in a voice low and comforting: "It's still the same old story . . ."

The completed movie will cut to Bogart, playing the namesake owner of the club, looking like he's on the verge of murder, entering the scene through a tall wooden door, resplendent in a double-breasted white dinner jacket. Walking slowly at first, then picking up speed, Rick makes a beeline for the piano.

Rick speaks through pursed lips, furious. "Sam, I thought I told you never to play—"

---

* Dooley Wilson did not know how to play the piano. Several musicians will later take credit for playing the actual notes to "As Time Goes By" for *Casablanca*. A friend of Wilson's named Elliot Carpenter is the individual most often given credit, although forensic musicologists have sided with a studio musician named Jean Plummer. Others give credit to another musician, William Ellfeldt. All three were on set during the two days it took to shoot the scene.

He stops short.

With a roll of his eyes and nod of the head, the piano player directs Rick's attention to Ilsa.

Curtiz yells, "Cut!" The camera is repositioned as the scene moves from the piano to a table in the corner. Other actors enter, among them Austria-Hungary–born Paul Henreid, who fled the Nazis and came to America before the war. As the new scene begins filming, the script contains dialogue about rationing and a curfew.

The new scene tells more about the main characters. Rick and Ilsa share their story in throwaway lines and short vignettes. They were a couple the day Paris fell. But the Nazi occupation marked the end of their love affair. Ilsa's husband, long thought dead, returned. Forlorn and angry, Rick has taken to drinking alone and refusing to let his saloon's piano player sing their favorite song.

"I remember every detail," Rick now tells Ilsa about June 1940. "The Germans wore gray. You wore blue."

"Yes," Ilsa replies, "I put that dress away. When the Germans march out I'll wear it again."

She wants him back. Someday. But not until Paris is free.

It's all pretend. A movie taking creative liberties. And yet, in the midst of a real-life war with no end in sight, Hollywood moviemakers with more belief in making money than making right are well aware that a Paris without Nazi occupation is a potent symbol of renewal, hope, and even true love that all the world will understand.

A fight for love and glory. A case of do or die.

That ideal keeps the men of Bir Hakeim fighting.

34

Erwin Rommel's surrender order comes at dawn.

It is one week since the Italians first attacked Bir Hakeim. Two unknown soldiers in desert khaki now slither through the perimeter minefield, pressing their bodies as flat as humanly possible against the earth, desperate to make it inside the safety of the fort without getting killed. French riflemen fire lazily at the intruders. The garrison's fourteen hours of withering sunshine are just beginning. Starting the day with potshots at anything that moves is a fine way to pass the time.

The intruders call out in English. They are British. Prisoners of war. Rommel has released them to deliver a message.

Slowly, rising to their feet, the unknown soldiers hold up a single yellow piece of paper.

· · ·

THE DEFENDERS OF Bir Hakeim are fearless—and thirsty.

And too familiar with all-out war.

The great Rommel has still not personally led an attack on the outpost, but the general sends waves of light Italian tanks and seemingly indestructible Panzer IVs to shell Bir Hakeim every day. The panzers have an effective range of 120 miles, can race across the sand at 25 miles an hour, and launch a 75mm shell with deadly accuracy from four miles away, allowing their gunners to fire at will, taking their time to zero in on the garrison without fear of reprisal.

And unlike Rommel's dash across France, where he never seemed to have enough air support, the Desert Fox has complete control of the Luftwaffe flying schedule. Squadrons of Stuka dive-bombers scream down from the sky, unable to see the camouflaged French positions but dropping their payloads nonetheless. The German pilots even slide back their cockpits to drop baskets of hand grenades to detonate on impact.

"The Stukas were the worst," one Legionnaire will write. "I could hear them several miles away, like a vast swarm of bees droning in the distance . . . They looked like a plague of silver locusts hovering above us, with nothing to prevent them from swooping down and picking at our bleached bones."

An ammunition dump was hit a few days ago, not just causing a ground-shaking explosion but destroying precious artillery stores so vital to keeping the enemy at bay. Perhaps just as alarming, Rommel is focusing his attack on British positions farther north. The supply line from Tobruk has been cut. Water is running out. A typical ration is now a half cup per day. It used to be a half gallon.

"Rommel used every weapon at his disposal to rain firepower down on Bir Hakeim. He had made our destruction a personal objective," the same Legionnaire will write. "'I'll get the French, I'll get them,' he vowed."

The truth of the matter is that Bir Hakeim is now completely surrounded. This is no longer a battle but a siege. Ammunition will soon run out. Food too. And water in the desert is clearly a finite resource. Yet the Legionnaires, refusing to allow imminent death to get in the way of cleanliness, are already washing clothes, dishes, and mugs in gasoline and sand.

The troops curse the English, who seem to be doing nothing to save them, while also fighting with the ingenuity of the desperate. When the poorly armed land mine technicians of the Jewish Brigade Group holding one edge of the fortress are overrun, they fearlessly stand in the open, light the cloth fuses sticking from glass bottles of gasoline, then hurl these Molotov cocktails toward the gun slits of the oncoming tanks. Burning and screaming, the enemy stumble out of their turret hatches, only to be shot.

And rather than cower in anticipation of the next round of panzers advancing through the minefields, General Koenig goes on the offensive, sending hit teams out in the night to raid enemy positions, steal supplies, and capture enemy soldiers for interrogation.

Hawker Hurricanes of the Royal Air Force eventually begin flying to the rescue when the sandstorms allow, reminding the French they are not forgotten and shooting dozens of the slower-moving Stukas from the sky. Enemy tanks cannot fire upon Bir Hakeim during aerial combat for fear of striking one of their own low-flying aircraft, allowing the defenders to push back their protective tarps and applaud the action. The tall, extremely thin Koenig does not grumble about how long it took for Bir Hakeim to receive aerial support. Instead, the general radios his thanks. "*Bravo! Merci pour la RAF.*"

To which the British pilots respond: "*Merci à vous pour le sport.*"

Thank you for the sport.

Koenig's élan earns the defenders of Bir Hakeim respect, just as their ongoing refusal to back down is slowly gaining the interest of the many journalists gathered to cover the hostilities. The desert war is the lead story in London and New York. Reporters often drive out into the desert and report the fighting from a hilltop three miles away. The unlikely French resistance at Bir Hakeim—the defenders outnumbered and outgunned two to one—is bringing worldwide attention to the Free French and the cause of General Charles de Gaulle.

But this cannot last forever. It is only a matter of time before the fort is overrun.

Yet the French still cling to hope.

. . .

THE NOTE FROM Rommel is brought to the small van concealed below the earth serving as Koenig's headquarters. Barbed wire coils around his dugout. The demand is written by hand on a single sheet of lined yellow graph paper.

"To the troops of Bir Hakeim," reads the message. "Further resistance will only lead to pointless blood-letting. You will suffer the same fate as the two brigades which were at Got el Ualeb and which were exterminated the day before yesterday—we will cease fighting as soon as you show the white flag and come towards us unarmed. Signed: Rommel, General Oberst."

Koenig's chauffeur and lover is a courageous Englishwoman named Susan Travers. She will report that her general is flattered by such attention from a legendary leader like Rommel.

But General Koenig is not afraid. Not in the slightest.

"I'm in contact with Rommel," Koenig writes in a note distributed to all his officers, hunkered down in their fighting positions on the edge of the garrison. "He says if we don't surrender he'll make mincemeat of us. I told him to take a running jump."

The general punctuates his response by ordering his commanders to open fire with the big 75mm guns.

Koenig then closes the letter by wishing every one of his soldiers a simple prayer:

"Godspeed."

. . .

THE SUBTLE HEADLINE detailing the subsequent German attack will be found in the *Times* of London the following morning: "Axis Repulse at Bir Hakeim."

Then the outcome in a single sentence:

"An attack by the enemy on Bir Hakeim, which continued throughout Tuesday, failed."

Godspeed.

35

General Erwin Rommel has come for Bir Hakeim.

Not that he expects the battle to last long.

Rommel is so sure the fortress is about to fall that he sends a message to his own headquarters: "I shall be in Bir Hakeim in the morning."

He will fail, but only by a day.

The siege of Bir Hakeim is two weeks old. General Marie-Pierre Koenig has repeatedly asked his superiors at Allied headquarters for permission to withdraw. Time and again the British command refuses this request. And still he pleads. "Water and ammunition virtually exhausted," Koenig now radios Allied headquarters. "Cannot hold out much longer."

All radio signals are made in the clear, with no attempt to add code or a cipher. Takes too long. German eavesdroppers listen to every communiqué, so adept at the task that they not only translate messages in an instant but are able to differentiate the signature transmission style of each command's radio operator. This allows them to know the precise location of each Allied unit.

So the Afrika Korps and Erwin Rommel are well aware of Bir Hakeim's debilitating hardship.

Reporters bearing eyewitness to the carnage marvel that anyone is still alive against such a massive fusillade. The *New York Times* describes the fighting as "the thunderous climax of the Axis offensive against the tiny, desolate outpost at Bir Hacheim [*sic*]."

The French are not ready to quit, but morale is understandably rock bottom. The soldiers keep up their spirits by dreaming of simple delights like slurping water from a cold mountain stream or a night in prewar Paris, strolling along the Champs-Élysées under bright streetlights with a special girl. "I took my place," one Legionnaire will fantasize about sitting down for a meal in a "chic Parisian brasserie," then "inhaled delicious scents of herbs and wine, garlic and roasting meats wafting towards us from the kitchen."

The men are sleep-deprived and on edge, always bracing for the next wave of Stukas and incoming rounds from the lethal and invulnerable 88s. Artillery kills when shell fragments send metal flying in every direction, tearing through skin and vital organs. The French are protected when they stay in their deep holes. But an 88 round also puts forth a blast wave, a percussive increase in air pressure that does incredible damage to soft tissue and eardrums when the round lands close. And there is a third cause of death when an artillery shell lands: the heat wave. A shell actually generates furnace-like temperatures upon explosion, burning flesh and hair if the round lands close enough.

Thus, life during any barrage is a complicated calculus of avoiding shell fragments, the blast wave, and an inferno while attempting to return fire, all the while knowing that even death will not bring peace. For there is no tending to the dead in the midst of battle. The mortally wounded sprawl out in the open, bloating in the sun until the shells

German Panzers grind through Belgium, blazing a bloody road to Paris.

National Archives

Field Marshal Erwin Rommel. Note the habit of wearing two Knight's Crosses at once.   *Getty Images*

A German soldier hoards a stolen phonograph and a bottle of champagne around the time Paris fell. *National Archives*

German Wehrmacht troops use inflatable rubber rafts to cross the Meuse.

National Archives

Hitler in Paris. *National Archives*

Winston Churchill and an observer watch for German air attacks in southern England in the wake of the fall of France.   *National Archives*

The defenders at Bir Hakeim.   *Getty Images*

U.S. troops on a transport bound for North Africa during Operation Torch.
National Archives

Stuka dive-bombers in action over North Africa. *National Archives*

Allied leaders at the Casablanca Conference. Left to right: Henri Giraud, Franklin Roosevelt, Charles de Gaulle, and Winston Churchill.

Getty Images

Winston Churchill and the large corona-format cigar he made famous, the Romeo y Julieta.   *Getty Images*

The relationship between Churchill and Charles de Gaulle was often complex, as seen in this candid moment. *Getty Images*

President Franklin Roosevelt, the political mastermind who openly questioned Charles de Gaulle's authority. *Getty Images*

General Dwight Eisenhower, seen here as a two-star general in the early days of World War II. By 1944 he would be promoted to the five-star rank known as General of the Army, one of only nine men in U.S. history to hold that rank. *Getty Images*

General George S. Patton, shown with four stars and a polished steel helmet. *Getty Images*

Resistance organizer Jean Moulin, seen here before his telltale neck scar forced him to wear the scarf that would become his trademark. *Getty Images*

Germaine Tillion, hero of the Resistance. *Getty Images*

Virginia Hall, the restless woman with one leg.
Getty Images

Charles de Gaulle standing before the Arc de Triomphe. *Getty Images*

stop falling. Swarms of black flies descend in an instant and then grow fat by gorging on French corpses.

But even when all is quiet, the Free French are physically aware of life-threatening hardship. Vicious heat is made more unbearable by lack of water. Lips are cracked. Tongues are chalk. Clothes are ringed with white salt lines, having not been washed for days. Dust cakes every last bit of flesh. Cockroaches and weevils infest the few biscuits that remain.

And everywhere, as far as the eye can see, the Afrika Korps.

"As the sun set low on the horizon, all we could see were the menacing silhouettes of the German and Italian tanks, pressed in so close around us that they could no longer open fire for fear of hitting each other," a Legionnaire writes. "I feared that none of us would survive another day."

A surprise telegram is received from General Charles de Gaulle in London: "General Koenig, be aware—and tell your troops that the entire France is watching you, and that you are its pride."

Surrender is still an option. Rommel sends an emissary to the fort almost every day. Time and again, General Koenig orders Legionnaires at the perimeter wire to tell Rommel no. On one occasion the German messenger veers into a minefield while driving away, his vehicle exploding as it runs over a mine, offering the defenders a rare moment of black comedy.

But the holdouts can only last so long. Even Koenig's upbeat style of leadership is done.

"We are surrounded," General Koenig responds to de Gaulle. "Our thoughts are always near you. We have confidence. Long Live Free France."

36

C harles de Gaulle and Winston Churchill share a bottle of Scotch. Not the whole bottle. It's Wednesday. Churchill has another meeting in an hour. Just a Johnnie Walker and soda to take the edge off a fragile and decaying partnership. The two men attempt to connect behind closed doors at 10 Downing. The tall, thin man and the squatty bulldog sit as divided as their two nations, the distance between armchairs an English Channel separating the human embodiments of France and England.

And yet, tonight brings hope.

It is with intent, not coincidence, that Winston Churchill and Charles de Gaulle sit together on this, of all evenings. History does not record what is said or how Churchill parses his words to deliver a delicious morsel of highly classified information to the general, but the evening of June 10, 1942, will forever be remembered in the history of France.

"5:30," bluntly notes Churchill's engagement calendar in blue ink and tight cursive. "De Gaulle."

No mention of agenda. No church bell tolls to mark the starting time on the half hour—that distinctive sound has been reserved as a warning that the Germans have begun an invasion. Thus, London—indeed, all of England—has not heard the welcoming peal of a church bell for two years. But Churchill's news this evening is almost as significant as an invasion warning—such vital knowledge that it was necessary to summon the recalcitrant de Gaulle. No servants or staff are allowed in the room to refresh their drinks or take minutes, a most unusual break with protocol. But there can be no worry about spies, leaks, or carelessly uttered revelations. The stakes are too high and thousands will die if this news gets out.

June started off scorching hot. There has been absolutely no rain. Three days ago temperatures hit almost 100 degrees—cool for the Libyan Desert yet almost incendiary for balmy London. But the weather has been refreshing since, making the seven-minute drive around St James's Park from de Gaulle's Carlton Gardens headquarters to Churchill's residence and office pleasant enough to walk instead. Despite this short distance, and the amazing fact that their two points of view might frame the future of Europe, the two great leaders rarely speak, let alone meet in person. Travel and schedule are not the reason. Instead, both are men with great egos.

And right now those egos are frustrated.

"I never ceased to feel a unity with France," Churchill will explain. "People who have not been subjected to the personal stresses which fell upon prominent Frenchmen in the awful ruin of their country should be careful in their judgments of individuals."

But the prime minister is far more direct when speaking of de Gaulle: "I knew he was no friend of England . . . I understood and I admired, while I resented, his arrogant demeanor. Here he was—a refugee, an exile from his country under sentence of death, in a position entirely dependent upon the goodwill of the British government, and also now of the United States. The Germans had conquered his country. He had no real foothold anywhere. Never mind. He defied all. Always."

De Gaulle is no less sanguine about his relationship with Churchill.

"I was nothing. Not the semblance of a force or an organization was behind me," the general will write. "Only if I acted as the inflexible champion of the nation and the state could I win support among the French and respect from foreigners . . . precisely because I was alone and without power I had to climb the peaks and never afterward descend from that level."

More whisky. More soda.

The Americans have not been invited to this summit. They play no role in the bold gambit unfolding tonight. Churchill and de Gaulle are free to sip their drinks and focus on their own special relationship.

Not that the Americans would attend. Somewhat incredulously, Franklin Roosevelt still favors the pro-Nazi Vichy government despite their persecution of the Jews and fealty to Adolf Hitler. He continues to refuse recognition of Charles de Gaulle as the true leader of French people everywhere. "Well, Roosevelt—you see, he would make a pronouncement and that would be like the laws of the Medes and the Persians," General Dwight Eisenhower will recall about serving under the president. The reference is to the biblical book of Daniel concerning a belief that cannot be altered. "He said to me, de Gaulle is not a sovereign. The sovereignty rests with the French people. I am not going to recognize him in anything until the French people do."

The good news from Washington is that Roosevelt has just asked Congress for the biggest war appropriations bill in American history. The president is requesting $10 billion in new expenditures, of which $3 billion is specifically designated for the nation's allies. Britain and the Soviet Union are first in line, but should de Gaulle finally convince Roosevelt of his government's legitimacy, the Free French cause would benefit substantially.*

Which is why this meeting is so vital. The prime minister's news could presage France standing on its own. Under Churchill's direction,

---

* The appropriations would be worth more than $186 billion in today's currency.

Britain continues to arm Free French troops. Agents of his Special Operations Executive units are working closely with the French Resistance to gather intelligence, rescue downed airmen, and commit sabotage against Nazi and Vichy targets. Of great relief to General de Gaulle, Jean Moulin, the dashing young man who wears a scarf to hide a failed suicide attempt while in Nazi custody, is on the ground in France, successfully organizing the various bands of resistance into a single cohesive force loyal only to de Gaulle. Coincidentally, Moulin is based in Lyon, also the center of operations for Virginia Hall, the woman with one leg who continues to evade Nazi detection.

But those successes are now left for another discussion on another day.

It is time to talk about Bir Hakeim.

. . .

THE *FIGHTING* FRENCH, as the defenders are now called, are making a run for it.

The breakout will take place at midnight. Tonight.

Roughly twenty-four hours ago, an order was issued by British lieutenant general Neil Ritchie, commander of the Eighth Army in North Africa and the man to whom General Marie-Pierre Koenig of the Free French force reports. The lengthy defense of Bir Hakeim forced the Nazis to shift the focus of their fighting long enough for the British to receive crucial new supplies and fall back toward Egypt, there to make a new stand.

So it is no longer necessary to hold Bir Hakeim.

General Ritchie is ordering the French to get out.

This highly clandestine order came to Churchill as part of the regular battlefield status updates he so voraciously consumes.

Charles de Gaulle does not receive these briefings. So it is left to the prime minister to pass along information that might be of interest to the French cause.

Winston Churchill and Charles de Gaulle raise a glass to the breakout.

37

T he Free French fighters of Bir Hakeim are sleeping.

Or so it appears.

There is no moon. Teeth chatter in the bone-cold desert night. This war is waged in daylight. Both sides sleep through the darkness and greet the day with an artillery salvo. In the desert beyond the wire, all around, the Afrika Korps and General Erwin Rommel slumber in peace, waiting for dawn to finally bring Bir Hakeim to its knees.

Tomorrow is the big day. Finally, the defenders will be slaughtered for the transgression of waging war without a trace of pusillanimity—particularly the Jewish Brigade, whose presence in Libya has now been noted by the highest authorities in Berlin.

That is, if the French are still here.

A jittery Susan Travers sits in the front seat of her Ford "Heavy Utility" staff car. Behind her stretches a long single file line of cars, trucks, armored vehicles, and artillery. The Ford's windscreen has been intentionally broken and the shards removed lest an enemy bullet do the same and send shattered glass into her eyes. Sandbags line the staff car's interior walls to stop bullets. Travers is worried about the radiator, recently repaired after being punctured by a Stuka bomb fragment. And the Ford has not been driven in three weeks, which is worrisome, given its tendency to stall.

But most concerning of all is the journey soon to come, a life-or-death dash to safety.

Travers is thirty-two and will go down in history as the only woman to ever serve in the French Foreign Legion. She is British, with dark hair, a sharp nose, and breasts small enough that she openly admits no need for a brassiere. Her lover is General Marie-Pierre Koenig, a married Catholic with whom she had a torrid affair in the Middle East in the early days of the war and has now followed to the desert.

Koenig returns her passion with abandon, though not at this outpost. Since their first day at Bir Hakeim—ironically, Valentine's Day—he has refused to share her dugout cot or even hold her hand, feeling he should not enjoy sensual comfort if his men cannot do the same. There is also the matter of appearances—a married Catholic sleeping with a female underling. Such lack of moral probity would surely undermine his authority.

Yet Susan Travers refuses to leave, despite not so much as a kiss from her lover. The two nurses evacuated weeks ago, so Travers is the only woman at Bir Hakeim. "Where you go," she tells Koenig of her decision to remain, "I will follow."

Koenig now steps toward the car, looking every part the general. His cleaned and pressed uniform looks brand-new. He has just shaved. Mustache clipped. Should he be taken prisoner, Koenig will present himself to Rommel as a man to be respected.

But surrender is not the plan. For tonight, the besieged garrison of Bir Hakeim is making a run for it.

Everyone. Each commander knows the rendezvous point. Even the wounded are being evacuated.

And every *thing*.

Not a gun, not a car, not a 75mm artillery piece, not a grenade—not a single usable item—is being left behind. War is not cheap. General Marie-Pierre Koenig and the men of Bir Hakeim will need all this equipment when it comes time to fight another day.

The convoy began lining up immediately after sunset. Travers and the general are near the front. Bomb-clearing specialists known as sappers wearing special headlamps that minimize light went out shortly after dusk to clear a new path through the minefields, the lane just wide enough for the convoy to rumble through. Deviating too far to the right or left will mean explosion and death. Even worse, the deafening noise will awaken the sleeping Germans. Instead of just one or two soldiers losing their lives, the entire brigade could be slaughtered within minutes, just as Erwin Rommel has promised.

The men are excited but take care to whisper.

Travers turns the ignition at midnight. Koenig, next to her, stands up and pokes his head out through a hatch in the roof to oversee the departure. The long line quietly snakes forward. The Englishwoman follows a group of small treaded vehicles known as Bren carriers. Headlights off. Sticking close together to find the way.

Suddenly, an explosion lights up the night.

Too late, Travers realizes that the anxious drivers in front of her have veered into a minefield. Burning vehicles illuminate everyone around them. The Germans awaken in an instant, hastily firing phosphorous flares into the sky. Some glow bright red as they burst, while others shine green. Night becomes day. Every last vehicle is illuminated. Panicked French drivers leap from their cars, only to be killed as land mines detonate. German machine guns and artillery open fire, pummeling the convoy. Afrika Korps gunners fire tracer rounds to lock on their targets. The bullets give off blue light as they sail through the nighttime air, almost elegant in their deadly arc.*

"Drive straight ahead as fast as you can," yells Koenig. "Quickly! Quickly!"

Travers steps hard on the gas. Driving through the desert by day is a challenge requiring specific compass headings, the angle of the sun, and extreme attention to staying on whatever rocky path constitutes a road. Travers has no precedent for racing through the unknown without moon or headlights to show the way. She cannot act, only react, pushing the Ford relentlessly forward because there is no going back. "We slithered from one hole to the next, our wheels skidding as I reached speeds of forty miles an hour," she will remember. "The din inside the car was awful. The engine was revving, the rocks beneath us were banging the underside of the car . . . and the sound of explosions and shooting reverberated around us."

Travers drives four straight hours like this. She and Koenig pause for a small break in the middle of the desert, where the couple suddenly realizes they are completely alone. There is no sign whatsoever of the French garrison.

Having no other choice, Koenig orders Travers to drive on.

The sun rises.

"We continued across the desert for several more hours without seeing another living thing—just a convoy of abandoned British cars in the morning fog, their seats empty, their fuel and water almost certainly stripped. We didn't dare touch the cars in case they'd been booby-trapped," Travers will write. "My eyeballs burned with tiredness."

Finally, in midafternoon, Travers and the general arrive at the rally

---

* Tracer bullets feature a small pyrotechnic charge in the base that illuminates upon being fired. This allows the shooter to follow the course of the bullet and make corrections to increase accuracy. Typically, every fifth bullet in a magazine or machine-gun belt is a tracer.

point, a remote British outpost twelve miles south of Bir Hakeim. There to greet them is the British 17th Motorized Brigade—and no one else. When a despondent Koenig asks for news from the garrison, there is none. Traveling onward to another outpost, they are once again told that there are no other survivors.

The exhausted chauffeur takes a nap.

.   .   .

IT IS 4:00 P.M. when Susan Travers wakes up. She has been asleep an hour. Her head aches. Then, looking out onto the horizon, she sees a vision.

"What I saw was a thin line of men and vehicles on the unbroken desert horizon," she remembers. "The mirage kept moving towards us. Jumping up, I cupped my hands over my eyes and strained to see what was in front of me. To my astonishment and delight, I suddenly recognized the raggle-taggle group winding towards us as the remaining survivors of Bir Hakeim."

Travers shouts for Koenig to come look.

"The general stood beside me, clasping his chest and trying to catch his breath," Travers writes. As the survivors finally arrive, "the general was embracing them all, shaking their hands vigorously and patting them on their backs."

Bir Hakeim has been taken, but at great cost to the Germans. Afrika Korps casualties number more than 3,000.

French losses are also formidable: early reports show 763 Free French are missing or captured. Seventy-two are confirmed dead, adding to the hundreds who died in the siege.

As for the remainder of the garrison, all 2,400 have escaped.

.   .   .

THE BERLIN HIGH COMMAND issues a statement the following day claiming the Afrika Korps "stormed" the fortress to finally end the siege. But the real story leaks. Adolf Hitler is furious yet forced to admit the truth. He continues his war of words with Winston Churchill by sharply insulting the British, who still display no sign of being able to defeat the German army. "This shows again," the Führer tells a reporter, "that the French are still, after us, the best soldiers in Europe. After this war, we will definitely have to set up a coalition that can militarily control a country of such impressive military feats."

Hitler's rage does not abate. The Afrika Korps has taken a substantial number of prisoners at Bir Hakeim, valiant men who stayed back to fight a rearguard delaying action so their comrades could escape. It is announced from Berlin that Hitler is ordering that "the white and colored Frenchmen made prisoner at Bir Hakeim, since they did not belong to any regular army, would not be subject to the laws of war and would be executed."

What follows marks the first direct confrontation between Charles de Gaulle and Adolf Hitler. Upon hearing that French prisoners will be shot, the general issues a threat of his own within the hour. The BBC broadcast is not just in French but also German and English so there can be no mistake:

"If Germany were to dishonor itself as to kill French soldiers fighting for their country, General de Gaulle would regrettably feel obliged to inflict the same fate on German prisoners."

Hitler backs down.

"On the subject of the members of the French forces who have just been captured in the fighting at Bir Hakeim, no misunderstanding is possible," the German radio announces. "General de Gaulle's soldiers will be treated as soldiers."

. . .

THE SURVIVORS OF Bir Hakeim are legend.

"After standing up for a fortnight to almost continual bombardment from the air and land, the Frenchmen were tired, hungry and dirty, but in the highest spirits," reports the *Times* of London.

The *Times* concludes: "After a day or so of rest they will be ready to get into battle again."

38

General Erwin Rommel is determined to increase the Nazi stranglehold on Fortress Europe.

Even if he has to get down on his hands and knees.

Rommel rides in the front passenger seat of his Horch 901 staff car. The dirt road unspooling through the desert is one sharp bump after another. A driver and two staff members share the vehicle. It is a week since Bir Hakeim fell. The French getaway is regrettable to Rommel, but he bears a grudging respect for the defenders. "Seldom in Africa was I given such a hard fought struggle," he admits.

Rommel has always been lean, but a year in the desert has chiseled his features and given his compact body the sleek countenance of a bantamweight boxer. His face is grizzled in a cowboy suntan: bronze cheeks and nose topped off by a lily-white forehead from tugging his cap down low. His haircut is an awkward concession to the desert, shaved on the sides with a short tuft of hair on top. The general's uniform, like his car's sand-covered bonnet, is coated in a fine layer of

Libya. Squint marks line the corners of his goggle-covered eyes. Binoculars dangle by a black leather strap from his sunburned neck.

The desert is never flat, but it is very often bare, alternately concealing and revealing a land of hostile sensation: cruel heat, savage winds, scorpions, vipers, biting flies, charred British Matilda and American-made M3 General Grant tanks painted with names of faraway girlfriends—like "Rosemary" with her turret blown off—escarpment, abandoned tents, blackened guns, spent casings, the trampled earth of a dozen recent battlefields.

And land mines.

Everywhere, unseen, land mines. Thousands upon thousands sown by the British to stop Rommel's amazing army, buried between sandy desert crust and the limestone beneath.

To most men, this is hell.

To Erwin Rommel, this is a kingdom.

His kingdom.

And like all great conquerors, his domain is never big enough.

Today's goal is the port city of Tobruk. The British own it. Rommel needs it. The capture of Bir Hakeim makes it possible for him to focus completely on expanding his realm. Only after taking the vital city with its square houses and flat roofs can Rommel advance on his ultimate goal, the Egyptian capital of Cairo.

Suddenly, across the desert, the general makes out the profile of German trucks parked in random fashion. Each vehicle is empty. No signs of drivers or soldiers. No one emerging from behind a rock after taking a relief break.

Erwin Rommel orders his driver to halt.

· · ·

It was February 1941 when Adolf Hitler summoned General Erwin Rommel to Berlin to name him commander of a new unit known as the Afrika Korps. They would fight in the desert, a type of warfare completely foreign to Rommel. These tanks and infantry would serve as a *Sperrband*—a forbidden zone—preventing a resurgent British Army from capturing Italy's colony of Libya.

The call to duty pleased Rommel. At the time, war was over in Europe. Opportunities to fight were few. As the general flew to Africa, his peers and adversaries in the panzer command languished, the glorious dash across France in the past and prospects of a future command highly unlikely.

No one could have foreseen what happened next. Rommel became the bully of North Africa, taking blitzkrieg to the British, ignoring orders to remain on the defensive. Time after time, the Afrika Korps prevails. Rommel's army became unbeatable, a crack unit pushing their mental, physical, and emotional limits to win battles. Rommel's men fight to exhaustion, often collapsing on the desert floor when a battle is won, so tired that enemy soldiers caught behind German lines and trying to make it back to safety will report walking directly through Rommel's sleeping army without anyone stirring.

The media pays attention. The "obscure German General Rommel" becomes famous, and not just to Berlin residents lapping up Nazi propaganda. Rommel grows so used to being filmed that he demands to repeat a scene if the camera angle used by the propaganda film crew is not flattering. He gets fan mail from German citizens and regularly responds with a signed photo. German Red Cross nurses stationed in the African desert regularly mob him for an autograph or snapshot.

It is the British press who dub Rommel the "Desert Fox" for his cunning. The *New York Times* will gush that Rommel is one of those "soldier's soldiers who win respect even from their enemies . . . the first military genius who has appeared in this war. He leads tank battles before lunch, air battles after lunch, and in the evening, like an umpire in a sham battle, explains to prisoners why they lost."

Time magazine is about to place him on the cover.

Perhaps the greatest acclaim is from Winston Churchill. The British prime minister was heavily criticized for praising a Nazi general in the House of Commons but will forever refuse to back down. "Rommel was a splendid military gambler," the prime minister will write in his memoirs. "Dominating the problems of supply and scornful of opposition . . . his ardor and daring inflicted grievous disasters upon us, but he deserves the salute I made him."

.　.　.

DESPITE THE GLORY, Rommel is racked by depression and self-doubt. One reason the Führer chose him for command in Africa was immense personal vigor. But now the general's health is declining from the long months of unrelenting sun, dust, and wind. "Field Marshal Rommel is suffering from chronic stomach and intestinal catarrh, nasal diphtheria and circulation trouble," his doctor will write. The general also appears jaundiced at times and suffers from boils on his face. "He is not in a fit condition to command."

To which Rommel will write home to wife Lucia, "Much too low blood pressure, state of exhaustion, six to eight weeks' rest cure recommended. I have requested the High Command to send a substitute."

General Erwin Rommel wants to go home.

Only he is not done here.

Rommel is garrulous when the cameras are filming but in fact has few friends. The general writes almost daily to Lucia, back home with their tall, bespectacled thirteen-year-old son, Manfred. The invasion of the Soviet Union one summer ago has led to moments of bitterness. Vital reinforcements, tanks, gas, and food he needs to win in Africa are being diverted to the Eastern Front. And until Rommel drives the British from Egypt by capturing Cairo and the vital Suez Canal, he well knows he is just one defeat away from falling out of favor with Adolf Hitler, a man with a very short memory.

. . .

ERWIN ROMMEL STEPS out of the Horch to deal with the baffling sight of the stalled and empty German trucks.

The general studies the ground. Carefully, Rommel gets down on his hands and knees. The sand has been disturbed. Using extreme caution, he brushes away the sediment.

A land mine takes shape.

Rommel's staff will not take the time to write down whether the general has chanced upon an anti-tank or antipersonnel mine. The British Mk series of antipersonnel devices are cylindrical in shape, the width of a bread plate and six inches tall. Britain's anti-tank explosives are the dimensions of a hefty hardcover novel and weigh in at five to twelve pounds. Both are made of steel and packed with TNT. Some versions add explosive barium nitrate or ammonium nitrate. Detonation takes place when the weight of an individual or vehicle applies pressure to the surface.

Whether the victim is a tank or a man, all it takes is four pounds of compression—the rough equivalent of a weak handshake—to make a land mine explode.

The explosive systems within the many styles of Mk are amazingly unique. There are few similarities, as if the munitions designers found one way to successfully build a land mine and then, realizing that long-term employment depended upon duplicating the process in a completely opposite fashion, moved on from the original design to start completely anew.

Yet they all blow up.

The blast range is thirty yards. Everything within that kill zone becomes a casualty. The outer casing of each land mine is steel. The explosion shatters the canister, sending thousands of shards of hot metal flying in every direction.

Rommel can clearly see what happened here: the drivers stopped when they realized they had entered a minefield. The British were waiting, having set the trap. The unlucky German drivers and soldiers are now prisoners.

Rommel would be wise to find a different road.

But the general's objective is to guide the attack on Tobruk, and that means getting to the other side of this minefield. He crawls forward. Upon locating an explosive device, Rommel determines its outlines and gingerly wipes away the sand. One by one, the general finds more mines and removes them from the road. His every point of contact with the earth—palms, knees, boots—has the potential to press down on a mine.

In fact, the general's life will indeed be cut short. The end will be sudden and unexpected, although he will have time to ponder his last thoughts.

But that tragedy is still two years away.

For now, Rommel thinks only of land mines. Not strategy, not Lucia, not biting black flies, not complete and utter exhaustion.

Land mines.

Rommel takes care. Great care. His touch is light. The Afrika Korps is beginning its final advance on Tobruk. Somewhere in the distance the general hears the percussive thud of artillery and longs to find the battle but knows this is not a time to rush.

Land mines.

A path in the sand. Rommel feels carefully, taking care not to miss even a single explosive device. He removes each bomb from the dirt and sets it to one side. Time means nothing.

Done.

The general stands. He wipes the desert grit from his hands.

Rommel orders his driver to find the battle.

39

Erwin Rommel gazes at his destruction.

Tobruk was once charming. Not this morning. The soft summer breeze smells of burning petroleum. Sunrise, normally a most beautiful time along the Mediterranean, is blotted out by a thick black cauldron of smoke rising from the far side of the harbor, the result of British troops detonating their fuel depots. Sunken ships rest in the shallow water, listing, hulls settled into the silt and superstructures poking above the waterline. Neighborhoods where extended families once made a life are sun-bleached rubble. Refugees. Stray dogs. Palm trees denuded by artillery.

And a hard truth: thirty-three thousand disarmed Allied soldiers mope in small listless packs, waiting to be taken into custody, each man privately coming to terms with his new life as a prisoner of war.

This is how a city looks when it has been bombed into submission. When the defenders have hung on until there is no choice but to surrender. This is how Paris will be reduced, should the Allies ever arrive to take it back. The Germans have the artillery to match any army gun for gun, and Hitler's forces certainly know a thing or two about doing battle amid rubble and ruins.

The defenders of Tobruk are lucky. When ancient Rome captured the city of Carthage at the end of the Punic Wars, its men were put to the sword, the women raped and then enslaved along with their children. The Romans leveled the prosperous city and salted the earth, ensuring that no living thing would grow from the ground. The five-hundred-year-old Carthaginian Empire, once located along the same African coastline west of modern-day Tobruk, ceased to exist.

The people of Tobruk are simply displaced. They will rebuild. Rommel will not stay. All the general wants from the city is for that precious gasoline to stop burning and a port closer to Egypt where German cargo vessels and oil tankers can replenish his army.

The Hotel Tobruk still stands, an air-conditioned miracle. Rommel makes it his headquarters. He'll accept the surrender in a few hours. No hurry.

Then on to Cairo.

. . .

SEVASTOPOL IS ALSO in ruins.

Colonel Dietrich von Choltitz is exhausted. A thousand miles northeast of Tobruk, this crucial Soviet port on the Black Sea has endured a nine-month German siege. It now looks like Tobruk in many ways: buildings leveled, sunken ships leaking oil into the harbor, and the smell of death, which has long since soaked into the stitching of Choltitz's battle-tattered uniform. Many of those casualties are the colonel's own German soldiers, his regiment reduced from 4,800 hardened veterans to just 349 during this long offensive. Severe winter weather also took its toll on Choltitz's personal health, a newly developed heart condition slowing the pudgy officer's movements and making it hard to breathe.

But this is the way of war. Choltitz has fought in Poland, harshly accepted the surrender of Rotterdam by refusing the handshake of the defeated garrison commander even after witnessing the carpet-bombing that leveled miles of city blocks, and can now look with grim satisfaction at the devastation of this once-beautiful Crimean harbor. In three years of fighting on many fronts since the war began, Choltitz has followed a steadfast path of doing whatever it takes, to whomever or whatever is needed. The colonel—soon to be promoted to general for his bravery—has absolutely no compunction about killing civilians and laying a city to waste in order to achieve victory.

None at all.

40

Paris sleeps.

The city is dark and quiet. A warm summer morning. Thin *pyjamas*, dreaming, snoring, the soft breathing of a child, a hand draped over a slumbering spouse's thigh, an hour too early or too late for making love.

Suddenly, a nightmare.

Fists pounding on apartment doors. Policemen shouting wake up. You're under arrest. Get your clothes on. Grab your belongings. Get out.

Right now.

Intentional chaos deprives the newly awakened of an ability to form quick rational thoughts. Almost no one dreams of fighting back. Paris knew this day was coming. But as thousands upon thousands open their doors to let in the gendarmes, this terror is unlike anything they could have imagined.

The police, numbering more than 4,000 and always traveling in pairs, take entire families into custody. Their orders are clear: "The teams charged with the arrests will have to proceed with the most possible speed, without useless words, and without comment," reads the circular defining the morning sweep. "Furthermore, at the moment of the arrest, the well-foundedness or ill-foundedness of this arrest is not to be discussed."

Everyone taken into custody is a Jew.

This is no surprise. Arrests of Jewish men are ongoing. Stories of life in the Drancy internment camp have trickled into the local community, telling of a multistory complex with watchtowers, no panes of glass in window frames, no place to wash, and minimal toilet facilities. Just three weeks ago, on June 22, 1,000 of those prisoners disappeared, packed into a train headed east.

Just east. That's all anyone knows.

But it is not just men this morning. For the first time ever, women and children are under arrest. All wear the yellow Star of David prominently sewn to their clothing, as required by law since June 1.* This marks them as Jews for one and all to see, just as this enduring symbol of their 4,000-year-old religion allows the police to enforce restrictions on riding the Métro, attending movies and concerts and relaxing in public spaces such as cafés, sitting on park benches, and even standing in line to buy food.

Families take only what they can carry. Some wrap belongings in a bedsheet. Others wrestle a small mattress to make life easier for a child. The quick thinking grab food.

"Parents were completely panic-stricken and looking haggard," a young Polish-born Jewish girl will remember. "They were holding little children, who were awake, crying, surrounded by policemen. It was a terrible shock."

---

* In a show of support for the Jewish population, many non-Jewish Parisians took to wearing yellow flowers, yellow handkerchiefs, and even yellow paper stars.

No time to bathe or brush teeth. Families are led onto the street, formed into lines, and walked to a waiting fleet of green-and-beige Renault public transit buses. Packed together tightly, unwashed, breath stale, the detained get their first minor sniff of the uncomfortable aromas that will soon become all too familiar.

Surprisingly, no one is French. As police herd the detained onto buses, these Jews speak in accents Polish, Austrian, Czech, German, and Russian. The Belgian and Dutch are being saved for another day. These arrests are a vestige of the war's first hours, when refugees flooded into Paris. It has taken two years, but this *rafle*—roundup, as Paris police are calling it—has finally arrived. And this is certainly not the Operation Roundup Winston Churchill and Franklin Roosevelt have planned for 1943.

If only it were. That proposed Allied invasion will come far too late to save these Jewish families.

A new Nazi plan named the Final Solution was just agreed upon at a gathering known as the Wannsee Conference, held outside Berlin in January. This "solution" is the systematic murder of every Jew in Europe.

Yet there is not a German soldier in sight this morning.

The Gestapo have planned this roundup with meticulous attention to detail.

But it is the Paris police who are executing not just a roundup, but the biggest mass arrest of all: *la Grande Rafle.*

. . .

FINDING THE JEWS is easy. Like all law-abiding citizens of Paris, families have done as they are told, and for the Jewish population this means registering their names and addresses with the local police. This information was placed in a special file maintained by the Commissariat General for Jewish Affairs in the 2nd arrondissement. The *fichier Tulard*—the Tulard File, named for the bureaucrat supervising each and every detail—was alphabetized and grouped according to nationality, profession, and home address. Louis Darquier de Pellepoix, the newly appointed

French collaborator in charge of the commissariat, then handed the registry over to the local Gestapo.

Such a high level of detail allows SS-captain Theodor Dannecker, a specialist in the Nazi answer to the Jewish question, to plan the roundup with precision. He is a man so loathsome that not even the Nazis trust him. This roundup will be the twenty-nine-year-old Dannecker's last grand act before being recalled to Berlin for looting. Local police and the French national train service, known as Société Nationale des Chemins de Fer Français—or just SNCF—are informed of their obligations.* Both comply as ordered. The arrests are such a high priority that Adolf Eichmann, the SS officer coordinating the deportation of Jews to death camps as part of the Final Solution, attends a July 10 planning meeting in Paris. The French make the minor suggestion of requesting that the raids not take place until after July 14, the national celebration of Bastille Day, a date in Paris history when citizens rose up in rebellion against an oppressive state. Comparisons with the German occupation being obvious, the Nazis agree to postpone the roundup rather than incite another great uprising.

The size and sweep of the arrests makes Adolf Hitler proud enough to shout it to the world. The United Press newspaper syndicate, relying on information provided by Berlin radio, reports that "all alien Jews living in Paris" have been arrested. The complete figure is 12,884. Women number 5,802 and children 4,051.

"All will be deported to the East," the Berlin report concludes with ominous self-congratulation.

. . .

THE FIRST ORDER OF BUSINESS after the arrests is separating men and women who do not have children from those who do. The childless are prodded into buses bound for Drancy, in a well-populated north-

---

* The literal translation of *chemin de fer* is "iron path" but the phrase is more often applied to a railway.

eastern suburb of Paris. Drivers deliver their first load of human cargo at dawn, then shuttle back and forth throughout the clear summer day. Each arrival's name is meticulously checked against the Tulard File. In all, 4,992 men and women are processed in the open-air court-yard before being confined in large group cells.

"Filth of a coal mine," one woman will describe Drancy. "Straw mattress full of lice and bedbugs. Horrid overcrowding. Eighty-six women, six water faucets, you don't have the time to wash . . . you can't go to the toilets more than once every sixteen hours."

So, three days later, it is with relief and curiosity that the Jewish prisoners of Drancy look down from the empty windowpanes of their prison barracks and see the return of the green-and-beige Renault buses.

One thousand men and women are selected to board. No one knows whether they are lucky or damned.

The answer comes five minutes after their departure. The Renaults arrive at Le Bourget train station, where the filthy and exhausted pris-oners are off-loaded for their mystery ride.

A train is waiting.

A train headed east.

. . .

FAMILIES WITH CHILDREN are not taken to Drancy. Not at first.

Instead, these 8,000 are driven into the posh heart of Paris. There, in the shadow of the Eiffel Tower, they are led into a legendary sport-ing arena. A high-banked wooden oval cycling track surrounded by rows of bleachers testifies to the building's roots as a velodrome. A great glass ceiling provides natural daylight. Fencing, weight-lifting, wrestling, and boxing matches were held in this great auditorium during the 1924 Olympics. Gold medals were awarded here. One hun-dred lions were once let loose on the arena floor as a circus act. Ernest Hemingway has written fondly about the thrill of witnessing six-day bicycle races on the smooth boards.

The Vel' d'Hiv—the Vélodrome d'Hiver, or Winter Velodrome—was once owned by Henri Desgrange, founder of the Tour de France. In a normal year without war, July 16 would likely have been the second Thursday of the three-week cycling competition.

But this is hardly a normal year.

Inside is chaos. Police block the exits but rarely venture within. No one is in charge. Space is a precious commodity, with parents staking out spots in the bleachers, on the track, and on the floor in the middle of the arena for their families to call their own.

The first thing the arrivals notice is the heat. The air is still and dense. The glass ceiling is painted blue as camouflage against an air raid. This darker color provides an odd sort of half shade. But just as the sun can pass through a shard of magnifying glass to fry an egg on a sidewalk, so the ceiling intensifies the stifling summer temperatures. Clothes grow damp from sweat. Morsels of shadow are precious.

Indignities increase as more families arrive. Windows are screwed shut to prevent escape. Water taps turned off. The Red Cross and local Quakers bring food but there is not enough. "The atmosphere was stuffy and nauseating," one Red Cross nurse will remember. "Nervous breakdowns, shouting, weeping of children and even of adults at the end of their tether. Several deranged individuals spread panic. All was helter-skelter, it was impossible to sleep."

Indignity turns to degradation. The velodrome has plenty of restrooms, but those with windows are locked shut. The few remaining toilets soon back up. The imprisoned Jews take to walking a few steps from their family area to relieve themselves in a corner. There is no place to hide. No place to wash out a cloth diaper. Piles and puddles grow and no one comes to clean them. Children defecate in the open, witnessed by hundreds of strangers.

So do their fathers.

And mothers.

And yet, although it seems unimaginable, life gets much worse.

Hours pass. Days. Escape is futile. Those making the attempt are shot. Desperate women slash the wrists of their young children, preferring them dead rather than enduring this suffering.

Outside, all is normal. Parisians stroll along the Seine, enjoying the warm weather. German soldiers on leave from the war gather at the Eiffel Tower to take tourist photos.

After three days, the green-and-beige Renaults pull up outside the Vel' d'Hiv.

. . .

THE TRAINS HEADED EAST—AND *all* trains carrying Jews head east—are traveling to the place known as Auschwitz. This is a death camp in Poland. Jewish men, women, and children will leave the train upon their arrival and step onto the platform. The groups will then be split into those who can work and those who are sentenced to immediate death. The condemned will be led to a gas chamber to be killed with a cyanide-based insecticide known as Zyklon B. They will walk to their murders without protest, having been told a Nazi lie that they are being sent to take a shower after their long exhausting journey.

Most of these Jewish refugees don't know any of this is coming as they board the train in Paris. Some do: the World Jewish Congress made headlines on June 29 by proclaiming that 1 million Jews have been murdered since the war began.

Small headlines. The *New York Times* ran the story in the middle of page seven.

The journey to Auschwitz is a little over eight hundred miles and can take up to four days on the busy wartime tracks. Although sometimes the Germans allow those being transported to sit in a third-class car to preserve the lie that the Jews are being transported to a new home somewhere in the east, most are crammed into a cattle car with a single barred window for ventilation and a single bucket for the entire group's ease. The Gestapo's suggested maximum number of individuals per cattle car is fifty, but the actual figure is most often double—or more.

At first the Nazis declare that Jewish children arrested in the roundup must remain in Paris. They are too young to ride the cattle cars to Auschwitz. These infants and adolescents are forcibly separated from their mothers and placed in temporary care.

But within two weeks of the roundup, on July 31, that policy is reversed. Boxcar loads of children unaccompanied by adults, some just toddlers, board the train.

Most are terrified.

Their only solace is the relief that they will soon be reunited with their parents.

41

The Resistance meets a most suspicious priest.

Germaine Tillion approaches the Café des Voutes on foot. The Colonne de Juillet towers over the Place de la Bastille. At more than a century old, it is familiar enough to ignore. Summer. Cobblestones. Mansard roofs above the roundabout. Germans in uniforms and civilian clothes lounging in sidewalk bistros. Parisians talking about food, because that's all anyone talks about. No meat. No butter. Everyone is hungry and too thin. Bistro coffee is not coffee at all but ground acorns and chicory.*

Tillion studies the crowd. She can't help herself. Bad form to wait

---

* The Place de la Bastille is built on the site of the infamous Paris fortress of the same name, stormed by a mob on July 14, 1789, as part of the French Revolution. This date is celebrated annually in France. The Colonne de Juillet—the July Column—is its centerpiece, commemorating Bastille Day. The column stands 154 feet high. Atop the monument is Le Génie de la Liberté, a winged figure representing the spirit of freedom.

too long in a public place. So she searches for signs of undercover Gestapo who might think she's conducting an illicit rendezvous. Even more, the Resistance leader with the kind face is an ethnographer, academically trained to observe human customs and behavior. She spent six years prior to the war in the Algerian desert, living with Berber nomads, a full immersion into scarcity and hardship, literally dwelling among murderers and thieves—a situation not so different than Occupied Paris.

Yet, Tillion's patience, fearlessness, friendly nature, and reluctance to grumble impressed the tribe as the behavior of an old soul. For even as she studied the Ah'Abderrahman, watching them herd their goats and sow their barley, the nomads were also studying her. Its leaders bequeathed upon Tillion the tribe's most distinguished title: *tamhurt*—"Old One."

Tillion is thirty-five.

Perhaps it is those same compassionate traits that allow Germaine Tillion to avoid suspicion while serving as a major Resistance leader. But as she waits for the priest who possesses a growing reputation for being sympathetic to the Resistance, she is well aware that someone is most likely studying her. Her cell has been compromised—of that she's almost positive. Too many have been arrested. Tillion would be naïve not to think she could be next.

"When a traitor penetrated part of the organism, like venom," Tillion will reflect on the perils of maintaining a Resistance network, "his ambition was to move up the arteries to the heart. This was only too easy to do and when it happened there was one network less and a few more deaths."

It is two years since Tillion returned from Algeria in May 1940, unaware Germany had invaded France. The ethnographer and her widowed sixty-four-year-old mother, Émilie, fled Paris before the city fell. But on their journey to the South, stuck in the morass of humanity also taking flight, she heard the voice of Marshal Pétain on the radio, stating that an armistice had been signed with Germany. The patriot within her was outraged. "When I heard Pétain's speech, I vomited. Literally," she writes. "It takes one second for the course of a life to change forever. Once the choice is made ... one must hold to it."

And for Germaine Tillion, that choice meant returning to Paris and joining the Resistance. The term now takes on many forms in Paris, from Gaullists to Socialists to men like Colonel Fabien and the Communists. But little was organized when Tillion and her mother first arrived home. Working first with a small French network assisting escaped prisoners of war, then as part of the band named for the Musée de l'Homme—which is also her place of employment—Tillion has avoided arrest. Tillion knows few contacts outside her close circle. Her contact with the SOE is the one-legged Virginia Hall in Lyon, whom Tillion knows only as "Marie." She regularly funnels information to Hall by courier, who then transmits that intelligence to London.

The priest arrives. Today he will take the three-hour train ride south to Lyon, carrying powerful information to Marie. Father Robert Alesch is a man of the cloth, but is today dressed in nondescript pants and a shirt. Mid-thirties. Powerful shoulders. Dimpled chin. Steel-blue eyes. Something in the priest's forward manner toward Tillion suggests he does not strictly follow his vow of celibacy. "I did not trust him and carefully kept him from knowing who I was," she will remember of this day.

But Father Robert Alesch, in fact, knows far more about Germaine Tillion than she would care to admit. The ethnographer and her mother, a noted writer and art critic, share a home in the suburb of Saint-Maur-des-Fossés. This is just one parish over from where Alesch says daily Mass. The mother and daughter secretly shelter airmen and prisoners of war within their three-story residence. Although Tillion had never before met the priest, one day not long ago he showed up at her home unbidden, dressed in black cassock, asking if he might be of help to her group. She was shocked that a complete stranger not only knew about her activities but also knew her home address. Tillion made inquiries. A trusted nun vouched for him. Tillion took a leap of faith and invited Alesch to work for her network.*

After all, it seems wrong not to trust a priest.

The credentials of Father Alesch, who most curiously speaks with a German accent, are actually impeccable. His courageous rants against Nazi Germany from the parish pulpit have earned him a loyal following among the Resistance. Alesch hands out photographs of Charles de Gaulle the way other priests hand out patron saint prayer cards. Many a resistant has kneeled in the confessional to confide in Alesch about their work against the Germans. As is the nature of their fight, these men and women are often later arrested. Alesch attacks the Nazis vehemently in his Sunday homilies when this happens, demanding to know what has become of the resistants.

Tillion and Alesch say their pleasantries. She slips the priest a matchbox containing microfilm laying out the defensive fortifications of a French port named Dieppe. Alesch is to deliver this package to "Marie."

Tillion and Alesch do not linger. Together, they walk fifteen minutes to the Gare de Lyon. It is on her way home. Alesch pays his fare. Tillion sees him to the platform. A conductor punches the priest's ticket. Only then, as Alesch is about to board, does Tillion turn to leave.

A man in plain clothes speaking with an accent taps her on the shoulder.

"German police. Follow me."

"You think perhaps I am Jewish," she says quickly.

"No," the policeman responds. "I knew right away that you are not. We only want to check your papers."

Suddenly, three men grab Tillion, pinning her arms to her sides

---

* The home of Germaine and Émilie Tillion still exists. A plaque in their honor marks the location of the yellow home with red shutters at 48 Avenue du Général Leclerc. The street was known as the Avenue d'Orléans during the war but afterward was renamed to honor Leclerc, the *nom de guerre* of a Free French leader.

and rushing her into the back seat of a waiting black Citroën. She has no way of knowing it, but police are also entering the Tillion home to arrest her mother.

Tillion turns to see if Alesch, with the precious matchbox in his possession, is also being detained. She is relieved that the priest is untouched. Oddly, he is not attempting to conceal himself. Instead, Alesch is a spectator to her arrest, the awful twist of his lips looking very much like a smirk.

Germaine Tillion realizes the truth.

Her Judas's blue eyes, Tillion will long remember, bear a look of triumph.

Tillion has no time to scream. Father Robert Alesch not only possesses vital information about the coastal defenses at Dieppe but is now leading German intelligence straight to Virginia Hall.

And Germaine Tillion has absolutely no way of warning her.

42

T he restless woman with one leg rushes to greet the German priest.

Virginia Hall was away when the courier came to visit two weeks ago. She still owes compensation for his last delivery. Grabbing an extremely large wad of francs from the hiding space behind her kitchen cupboard, the spy walks the most direct route to their meeting. Hall crosses the broad blue-green Rhône River via the Pont de l'Université, makes a right on the Quai du Docteur Gailleton—where the bronze bust of the former town mayor of the same name has recently been removed and melted down for the war—then left onto Place Antonin Poncet and, finally, ducking into the yellow stone building housing the gynecology practice of her good friend and Resistance confidant, the wily Dr. Jean Rousset.

Hall is now a veteran spy, having been under cover in France for over a year. Evading surveillance has become second nature. Even during a brisk walk she glances down alleys, checks her reflection in windows, doubles back to see who might be following her. No detail is too small. No stranger goes unscrutinized. Shoes are always a giveaway: a dedicated watcher might change a coat or a hat to affect disguise but rarely does anyone change their shoes. Hall pays attention. One sloppy mistake could be the end.

And that demise will be horrible. Stopping the Resistance is top priority to the three primary law enforcement agencies operating officially and unofficially in Unoccupied France: the Gestapo, the Vichy police, and the Abwehr. Their methods of torture are medieval, particularly for women: rape, sometimes by a German shepherd; nipples ripped off with pliers; fingernails and toenails slowly pulled out one by one by one by sliding hot needles between soft pink flesh and nail.

And much more. Nazi creativity for breaking the human will has no limits.

Hall is the heart and soul of SOE Section F—F for *France*—underground activity, not only coordinating a complete resistance network of dead drops and surveillance outposts but even, somewhat miraculously, managing to break captured SOE agents out of prison. British records will show that almost every one of their agents working under cover in France receives some sort of assistance or guidance from Hall's network.

Hall has also taken greater control of her destiny by maintaining contact with London whenever she needs. She travels cautiously but often, altering her appearance with scarves, hats, glasses, and accents, and puffing out her face by stuffing pieces of rubber into her cheeks. Virginia Hall goes by many names. The Germans have deduced that she is either English or Canadian but do not know what she looks like. "Cuthbert," her wooden leg, is her only distinguishing feature.

Yet, babysitting the countless resistants who seek out Hall to ask for money, radio transmissions, and a safe house to lay low for a few days is exhausting. There are too many details. Too many judgment calls about whether or not to trust the total stranger coming through the door claiming to be a friend.

This priest is such a man. Hall is meeting Father Alesch for the first time. He claims to be a Resistance courier from Paris. The chubby, mustachioed Dr. Rousset—who risks his own life every day by using his practice as a conduit for information, hides downed Allied pilots in an upstairs room that he has disguised as an insane asylum, and uses his knowledge of gynecology to cure local prostitutes of venereal disease (but only after they have shared their infection with German soldiers)—has total faith in Alesch.

But Rousset is a devout Catholic. Hall knows this. Of course he believes a priest.

Hall needs to decide for herself.

She pushes open the large wooden doors of Number Seven and marches through the waiting room without pausing. Her limp, the one telltale mark of her identity the Nazis know for sure, is barely noticeable.

The priest waits in a small office.

Father Robert Alesch has removed his beret. He carries a handbag. Normal clothes. Speaking in his thick German accent, the abbé asks if Hall is the one and only Marie Monin—"*la personne principale*" to the Resistance movement.

Hall knows better than to answer.

Alesch has come from Paris. He claims the Germans shot his father, fueling him with the rage needed to risk his life for the Resistance. The prior courier, a chemical engineer named Jacques Legrand, can no longer safely travel to Lyon, but has assigned him the task. As proof, the priest presents a letter in Legrand's handwriting.

Hall studies the note. She recognizes the script.

But still has her doubts.

.　.　.

WITH GOOD REASON: the priest is a liar.

The father of Robert Alesch is very much alive.

Jacques Legrand is currently in Gestapo custody, betrayed by Father Alesch.

Germaine Tillion, arrested twelve days ago, languishes in La Santé Prison.

The Abwehr pays Alesch 12,000 francs each month to spy, with bonuses for each arrest.

The priest maintains a lavish Paris apartment and several mistresses.

Those resistants arrested after making their Catholic confession to Alesch disappeared because the priest broke his clerical vow of confidentiality and spilled that information to his Nazi handlers.

The vital microfilm information about the defenses at Dieppe has been handed over to the Abwehr in Paris. The intelligence never reaches London. A most rudimentary form of invasion planning takes place as a result, embarrassing in its ineptitude, with prewar picture postcards of the beaches used as photographic references to plan the invasion. The August 19 commando raid by 6,086 Canadian soldiers, U.S. Army Rangers, British soldiers, and Free French fighters ends in a bloodbath. Half are killed, wounded, or taken prisoner within the first twelve hours. In addition, more than one hundred British Royal Air Force planes are shot down and the Royal Navy suffers the sinking of a destroyer.

All because of Father Robert Alesch.

. . .

VIRGINIA HALL FINDS it uncomfortable to trust the priest, despite Dr. Rousset's encouragement. The German accent, which Alesch explains came as a result of growing up in Alsace, is unlike any she has heard in France.* Recruiting a resistant with a German accent—and a priest at that—would be a brilliant method of diverting suspicion.

Yet, Father Alesch comes strangely empty-handed for a courier.

---

* The Alsace-Lorraine region is the borderland between France and Germany.

And his demand to know her identity is a clear violation of Resistance protocol, as anonymity means longevity. The priest does not appear to be an audacious man, just confident, but boldly requests that Hall provide him a shortwave radio. This is yet another enormous security breach. If Alesch is a Nazi spy, he could have her arrested immediately for possessing a transmitter. The priest could also send messages of his own to London, knowing that the SOE will mistakenly believe they are coming from the radio's true owner, Virginia Hall. In this scenario, Alesch and his Nazi handlers could transmit false information in her name to compromise the SOE cause.

Hall says she'll see what she can do about the radio. Despite her ambivalence, Hall hands Alesch an envelope stuffed with the 200,000 francs as payment for the matchbox of microfilm delivered on his last trip.*

Father Alesch bids Virginia Hall *au revoir* and begins his journey back to Paris.

He will return. She knows this.

Or a Nazi arrest team will come instead.

London has been pressing Hall to come home for some time. The average SOE operative stays in place four months. Hall is overdue. She could leave this instant. No questions asked. But while the SOE agent may have given Robert Alesch money, she has given him no information about herself. Hall knows she has two things going for her: the Germans still don't know what she looks like, and the Germans still don't know where she lives.

The restless woman with one leg makes her decision.

She is staying in France.

---

* A little over $100,000 in modern currency. It's worth noting that much of Hall's currency was counterfeited by the SOE in London, meaning the actual worth is nothing. Also, France has devalued the franc several times, so establishing a legitimate comparison is difficult.

43

The British are coming.

Erwin Rommel runs for his life. The Desert Fox oversees retreat from his staff car, desperately guiding a battered column of Afrika Korps tanks and troop transports west to Libya. The British Eighth Army is hard on his tail. Inky-blue Mediterranean on the right, dun-colored desert to the left. Wind up and Egyptian sky threatening rain. Rommel's long leather uniform coat is buttoned to the throat, where a scarf covers his Knight's Cross. Peaked cap. Goggles. Binoculars. Jaundiced, exhausted, deeply disillusioned, defiant, desperate.

The great Desert Fox is also disobeying a direct order from Adolf Hitler in a desperate quest to avoid annihilation. This could get Rommel shot, but he has no choice.

The field marshal studies the storm. Heavy rain would make a nice distraction—or at the very least keep those Royal Air Force Spitfires out of the sky. He sweeps his binoculars across the desert, searching

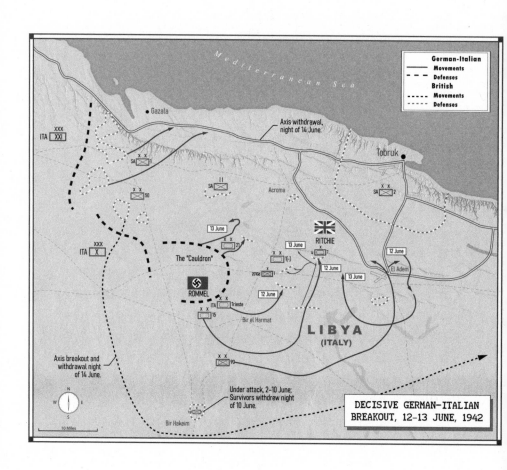

Mediterranean Sea

Gazala

Tobruk

ITA XXX XXI

SA X X 1

SA II

Acroma

SA X X 2

X X 50

ITA XXX X

13 June

X X 21

The "Cauldron"

RITCHIE

13 June

X 4 7

12 June

El Adem

13 June

X X 1(-)

12 June

ROMMEL

2/10d X 1

12 June

ITA Trieste

X X 15

Bir el Harmat

LIBYA
(ITALY)

X X 90

Axis withdrawal,
night of 14 June.

Axis breakout and
withdrawal night
of 14 June.

Under attack, 2–10 June;
Survivors withdrew night
of 10 June.

Bir Hakeim

N
W   E
S

10 Miles

German-Italian
——— Movements
– – – Defenses
British
· · · · Movements
· · · · Defenses

DECISIVE GERMAN–ITALIAN
BREAKOUT, 12–13 JUNE, 1942

for distant clouds of dust. Rommel was once unbeatable. Now he has fallen. Retreat, however, can salvage everything—ammunition, gasoline, soldiers, and panzers. But first he must get away.

And so the Desert Fox runs from the pack of British hounds close on his trail.

Yet this is not the beginning of the end.

That moment took place three nights ago.

. . .

"THE ANTICIPATED BRITISH main attack came on the night of 1st November," Rommel will remember. "For three hours, hundreds of British guns rained down shells on our positions, while rolling British night air raids on our German-Italian troops followed. Then massed British infantry and tanks advanced westwards through a curtain of fire and behind a screen of smoke."

It's almost unfair. The British fire unlimited rounds of ammunition but the Afrika Korps have almost none left. Royal Air Force Spitfires and Hurricanes control the skies, knocking down the far slower Luftwaffe Stukas with such impunity that they will become obsolete and rarely flown at all. The American Grant and Lee medium tanks now utilized by the British, with their thick two-inch hull armor and 75mm guns, are almost the equal of Rommel's Panzer IV—until now the best tank in the desert.*

Even more daunting, a juggernaut known as the Sherman has arrived from America. The state-of-the-art tank has an operational range

---

* The Grant and Lee are the same tank but with different turret configurations. Elements of the French Char B1 were introduced in the design process. The design initially featured a crew of seven—driver, commander, upper gunner, gunner, loader, machine-gun assistant, and radio operator. In time, crew size would be reduced as one of the gunners took on radio operation duties. Despite this, the interior is relatively roomy and the tank is ten feet tall, earning it the nickname "iron cathedral."

of 150 miles, a top speed of 30 miles per hour, a two-inch steel hull, and a 75mm M3 gun capable of penetrating enemy armor from almost two miles away. The Sherman is the Panzer IV's equal in every way.

The only difference is that the British have hundreds more Shermans than Rommel has panzers.

Field Marshal Rommel has no way of knowing about the long-ago May 1940 meeting in a Louisiana high school basement to discuss the future of American armor. Or how that gathering of light generals and bird colonels took the German army's blitzkrieg across France as inspiration, subsequently marveling at Rommel's daring tank escapades in North Africa. The Sherman, Grant, and Lee are a result of the United States' new commitment to mobility in the form of tank warfare, designed and placed into production just months after that Louisiana conference.

And for that, Erwin Rommel has only himself to blame.

Tobruk was secured five months ago. Cairo seemed won. On October 1, Hitler promoted Rommel to field marshal, the highest rank in the German army.

But as Rommel writes in his journal, "It is easy to see how the clouds of disaster were gathering for my army." Tobruk garnered the Germans an enormous bounty of gas, food, and ammunition, giving rise to the false sensation of plenty. But logistics are everything in desert warfare, and those supplies are inevitably exhausted as the Germans leave Tobruk and advance hundreds of miles into Egypt...

... where their advance grinds to a halt.

The roadblock is a lovely seaside town named El Alamein.

Anchored on one side by the Mediterranean and on the other by the Qattara Depression, with its impassable salt marshes and groves of umbrella thorn acacia, El Alamein is a choke point on the coastal road through which advancing armies must pass. The British Army chose this spot to dig in after their loss at Tobruk, clinging to the singular hope of saving Cairo.*

Rommel spends the last week of June prowling the Egyptian desert in his staff car, observing these new enemy fortifications. He travels unprotected and alone, save for his driver and small loyal staff, coming under fire from the RAF by day and sleeping under the stars each night. The results are depressing. The Afrika Korps cannot win. Rommel lacks the resources to attack in strength.

And yet, an impatient Rommel has no choice. On August 30 the field marshal sends his army in a southern sweep around El Alamein, trying to bypass British defenses. For the first time, the Desert Fox wages war against a newly appointed British commander named Bernard Law Montgomery. Knowing in advance of Rommel's offensive due to intercepted German intelligence, Montgomery digs in and waits, ultimately winning a defensive battle. Rommel retreats.

As summer gives way to fall, Rommel endures stalemate rather than blitzkrieg. "The swine isn't attacking," Rommel fumes about Montgomery to fellow German field marshal Albert Kesselring. Throughout September and into October, Afrika Korps resources dwindle while the British receive an amazing surplus of supplies, including three hundred new Sherman tanks and one hundred self-propelled guns sent directly from America to Cairo. In all, the British now have seven brigades possessing more than 1,000 tanks and more than 1,200 fighters and bomber aircraft.

Meanwhile, the Mediterranean is a British lake. German cargo ships and oil tankers trying to resupply the Afrika Korps through Tobruk are sunk by British warships and warplanes at an alarming rate.

---

* The Qattara Depression descends to 436 feet below sea level and covers an area of more than 7,000 square miles. In addition to its salt marshes and dry lake beds, the depression is a vital habitat for cheetah and gazelle.

In the month of September, 30 percent of Axis shipping bound for North Africa is sunk. In October, that figure rises to 40 percent. Most crucially, 66 percent of all petroleum bound for the Afrika Korps now rests at the bottom of the Mediterranean.

By late September, Rommel has had enough. The desert war cannot be won. Suffering from traveler's belly and jaundice, the field marshal requests permission to fly home on sick leave. Rommel's successor, General Wilhelm Ritter von Thoma, newly arrived from the Russian front, assesses the situation and almost immediately requests permission from the Führer to retreat, seeing no hope of victory.

Adolf Hitler says no.

So the doomed Afrika Korps holds the line.

And waits to die.

Montgomery finally attacks October 23. Almost 1,000 British artillery guns open fire under a full moon, attacking first the entrenched German batteries and then shifting focus to infantry positions.

Rommel is sick in Austria. Two days later, still unwell, the field marshal is flown back to Africa by direct order of Hitler. Retreat is already on Rommel's mind, yet he delays out of loyalty to his Führer. He orders a counterattack for October 28. Yet, even before the assault can begin, Afrika Korps units are destroyed by Royal Air Force bombers as they assemble. The RAF drops eighty tons of bombs on Rommel's tanks and men, scattered over six square miles. The counterattack never takes place.

"This was the last occasion on which the enemy attempted to take the initiative," the British battle report will read.

One week after returning to the desert, Rommel is convinced it is time to run.

"By evening I was receiving reports from the Panzer Army that its supply situation was totally desperate," he writes on November 2. "We had already let loose four hundred and fifty tons of ammunition that day, while three destroyers had brought only one hundred and ninety tons into Tobruk. The British had as good as complete control over the air and sea to Tobruk and beyond, and were constantly bombing the town and port . . . the fuel situation was becoming critical and the worst of the fighting was yet to come."

Rommel adds: "Thus, we faced total annihilation. The Afrika Korps had barely thirty-five serviceable tanks remaining.

"Here was the moment to slip away."

.　.　.

ROMMEL TELEGRAPHS Adolf Hitler for permission. The message is wordy and vague, couched in a desire to avoid delivering bad news to a man he aims to please above all others. The writing is a far cry from the taut, cocky surrender order delivered to the defenders at Bir Hakeim. Rommel even refers to the Afrika Korps from a remove, as if he were nothing more than a studied observer.

"The army's strength was so exhausted that after its ten days of battle that it was not now capable of offering any effective opposition to the enemy's next breakthrough attempt . . . With our shortage of vehicles an orderly withdrawal of the non-motorized forces appeared impossible . . . In these circumstances, we had to reckon, at the least, with the gradual destruction of the army."

Then Rommel waits.

The field marshal overrides his innate cunning, losing precious time to run but not wishing to endure the Führer's wrath by falling back without consent. With every passing hour, the damage inflicted upon the Afrika Korps by the British—and a lack of German supplies to engage Montgomery's army in meaningful combat—leads to more casualties and prisoners. By the end of the battle, more than 59,000 German and Italian soldiers are either listed as dead, missing, or captured.

"To Field Marshal Rommel," comes the Führer's reply on November 3. Hitler's response is scathing and deluded.

". . . In the situation in which you find yourself, there can be no consideration other than to stand firm and throw every gun and every man into the fight. Everything possible is being done to help you. Notwithstanding his superior numbers, the enemy must also be worn out. It will not be for the first time that strength of will shall have triumphed over larger forces. As for your men, you can offer them no path but victory or death."

.   .   .

ERWIN ROMMEL HAS never defied Adolf Hitler. It is very much in Rommel's nature to be insubordinate to lesser authority figures—even fellow generals, in particular, anyone Italian—but his reverence for the Führer is all-powerful.

No more.

The Afrika Korps will not stand fast. There will be no victory or death.

But the delay while waiting for Hitler's reply is already proving costly.

"So it had come about, the thing we had been trying with all our might to prevent: the front was broken through, with fully motorized enemy streaming through into our hinterland," Rommel will write. "I immediately ordered retreat forthwith, and to save what could be saved . . . Nevertheless, so much had already been lost by postponing the retreat twenty-four hours."

Rommel concludes in his own defense: "Anything that didn't immediately make it onto the road and flee was lost, as the enemy swept on across a wide front and overtook everything in its path."

Now, retreating along the Mediterranean coastal road, Rommel is shocked to see that Montgomery has sent his armor on a sweep around the German column.

The Afrika Korps' escape route is almost blocked.

The storm hits just as all seems lost. Thick rain lashes the desert, flooding the low wadis and turning sand into mud, bogging down British tanks and grounding Spitfires. As always, Rommel demands that his men press on despite this new obstacle, desperate to put more miles between himself and his pursuers. After that will come the reckoning with Adolf Hitler.

So it is that the Desert Fox gets away.

For now.

Field Marshal Erwin Rommel races west with the few remaining men and tanks under his command. His goal is Tripoli, 1,000 miles to the west—or maybe farther, if need be. There are no British troops in that direction.

The Americans, however, are a much different story.

44

Major General George S. Patton is eager to fight.

No more Louisiana war games. H hour for Operation Torch is two hours away. The enemy is Vichy France, not Nazi Germany. For the first time in twenty-four years, Patton will taste real combat. He is up and wide awake, showering, shaving, and dressing in his tailored battle uniform. Eager. Impatient.

Ready.

The steel deck is steady beneath Patton's polished boots. USS *Augusta* is six hundred feet long and just sixty-six feet at the beam, yet barely sways from side to side. This is extraordinary news.

The general is trim, maintaining fitness during the Atlantic crossing by running in place in his quarters. Patton's custom holster belt will still buckle easily over his hips. Though known for his personal eccentricities, the donning of the pistols can wait until just before going ashore at 0800. Strolling the decks of a warship wearing ivory-handled revolvers is too much, even for the idiosyncratic George S. Patton.

Days ago, swells were running at eight feet, the breakers crashing onto beaches far too high for putting men and equipment ashore safely. With winter storms coming, today's landing date is as late in the year as war planners dare schedule the invasion. Poor weather would mean pushing to spring. So these flat seas elate the general. "Dead calm, no swell—God is with us," he writes in his journal.

The *Augusta* cruises eight miles out to sea. Patton's stateroom for the Atlantic crossing is among the most well-appointed in the Navy, once even used by President Roosevelt for a 1941 meeting off the Newfoundland coast with Winston Churchill. But after two weeks of relative luxury, the general is impatient for the Spartan rigor of battle.

Patton strides onto the main deck and stands at the rail. A new moon makes for a dark night on the water. He studies the silhouette of Casablanca. "Lights at Casa burning," Patton notes, gazing toward land. The city's profile is low, save for the towering El Hank Lighthouse rising from a rocky bluff like a towering waterfront minaret. Its glaring searchlight still guides ships into port, Casablanca's defenders having no idea that over one hundred Allied vessels bob unseen offshore.

The Moroccan city's population is just over a quarter million, not including the European refugees filling its hotels and guesthouses. These transients are exotic and pedestrian, Jew and Gentile, giving the city a vibe one Operation Torch planner describes as "half-Arabian, half-European, and half-Hollywood." Pleasure craft anchor in the protected harbor. French warships such as the *Jean Bart* dock quayside. Somewhere in the darkness bristles a hidden thicket of coastal artillery batteries. El Hank, given its strategic location, has a battery all its own, perhaps the most formidable in all Casablanca—every single onshore gun pointed straight out to sea.

Mysteriously, the lighthouse's powerful beam goes dark at 0300.

. . .

OPERATION TORCH WILL simultaneously drop 100,000 American troops on landing beaches in Morocco, Algeria, and Tunisia. General

Dwight Eisenhower, newly appointed supreme commander of the Allied Expeditionary Force in North Africa, supervises the overall operation.

Patton commands the western sector, focused on Morocco's Atlantic coast. The landing beaches at Oran and Algiers in the Mediterranean will require British assistance, but Patton's force of 33,843 is all American.

Although Morocco is a colony of France, none of Charles de Gaulle's Fighting French troops are taking part. General de Gaulle has long suspected the Allies of planning this invasion. Yet he has been kept in the dark, given absolutely no information about when or where Torch might occur, for the Americans are backing a very different Frenchman to take charge of all those Vichy forces in North Africa who might choose to surrender and change sides.

The suave, undeniably brave, and equally dimwitted General Henri Giraud was Charles de Gaulle's commanding officer just prior to the war during a posting to the garrison at Metz in eastern France. Giraud still considers the Fighting French leader his subordinate, showing superiority by using the less formal "Gaulle" when addressing him, rather than full name or rank.

But Charles de Gaulle is not cowed.

On May 13, 1940, just three days into the war, the sixty-one-year-old Giraud, a square-shouldered, balding man with a thick black mustache, blundered into a German patrol while conducting reconnaissance in the Ardennes. He was taken captive and imprisoned in Germany's Königstein Fortress, a four-century-old castle on the river Elbe. After two years of planning he escaped by lowering himself down steep castle walls using a rope he wove in secret from bedsheets and strands of wire, then leapt onto a moving train. He connected with the British SOE. The commandos provided Giraud with money, clothes, and identity papers, allowing him to finally reach the safety of Gibraltar. Giraud's escape is a courageous tale, most appealing to an

American president hitching his wagon to a genuine French hero. Not surprisingly, like an ancient storyteller again and again spinning an epic saga, Giraud never tires of sharing his story in dramatic detail. For good measure, he sometimes tells the story of his World War I POW escape involving a circus and legendary nurse Edith Cavell.

But it is not solely General Giraud's bravery that so enamors the Americans—and, to a lesser extent, an increasingly exasperated Winston Churchill. It is de Gaulle himself. The general has grown intractable in the defense of his Fighting French, even smashing a chair during a Downing Street meeting with the prime minister. De Gaulle's fondness for comparing himself with Joan of Arc, whom he claims to be a distant relative, strikes many in Allied leadership as pretentious and off-putting.*

General de Gaulle has many things going for him, including a Fighting French army of 50,000 men stationed throughout Africa and the Middle East. He also enjoys increasing loyalty from the French Resistance, now nearly unified under the leadership of Jean Moulin. But no one really likes him. General Henri Giraud—pliable, vainglorious, and all too eager to accept any compliment sent his way—is much easier for the Allies to manage.

So, as far as the Americans are concerned, General Charles de Gaulle should just go away.

If not for Winston Churchill's support, the general might already be gone.

. . .

GENERAL GEORGE S. PATTON's infantry will land on a broad sandy beach eighteen miles north of Casablanca, at a resort known as Fedhala. Paratroopers will secure the main airfield. Three columns of

---

* Joan of Arc was a teenaged French heroine who inspired French victories over the British during the Hundred Years' War. She was later captured and burned at the stake. Jeanne d'Arc, as she is known in France, was nineteen at the time of her death.

mighty M4 Sherman tanks will put ashore at Safi, 140 miles south. Infantry and armor will then race to capture the heavily defended naval base at Casablanca, attacking from opposite directions.

The conquest will not be easy. Vichy defenders number more than 55,000, armed with a complement of 120 tanks and almost 200 fighter and bomber aircraft—of which more than half were manufactured in the United States and purchased before the war.

In addition, Casablanca is defended by submarines, destroyers, lightweight cruisers, and the half-built *Jean Bart*. The warship was still under construction as France fell. In a dramatic getaway, *Jean Bart* survived an unintentional grounding in shallow waters and then bombing by German Heinkel bombers while fleeing the shipyard at Saint-Nazaire. She limped across the Mediterranean into the Atlantic, still missing her primary turrets. Yet, unfinished as she might be, *Jean Bart* is still quite capable of opening fire from her main battery on the bow, four-barrel fifteen-inch guns with an accurate range of twenty-five miles, more than capable of pulverizing the American landing force all the way north on Fedhala beach with two one-ton shells per minute.*

Patton has drilled his men relentlessly in the eleven months since America entered the war. His new style of tank warfare is his own version of blitzkrieg. Tanks and other vehicles are always on the move, remaining fifty yards apart to prevent a bunched target. Infantry follows close behind. This style has worked splendidly for Erwin Rommel and the German panzers but remains unproven by an American force.

Thus, Patton has prepared for this morning with furious attention to detail. Training took place in the searing heat of California's Mojave Desert, offering the best available simulation of North Africa. Troops were instructed to protect their skin from the sun's debilitating rays by keeping sleeves rolled down at all times. Patton rationed

---

* For those wishing to make the journey to see the landing beach, it's worth noting that Fedhala was renamed Mohammedia in 1960.

water so his men would train their bodies to do without. Over and over, he repeated that movement is vital. Digging a foxhole is no different from digging a grave.

"When the great day of battle comes," he writes in a letter to his troops during the Atlantic crossing, "remember your training."

To avoid enemy detection, the task force has sailed from several American ports, traveling 4,000 nerve-racking miles across ocean prowled and dominated by German U-boats.* These submarines have devastated convoys of merchant marine vessels carrying vital war supplies to England and are more than capable of sinking all 102 aircraft carriers, cruisers, destroyers, tenders, and assorted other vessels of the naval task force.

"And remember above all that speed and vigor of attack are the sure roads to success and you must succeed—for retreat is as cowardly as it is fatal. Indeed, once landed, retreat is impossible. Americans do not surrender," the general admonishes his men.

And yet, Patton has long been unsure Operation Torch will succeed. The enormity of transporting an invasion force across thousands of miles of dangerous ocean, the determination of a defensive army fighting for territory they call their own, and temperamental autumn weather has him fearing this could be "a very desperate venture."

But as the general himself writes, there is no turning back.

---

* U-boat is German for *Unterseeboot*—"undersea boat."

45

H hour is delayed for reasons beyond Patton's control.

This is the Navy's ball game. The general won't assume total command until he steps onto African sand.

Another delay. The darkness is still complete, but sunrise will soon unveil the eastern horizon. Landing craft will be completely visible to enemy gunners. Transports loaded with American troops wriggle closer to shore through the armada, each vessel marked by colored lights denoting center, left, or right in the carefully orchestrated approach to landfall. Finally, just before morning's first orange rays of sunshine, the landing craft dash to the coast.

Patton frets, though not for the reason most commanders grow anxious about engaging the enemy.

Quite the opposite.

The general's wariness about Operation Torch extends to the true motivations of his Vichy opponent. Patton is unclear whether the French will fight fiercely or not at all, embracing the Americans as enemy or ally. Patton much prefers the former. The general has written just-in-case farewell letters to old friends during the many hours at sea, but he is far more conflicted about not fighting than about dying.

"From some messages we have," Patton writes his wife, Bea, on November 2—their thirty-three years of marriage have often been contentious, strained by duty separations and the general's infidelities— "it seems that there is a good chance the French Army and Air will join us. I hope not, for it would sort of pull the cork [out] of the men— all steamed up to fight and not have to—also it would be better for me to have a battle."

Those fears are allayed at 0455. The code words *Batter Up* are received from the landing site at Safi, signifying that the Vichy French are firing upon the Americans. The sun is rising. Patton bears witness as the distant red-tile roofs and towering date palms of Casablanca make themselves known. In turn, the city's defenders gaze out upon the breathtaking sight of an American fighting force of uncountable magnitude that has somehow appeared off their coastline in the few short hours between a late dinner and an early breakfast.

The United States Navy lets loose a thunderous barrage. Casablanca's coastal batteries quickly return fire.

USS *Ranger*, an aircraft carrier safely positioned thirty miles northwest of Casablanca, launches its first wave of F4F Wildcats at 0615. Four *Sangamon*-class escort carriers—tankers converted into carriers with the addition of a flight deck—soon send their own contingent of Wildcats, Dauntless dive-bombers, and TBF Avenger torpedo bombers aloft.* These aircraft will attack Vichy airfields, hopefully destroying the enemy air force on the ground. Should French planes take off,

---

* One of these converted tankers, USS *Suwannee*, is commanded by Captain J. J. "Jocko" Clark, the first Native American to graduate from the U.S. Naval Academy at Annapolis, in the Class of 1917.

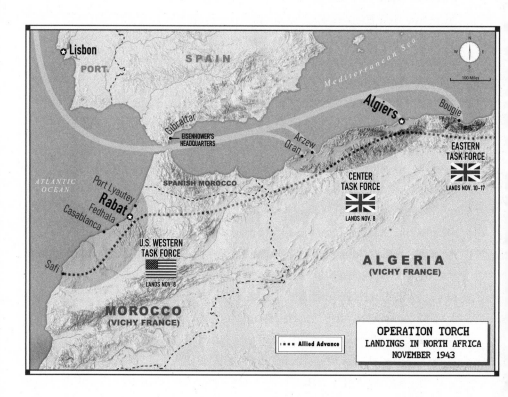

Lisbon
PORT.
SPAIN
Mediterranean Sea
N
W ● E
S
100 Miles
Algiers
Bougie
Gibraltar
EISENHOWER'S
HEADQUARTERS
Arzew
Oran
EASTERN
TASK FORCE
LANDS NOV. 10-17
ATLANTIC
OCEAN
Port Lyautey
SPANISH MOROCCO
CENTER
TASK FORCE
Rabat
Fedhala
Casablanca
LANDS NOV. 8
Safi
U.S. WESTERN
TASK FORCE
ALGERIA
(VICHY FRANCE)
LANDS NOV. 8
MOROCCO
(VICHY FRANCE)
▪▪▪▪ Allied Advance
OPERATION TORCH
LANDINGS IN NORTH AFRICA
NOVEMBER 1943

warplanes of the Navy "Fighting Nine" Wildcat squadron will be in the unlikely situation of midair dogfights pitting the American-made planes flown by both sides against one another. What would normally feel like a training exercise will prove all too deadly.*

At 0715, Patton receives a telegram from General Dwight Eisenhower. The simple message is typed onto a form headlined "Naval Message," authorizing Patton in capital letters to PLAY BALL. This is the signal to return fire.

Patton already knows.

The general hands the missive to an aide, telling him to keep it. The instantly precious historical artifact marks the precise moment when George S. Patton initiates hostilities against Adolf Hitler. Patton tells the aide it will make a great souvenir.

Finally, 0800.

The Higgins boat (designated "landing craft, vehicle, personnel") transporting Patton to Fedhala beach still swings from davits hanging over the aft section of the *Augusta*'s slender hull. Patton's orderly, Sergeant William George Meeks, moves the general's personal possessions from his stateroom to the landing craft.†

But Patton remembers almost too late that his pistols are stored in a valise just placed on board. He is extremely particular about these handguns, a .45 Colt revolver owned since his service in Mexico in 1916 and a .357 Magnum Smith & Wesson purchased in the 1930s.

---

* French aerial units in Morocco flew the Douglas DB-7 medium bomber, the Martin Model 167 bomber, and the Curtiss H-75A-4 fighter—which was instead named the P-36 Hawk when flown by American forces. The French purchased these aircraft before the start of the war. When it became clear that France would fall to Germany, to keep them out of Nazi hands these units were ordered to North Africa, where they were incorporated into the air force of Vichy France—l'Armeé de l'Air de Vichy.

† Named after Andrew Higgins, a lumber businessman turned ship builder, these landing craft are thirty-six feet long and ten feet wide, designed to carry thirty-six soldiers to a foreign beach at the rate of nine knots per hour. The boats proved so successful in amphibious landings that Adolf Hitler dubbed Higgins the "new Noah."

Patton chafes when others mistakenly believe the unique white hand-grips are made of pearl. "Only a pimp in a Louisiana whorehouse carries pearl-handled revolvers," Patton corrects. "These are ivory."

On board, photographers are chronicling the invasion. There is no way General Patton is getting his picture taken without those pistols. The loyal and patient Sergeant Meeks, a forty-six-year-old African American who well knows the general's eccentricities, retrieves the weapons. Patton takes a moment to wrap his custom-made leather S. D. Myres holster belt around his waist and couple the interlocking brass "US" buckle.

"At that moment, a light cruiser and two big destroyers came out of Casa, tearing up the coast close to shore to try to get our transports," Patton notes in his journal. "At once, Augusta speeded up to 20 knots and opened fire. The first blast from the rear turret blew the landing boat to hell and we lost all our things except my pistols."

The French soon fire marker rounds—shells filled with pink and green dye to make the *Augusta* easier to see from a distance. "I was on main deck just back of number two turret leaning on the rail when one hit so close that it splashed water all over me," Patton writes. The general is not only drenched, but bright dye coats his combat jacket. Meeks attempts to wipe it off.

Patton stops him. "Leave it there. This will stay on the fucking jacket as long as I am able to wear it."

The naval battle is a pitched fight between a vastly superior U.S. force and a valiant and professional Vichy navy that will not back down. The ocean battles will continue on and off until Casablanca falls in three days. Five French destroyers—*Fougueux, Brestois, Boulonnais, Frondeur, Alcyon*—will be sunk, along with the submarines *Sidi-Ferruch, Oréade, Psyché*, and *Amphitrite*. The American ships USS *Massachusetts*, USS *Wichita*, and USS *Brooklyn* are hit but stay afloat. USS *Edward Rutledge* is struck amidships by a torpedo and sinks, as do USS *Hugh L. Scott* and USS *Tasker H. Bliss*.

The beach landings, as epic and courageous as taking fire while bringing so many men and vehicles ashore might be, are no matches for the fury of two fully engaged navies.

The air is rent with chaos and cacophony. A trembling and quaking Atlantic, ringing in the ears, that nail polish smell of cordite, geysers pouring down water, black pillars of smoke, ships pierced, boilers exploding, oil slicks, good men too far from shore to swim for it.

Good men drowning.

And throughout the fight, lightning and thunder and percussion as those enormous naval guns propel round after round, the loosing of each shot a punch to the solar plexus so powerful and immediate and personal that every man feels it travel down into the deepest pit of his belly.

And that subtle unspoken fear, on steel decks where sailors speak English and steel decks where sailors speak French, as torpedoes and ships' guns and shore batteries send the Atlantic rushing into the galleys and sleeping quarters and engine rooms they call home, killing men anonymously and without giving them time to ask themselves:

Am I next?

. . .

FINALLY, PATTON SETS FOOT on African soil. The time is 1320. Sandy beach. Tide coming in. American troops and equipment occupying the inland berms. German officers unlucky enough to have visited Morocco on the eve of invasion now taken prisoner and being questioned, their haughty Nazi-ness replaced by disheveled and deflated men looking all too ordinary in rumpled uniforms blousing one size too big.

"Got very wet in the surf," the general writes of his first steps onto Fedhala beach. As a young military cadet Patton often walked to the far end of the rifle range during target practice to desensitize himself to bullets whizzing past his head. Some said he was suicidal. Patton called it preparation.

To the general's great disappointment, that training is not put to the test after rusting for a quarter century. "There was still quite a fight going on but I had no bullets [shot my way]," he laments.

Casablanca does not surrender today. Patton's first battle—and victory—of the Second World War is not complete. Yet the defeated Vichy soldiers of Fedhala salute the general as he inspects the town, some even grinning at their new American conqueror.

Back in America, Bea Patton is besieged with interview requests as the nation learns about Operation Torch. "All I can think of is your triumph," she writes to her husband, years of heartache momentarily set aside. "And the thought that rings through my head like a peal of bells is that the first jump is taken and that you will never have to take it again. And I know that it is a success."

Time magazine writes that Patton is "tough" and "muscular."

The *New York Times* instantly renders the general iconic, labeling Patton "America's two-gun general."

Ivory-handled pistols nestled snugly against his thighs, General George S. Patton breathes a sigh of relief and revels in the reportage.

. . .

IN LONDON, a manic Charles de Gaulle screams as he learns of Operation Torch upon rising from bed on the morning of invasion. "I hope the Vichy people throw them back in the sea!" the general seethes.

Once again, Winston Churchill has foreseen the need to speak in confidence with the Fighting French leader at a delicate time. The prime minister has already taken the precaution of scheduling a luncheon to explain Allied thinking. De Gaulle, in turn, is aware that he may soon lose Churchill's backing for the arms, broadcasting power, and London sanctuary so vital to leading his Fighting French cause— and thus any chance to realize the personal ideal of France he cherishes almost as devoutly as the Father, the Son, and the Holy Spirit.

Surprisingly, during the lunch, as Churchill reassures de Gaulle that Britain still backs him as "the only authority" to lead the French struggle despite Franklin Roosevelt's misgivings, the general mumbles that France comes first and that it is "right to choose General Giraud for this."

A hurt Charles de Gaulle is not telling the complete truth; he is buying time to make his next move. These many months working with Winston Churchill have taught Charles de Gaulle a thing or two about politics.

. . .

GENERAL GEORGE S. PATTON's first long day of war comes to an end.

"Spent night at Hotel Miramar," Patton journals about his new waterfront headquarters in Fedhala. In three days' time he will accept the surrender of Casablanca in the Miramar's restaurant—coincidentally, on November 11, the date of the World War I armistice. But for now it is enough to be ashore.

"Very nice," the general writes of the hotel. "But it had been hit several times so there was no water, nor light, and only cheese and fish to eat and champagne to drink.

"God was very good to me today."

46

Winston Churchill savors victory.

Finally.

Mansion House is electric with patriotism and bacchanal. Today is the annual Lord Mayor's luncheon, a London tradition for eight centuries. William Shakespeare himself described the feast in *Henry V.* Clementine Churchill arrives wearing a hat colored in the bold palette of triumph: bright red. Long tables with twenty-four place settings. Ironed white tablecloths, gold-plated china, celebratory red and white carnations. Baking bread, roasting turkey, and a simmering perfume of thyme, allspice, and bay leaves from today's tender first course, hot turtle soup. Old friends and old enemies make nice, succored by sherry and sweet white hock.

And a surprise to mark this very special day: every guest receives a box of matches, a keepsake as scarce as hen's teeth in wartime.

Luncheon is held in the Egyptian Hall here at the Lord Mayor's official residence rather than the traditional site at London's cavern-ous Guildhall a half mile away. There, the great room has the high ceilings of a cathedral and stone walls five feet thick, a space of medieval splendor recalling a day when the thick oak doors might be flung open and an army on horseback free to gallop their mounts over the threshold to hail an all-powerful king—or, if not soldiers and horses, an army of jesters and courtesans parading through that same massive entry to please a profligate ruler and his court.

But the Guildhall was seriously damaged by Luftwaffe bombs during what has become known as the Second Great Fire of London. Thus, the relatively smaller but more stately Egyptian Hall.*

The newly elected Lord Mayor, Sir Samuel Joseph, enters to the sound of trumpets. Winston Churchill sits in the seat of honor at the head table as Joseph makes his opening remarks. Churchill will speak next.

The prime minister is loose, smiling, clad in his now-familiar black suit, waistcoat, bow tie, and pocket square. A few months ago, in Cairo, that uniform was nowhere to be seen. Churchill greeted Britain's Egyptian command in a weathered pith helmet, loose necktie, and a wrinkled tropical suit that rode up over his wide rump. He flashed two fingers in a V to show his personal victory sign for the newsreel cameras and pretended to be jovial.

In fact, a grim Churchill flew to Cairo because the city was all but lost. The Afrika Korps was less than one hundred miles away. British bases evacuated. Intelligence files hastily incinerated in a last-minute inferno of all things English. German radio operators taunting the Egyptian capital, sending messages telling the women of Cairo to be ready and willing for the Afrika Korps.

---

* The night of December 29, 1940, was the worst night of bombing during the London Blitz. From 6:15 in the evening until 4:00 a.m. more than 100,000 bombs fell on London. The city's water main was destroyed, hampering firefighting efforts. Flames destroyed a larger portion of London than the First Great Fire in 1666.

"It was absolutely necessary that I should come here," Churchill writes Clementine from Cairo on August 9. "This splendid army, about double as strong as the enemy, is baffled and bewildered by its defeats. Rommel is living almost entirely on transport and food and fuel captured from us. He is living from hand to mouth, his army's life hangs on by a thread, but meanwhile a kind of apathy and exhaustion of the mind rather than the body has stolen over our troops which only new strong hands, and above all the gleam of victory, can dispel."

Churchill, believing that drastic times call for drastic measures, relieved his commanding officer, Field Marshal Claude Auchinleck. Lieutenant General William Gott was appointed successor to the "Auk," only to die one day later in a plane crash.

Desperately casting about for a general who might actually win a battle, Churchill settled on General Harold Alexander as his overall commander. The prime minister then selected a relative unknown to lead the Eighth Army, the meticulous, fidgety General Bernard Law Montgomery, a man of surprising charisma and the bones of a sparrow. "I don't drink or smoke and I am one hundred percent fit," Montgomery boasts to Churchill. Without hesitation, the prime minister responds: "I drink and I smoke and I am two hundred percent fit."

Despite their differences, the impulsive politician and the persnickety warrior begin a relationship that will alter both their lives.

Churchill has now been in office twenty-eight months, "during which we had an almost unbroken series of military defeats," he will frankly admit. "A chain of misfortune and frustration to which no parallel could be found in our history . . . [i]t is indeed remarkable that I was not in this bleak lull dismissed from power."

And now, finally, thanks to Montgomery, El Alamein.

And Torch. American ships dropped Patton's forces off Morocco, but it was the Royal Navy that brilliantly handled the Mediterranean landings.

Winston Churchill's insistence on waging war in North Africa is vindicated in most glorious fashion. The American invasions of Operation Torch place Rommel's depleted Afrika Korps between two powerful Allied armies with nowhere to run and soon to be squeezed.

And as soon as the Lord Mayor finishes speaking, the prime minister intends to share this victory with the people of Britain.

. . .

LONDON CITIZENS PRESS against a rope line in the open square outside the Bank of England, patiently waiting on Churchill. Time and location have been kept secret due to fears of a German aerial attack. At 1:00 p.m., loudspeakers atop the bank informed passersby that Churchill would soon be speaking. Town criers walked the city spreading the news.

The prime minister's voice will be broadcast through those same oversized rooftop speakers. It is a bitter gray November Tuesday, certainly not a time for standing too long in the cold. Long winter coats. Hats. Scarves. Women clutching pocketbooks in front of their waistlines with both hands. The sudden news about the speech caught pedestrians as they went about their workday business. There are no children here to fuss or fidget, for they remain in school. Just a collection of strangers facing in the same direction, not talking, gazing at the loudspeakers with the solemn patience that has become a cornerstone of life in wartime London.

These people have listened to Churchill's broadcasted speeches in times of trouble.

And there have been many.

Now these men and women want to hear his voice in a time of triumph. The war is hardly over. Of that, everyone gathered is extremely well aware. They are far beyond delusion but still succored by hope. Thus, the people of London need *something*—as little as a word or two—describing the distant light at the end of this very dark tunnel.

Or something, if only for an hour or a week, for Britain to celebrate.

. . .

MEN WHOM WINSTON CHURCHILL knows well are dining this afternoon in the Egyptian Hall. Each has received an invitation to attend this great feast, along with London's aldermen and the archbishop of Canterbury—a summons that advised them to keep the location and time of luncheon secret. These are the wealthy, the influencers, the connected, the powerful. And although Churchill has often gone deeply in debt to maintain this level of societal status, he will forever struggle to remain one of them, even when the day comes that he no longer holds public office. Many a man in this room has publicly bashed the prime minister, in particular questioning his leadership after the disaster at Tobruk. But as Churchill pushes himself up from the table to speak, these same men now rise and rain down applause.

Not the stiff, beleaguered clapping that has greeted Churchill before so many taut speeches about failure and death.

Instead, radiant affection. Gentlemen celebrating one of their own. Smiles. Private jokes. A standing ovation continuing a beat too long.

The diners sit and grow silent. Churchill waits.

"I have never promised anything but blood, tears, toil, and sweat," the prime minister reminds the audience, transitioning into the heart of his speech after short opening remarks. "Now, however, we have a new experience.

"We have victory."

Churchill lets the words ring over the room.

In the shadow of the bombed-out Guildhall and along the streets near Mansion House, the only sound is Churchill's voice floating down onto the crowd.

"—a remarkable and definite victory. A bright gleam has caught the helmets of our soldiers, and warmed and cheered all our hearts."

Churchill is forced to pause as Britain's better palms pound on the wooden tables like schoolboys'.

"Britain," the prime minister resumes, "always wins one battle—the last.

"We seem to have begun rather earlier this time."

Churchill speaks slowly and with great deliberation. Every sentence is followed by a dramatic pause.

"Rommel's army has been defeated.

"It has been routed.

"It has been very largely destroyed as a fighting force.

"This battle was not fought for the sake of gaining positions or so many square miles of desert territory. General Alexander and General Montgomery fought it with one single idea. They meant to destroy the armed force of the enemy, and to destroy it at the place where the disaster would be most far-reaching and irrecoverable . . .

"Now, this is not the end.

"It is even not the beginning of the end."

Here, Churchill waves his right arm up in the air and brings it down with a flourish, the conductor announcing the dramatic finale to a great symphony.

The prime minister then lowers his voice and sweeps his gaze over the room.

"But it is, perhaps, the end of the beginning."

. . .

Church bells.

For the first time in twenty-eight months, church bells.

From St Paul's to Westminster Abbey to parishes in the distant bosom of the green British countryside, church bells.

Defiant, celebratory, Divine, pealing at Churchill's request.

Announcing celebration, not invasion.

The tide is turning.

Britain, finally, has something to cheer.

47

The restless woman with one leg has nothing to celebrate.

As Winston Churchill wraps up his Mayor's Day speech in London, Britain's top Special Operations Executive agent is in mortal danger, her suppressed terror a diametric opposite to the prime minister's momentary glow.

Virginia Hall hides in her room at the Hôtel de la Cloche, waiting. Tall windows. Long curtains. Wrought iron. A bunker twenty miles from the Spanish border owned by Resistance sympathizers. Alerted in advance by the American consulate in Lyon that the Germans would soon take control of Unoccupied France, she fled the city in a controlled panic.

"The Enemy's Most Dangerous Spy," screams handbills being posted on kiosks throughout France. "We Must Find Her and Destroy Her!'

An accurate drawing of Virginia Hall's likeness, provided to the Gestapo by Father Robert Alesch, also adorns the wanted poster.

Unoccupied France is no more. The myth of French self-determination is gone. Nazi Germany controls every last hectare of French soil.

Three weeks ago, on October 18, Adolf Hitler issued his "Commando Order," an acknowledgment of Resistance and SOE success in sabotaging the German war effort. The directive states that all captured commandos are to be shot immediately.

But a firing squad is too quick a death for the Gestapo. Information must first be extracted. In Lyon, the German secret police have set up headquarters at the Hôtel Terminus. There, Commander Klaus Barbie is making it his personal mission to capture and torture "that limping Canadian bitch."

The Gestapo have not arrived in Perpignan. Not yet. But they are coming.

Hall is on the run—almost too late but dashing toward freedom nonetheless. She felt the heat long before Torch, requesting permission from London to fly to the SOE's Baker Street headquarters by way of Lisbon. Despite their approval, Hall had a change of heart and remained. There was still work to be done.

But now Virginia Hall is famous. And famous gets her a free return ticket to Klaus Barbie.

If only Hall had fled. It would have been easy, almost pleasant, a wistful farewell to the French countryside she has come to know so well. A series of trains: French border, Spain, Portugal. A loud but relatively leisurely flight on the four-times-a-week BOAC DC-3 service from Lisbon to Whitchurch Airfield, outside Bristol. No haste. No rapid pulse at passport controls. No terrified realization that every man, woman, and child in France is looking straight at her, completely certain they are staring into the eyes of the woman on the "Wanted" poster.*

---

* BOAC stands for British Overseas Airways Corporation. The airline was formed in 1939 by the merger of Imperial Airways and British Airways. BOAC ceased

Hall slept not at all on the overnight ride from Lyon. Gestapo prowled the platforms during a tense change of trains in Marseille. Further travel by rail is out of the question. This cannot be a random act of flight, but a carefully coordinated use of networks she has set in place.

The first step was fleeing Lyon. The next was connecting with an operator here in Perpignan code-named "Gilbert" whose daily routine for the SOE includes lingering in the village square every afternoon between two and three.

Just in case.

Hall made the connection. She requested that Gilbert arrange a guide to walk her over the Pyrenees. This is step three. A spindly network of the Chemin de la Liberté (Freedom Trail) used to funnel downed fliers out of France threads through the rugged mountain terrain. The way is craggy and vertical. Winter is coming. The trails will be watched by police and their tracking dogs.

And Virginia Hall has just one leg.

Amputee or not, Hall has to get over these mountains. There is no other choice.

Gilbert does need to know about Cuthbert. Most people can't tell. Finding a local *passeur* to guide her would be harrowing in the best of times. Expecting that individual to risk his freedom for someone literally unable to run for their own life is ludicrous.

So the restless woman with one leg keeps her secret to herself.

But she well knows that she'd better not complain—and she'd better keep up.

Her guide arrives just after dark.

---

operations on March 31, 1974, when it became part of another merger that formed the modern entity of British Airways.

. . .

VIRGINIA HALL'S TRAIL to freedom begins thirty miles inland from Perpignan, in a thousand-year-old village in the Pyrenees foothills known as Villefranche-de-Conflent.

Dawn. Stone ramparts of an eighteenth-century fortress overlook the town, dwarfed by a towering peak rising abruptly to the south. The party is one *passeur*, Virginia Hall, a Polish Jew, and a Frenchman. The two other travelers are impoverished and request a delay to come up with the guide's fee. An impatient Hall has no time to wait. She hands over 50,000 francs to cover all three.

The path travels southward through pine forest along the snow-fed Rio Oja up to a mountain pass, all the way down into a valley, and then up and up and up again over another pass. The descents are as precarious as the ascents are rigorous. Hall carries her belongings and a radio in a bag slung over her shoulder, disguising her limp by pretending the heavy carryall is disrupting her gait. The others don't catch on.

The journey will be more than fifty miles and last two days. Elevation gain in the first fourteen miles alone is more than 5,000 feet. The highest pass is almost twice that. Rocks and pine trees define the path at first, then ice, loose rocks, a stiff wind, snowdrifts three feet deep, and random drop-offs several hundred sheer feet straight down.

Hall will call this trek the "scariest moment of my life."

Cuthbert makes her stump bleed. The blood drenching Hall's sock freezes when the group pauses to rest for the night. She radios back to England that she is en route but that Cuthbert is giving her trouble.

"If Cuthbert is tiresome," comes the reply from a radio operator with no knowledge of the wooden leg, "have him eliminated."

In Lyon, Hall's undercover colleague, Dr. Jean Rousset, is soon to be arrested in a Gestapo roundup. He will be taken from his home in the middle of the night, wearing his pajamas. Rousset will be tortured at the Montluc prison in Lyon and condemned to the Buchenwald concentration camp in Germany.

Virginia Hall knows none of this. She is on her way out. But the Spanish authorities are sympathetic to Nazi Germany and will surely repatriate her to France unless she evades police even after completing her mountain crossing.

Two days after entering the mountains—exhausted, filthy, and famished—Virginia Hall safely arrives in Spain.

Where she is promptly arrested.

48

asablanca is released early.

New Yorkers can't wait to see this tale of wartime intrigue, even on Thanksgiving. Opening day. First show. Sidewalk line snaking outside the Hollywood Theatre. Broadway and Fifty-First. Doors open at 11:30. Inside, the Hollywood is lavish: floor-to-ceiling columns, plush carpeting, hand-painted murals, glass chandeliers, fifteen hundred seats spread out between lower level and balcony, plus standing room. No better place for a holiday escape to tropical Morocco.

Macy's Thanksgiving Day Parade would normally be passing by right about now, but that eighteen-year-old tradition has been canceled due to the war. Rubber and helium used to form and float the giant character balloons have been donated to the cause. Instead, soldiers and sailors march down Broadway in a patriotic parade, eager to break formation when it comes to an end on Thirty-Fourth Street and revel in this day of feasting and drinking. Restaurants throughout the city are answering an appeal by Mayor Fiorello La Guardia that every man in uniform receive a hot turkey dinner. No one wants to miss out.*

The same holds true for *Casablanca*. America is finally in the European war. The coincidental timing of the film and the American landings could not have been better planned. The movie was supposed to be released seven months from now, in June, but studio bosses Jack and Harry Warner rushed *Casablanca* into theaters to take advantage of Operation Torch—a marketing ploy they freely admit. "As exciting as the landing at Casablanca!" cries one ad.

"Remember that it was completed and ready weeks before our forces invaded North Africa and that, almost on the heels of the first invasion barge to touch African soil with our soldiers, it was on the screen, helping in its definite way to interpret the action for you, to explain Vichy France to you," Harry Warner explains to *Variety* magazine.

New Yorkers have followed the exploits of General George S. Patton in the *Times* for the past nineteen days. They now fill every seat in the Hollywood, a movie palace specially built by Warner Bros. to showcase their top films. Thirty-one thousand tickets will be sold in the first week, an amazing figure in light of the fact that superstars Cary Grant, Ginger Rogers, Judy Garland, and Errol Flynn all have films screening within blocks of the Hollywood.

The difference is that none of them possesses the timely novelty of *Casablanca*. This new war against Hitler is taking place in far-off countries foreign to Americans in every way. Most citizens have never traveled outside the United States, let alone to Africa. Names like Morocco, Libya, and Tunisia are mysterious, alluring, and a little bit dangerous.

Casablanca explains it all. The audience hears the name de Gaulle.

---

* The Hollywood Theatre and its luxury appointments still stand. It is now the home of the nondenominational Times Square Church.

They see for themselves the Cross of Lorraine. They witness the desperation of refugees willing to steal, to cheat, to lie—anything to flee. And for moviegoers who didn't understand the difference between Free French and Vichy French before settling into their plush maroon movie seats this morning, the full-throated singing of "La Marseillaise" to drown out Nazi officers bellowing "Die Wacht am Rhein" in Rick's Café makes that gulf very clear.*

The camera cuts to actress Madeleine Lebeau shedding tears of rage as she belts out the words. Her look of anguish is real, for Lebeau is French. The nineteen-year-old fled Paris with her Jewish husband in June 1940. Every member of his family will die in a concentration camp. "*Vive la France!*" she cries when the on-screen Germans give up the competition. "*Vive la démocratie!*"†

Americans get it.

"Against the electric background of a sleek café in a North African port, through which swirls a backwash of connivers, crooks and fleeing European refugees, the Warner Brothers are telling a rich, suave, exciting, and moving tale in their new film *Casablanca*," lauds the *New York Times* in a lengthy review. "[T]he Warners here have a picture that makes the spine tingle and the heart take a leap."

The first screening ends midafternoon. *Casablanca* is deeply quotable. As with most such movies, the best lines are repeated by members of the audience as they file out of the Hollywood and head home

---

* "Die Wacht am Rhein" translates to "Watch on the Rhine." The song alludes to the many wars between Germany and France through the centuries. "Dear Fatherland, put your mind at rest . . . Firm and true stands the watch on the Rhine . . . And if my heart breaks in death, / You won't become a Frenchman yet, / As abundant with water is your flood, / So is Germany in heroes' blood."

† Lebeau's husband, forty-three-year-old Marcel Dalio, plays the role of the croupier in *Casablanca*. He was so well known for his acting in French films before the war that the Nazis distributed posters of his likeness to show France what a "typical Jew" looks like.

to give thanks. In the film's final scene Humphrey Bogart is off to join the Free French in Brazzaville. Speaking to Claude Rains, portraying a Vichy administrator, Captain Louis Renault, who has decided to change sides and join him, Bogart as Rick closes the movie with the iconic line: "Louis, I think this is the beginning of a beautiful friendship."*

Oh, that Charles de Gaulle could say the same about Franklin Delano Roosevelt.

---

* The final scene was filmed at what was then known as Metropolitan Airport (now Van Nuys Airport) in Southern California and on Stage One at the Warner Bros. lot. The set was too small to accommodate a life-sized Lockheed Electra 12A aircraft, so the plane used in the film was actually an undersized prop made of plywood. A fog machine and the use of little people as extras were utilized to give the aircraft greater scale.

THE AMERICANS

49

Winston Churchill's secret mission will change the course of the war.

If the prime minister doesn't get blown up first.

In the spirit of resistance, Churchill has nicknamed his personal aircraft *Commando*. The American-made Liberator Mark II bomber, serial number AL504, flies at 8,000 feet over the Atlantic—"five hundred miles from anywhere," in Churchill's explanation. Exterior painted black for stealth. No windows except flight deck and nose bubble. Four Pratt & Whitney R-1830 "Twin Wasp" engines thrumming with steady and deafening power that only cotton balls in each ear can suppress, the droning din jarring yet reassuring during a nine-hour flight so far from land.

The prime minister cautiously navigates the narrow catwalk over the empty bomb bays when the mood strikes, those big doors looming several feet below his precarious tiptoeing sealed shut for safety. He is fond of taking a Scotch up to the cockpit, there to smoke a cigar and kibitz with pilot and copilot, who surreptitiously open a vent for just this occasion. Churchill, himself a former aviator, indulges his curiosity with questions about flight and length of time to destination as the crew navigates by map, sextant, and stars. Even without a drink, Churchill very often wakes in the middle of the night to inquire about *Commando*'s location, dressed only in slippers, robe, and silk nightshirt.

Or sometimes just the nightshirt.

Right now Churchill is sleeping. The prime minister wishes to be fresh upon touching down in Africa. His king-sized berth is built into a strongpoint below the fuel tanks and high-aspect-ratio Davis wings that allow Liberators to fly farther and faster than the Allies' better-known B-17 bomber. Heaters specially installed for Churchill's personal comfort make it cozy enough in the main fuselage to sleep comfortably, even at this altitude in a minimally insulated aircraft.*

Not quite as restful is the fitful slumber attained by Churchill's staff and some of Britain's highest-ranking military officials who now sleep sitting up in chairs directly below, dressed in full uniform and whatever extra clothing they can find.

Such are the benefits of being prime minister.

Yet, something is wrong.

Churchill wakes up, toes melting.

His nose wrinkles at the strong smell of kerosene.

Churchill looks to the bottom of the bed, where his feet are uncomfortably close to a heater. Which is too near his blanket. Which, in turn, might soon be set ablaze. Inevitably, the fire and that flammable

---

* The Davis wing is named for its designer, freelance aeronautical engineer David R. Davis. This design was used prominently on many American bombers and featured a long, narrow wing and teardrop airfoil designed to reduce drag, increase lift, and allow higher speeds. The wing is thicker than most, allowing for fuel storage within the wing itself. The aspect ratio is the square of the wingspan divided by the wing area, meaning that a long, narrow wing has a higher aspect ratio.

kerosene in the air will combust. Churchill's sleeping location directly beneath the fuel tanks ensures a most grisly demise.

The prime minister climbs down from the bed.

Quickly.

Among those sleeping upright is Sir Charles Frederick Algernon Portal, known simply as Peter. The forty-nine-year-old Oxford graduate worked his way up from the lowest enlisted ranks to become chief of air staff, the most powerful man in the Royal Air Force. He joins Churchill on this secret mission due to his belief in the power of bomber aircraft, which many Allies see as key to winning the war.

All that matters to Winston Churchill right now is that Portal knows his way around the inside of a big airplane. So the prime minister ignores the other sleeping aides and functionaries as he rouses Britain's top pilot. "I therefore climbed out of my bunk and woke up Peter Portal," Churchill will write, "and drew his attention to this very hot point. We looked around the cabin and found two others, which equally seemed on the verge of becoming red hot."

Should *Commando* explode, the sudden and horrific destruction will not only vaporize everyone on board but also render the death of Winston Churchill a mystery for the ages, the corpse of Britain's indefatigable wartime leader never to be found and thus consigned to legend. *Commando*'s wreckage—should there be any—will be too far from land for search or rescue.

This is more prophetic than far-fetched. Two years from now, on March 27, 1945, *Commando* will disappear just before a routine landing in the Azores. Churchill is not on board but will describe recovery efforts to the House of Commons the following day. Fragments of wreckage, empty yellow inflatable rafts, and an oil slick will be the only findings.

So *Commando* has the capacity to detonate. Such a tragedy is disconcerting at any time, but for it to occur at this critical juncture in the war will literally change world history. There will no longer be a Winston Churchill to alternately berate and kowtow to the all-important Americans. A new prime minister might not understand the British soul and thus lose the people's confidence at a time when the nation cannot afford to lack faith in leadership. But most all, Churchill has a vision for what the rest of this war looks like. It is his own distinct concept, favoring a British invasion of Italy over a cross-Channel landing in France. This will seal Britain's continuing role as a global superpower and humiliate "that man" in the process.

The prime minister will share those hopes with Franklin Roosevelt at his top secret destination, for the president has also embarked on a flight over the Atlantic, a roundabout five-day journey marking the first time a sitting U.S. president has flown internationally.*

Their destination is Casablanca.

No one is to know. Not yet. And certainly not the media.

The guest of honor, should he decide to attend, is an extremely angry General Charles de Gaulle.

General Henri Giraud, Roosevelt's personal choice to govern the French people, will also be present.

Churchill envisions the two men forming a partnership.

Roosevelt prefers to call the French affair a "shotgun wedding."

. . .

"WE WENT INTO the bomb alley," Churchill will write of his nighttime journey through *Commando* with Peter Portal, "and found two men industriously keeping alive this petrol heater. From every point of view I thought this was most dangerous. The hot points might start a conflagration and the atmosphere of petrol would make an explosion imminent.

---

* Roosevelt's aircraft was a Boeing 314 Clipper flying boat named the *Dixie Clipper*. The entire journey covered 17,000 miles. Boarding the aircraft in Florida, Roosevelt made stops in the Caribbean, Brazil, and then across the Atlantic in Gambia before pushing on to Casablanca. The route was repeated in reverse as Roosevelt flew home.

"Portal took the same view. I decided it was better to freeze than to burn."

Churchill orders all heaters turned off.

But the prime minister's exploration does not go unnoticed. "The P.M. is at a disadvantage in this kind of travel because he never wears anything at night but a silk vest," writes Sir Charles McMoran Wilson, also known as Lord Moran, Churchill's personal physician and among the men attempting to sleep upright. "On his hands and knees he cut a quaint figure with his big, bare bottom."

So it is that Winston Churchill retreats to his lofty bunk and swaddles himself in extra blankets.

"We went back to rest shivering in the ice-cold winter air," he will later recall.

"I am bound to say this struck me as a rather unpleasant moment."

50

General Charles de Gaulle finds *this* moment rather unpleasant. The general slouches in a padded armchair, one of four lined up side by side in the garden outside President Franklin Roosevelt's whitewashed Moroccan villa. From uniform to haircut, everything about de Gaulle is military, save for the thin, dark cigarette smoldering in his left hand and eye-rolling insolence writ large on the long, narrow face that once earned comparisons with a stalk of asparagus.

Glaring sunshine. Olive trees as tall as the Anfa Hotel's third story. Manicured gardens. Big grassy lawn. Perimeter barbed wire strung with tin cans to announce intruders. Armed American military guards with a shoot-to-kill order. And "desert heat," reports *Time* magazine—a description disregarding the fact that the distance between the Atlantic coast and Saharan sands is almost four hundred miles.

A gaggle of fifty journalists, photographers, and newsreel crews cluster ten feet in front of de Gaulle and the three other dignitaries. Until now, no one in the media knew the Allied leadership was anywhere near North Africa. The handpicked press were flown in from Tangiers this morning and ushered to this lawn without being told why. Their audible gasp at the sight of these assembled dignitaries confirms that this clandestine planning meeting has indeed been conducted in complete secrecy.

Winston Churchill sits to de Gaulle's left, looking like a prosperous gangster in homburg and familiar black chalk stripe three-piece, close enough that the French and English leaders' elbows touch. Franklin Roosevelt is to the general's right in gray suit and dark tie, knees crossed, carefully pressing sweat off the top of his eyelids with the back of his hand as the Moroccan noon gets the best of him.

At the far left, resplendent in French dress uniform and knee-high riding boots, basking in the full benefit of the American president's attention, is de Gaulle's rival, General Henri Honoré Giraud, newly appointed high commissioner for French North Africa.

"Out of the meeting," one British broadcaster will describe the hoped-for French power merger, is the ambition "to grow the union of the Fighting French who had never lost hope, and the [Vichy] French for whom hope had been reborn."

Operation Torch was two months ago. Whatever sly niceties de Gaulle once remarked about his former commanding officer have turned to cynicism. When General Giraud captivated Friday's lunch here at the Anfa with the saga of his Nazi prison escape, de Gaulle waited until the very end to add his own biting coda: "And now, General, perhaps you could recount to us the circumstances in which you were taken prisoner."

That was forty-eight hours ago. The ice between the two men has yet to melt. This Casablanca Conference has resolved so many potentially divisive Allied issues, but the problem of who will lead France remains prickly.

"Mr. President," cries out photographer Sammy Schulman of the International News Photos agency. "Can we have a photo of the two generals shaking hands?"

"*Mais oui*," says Giraud, bouncing out of his chair.

Franklin Roosevelt grins with expectation. It was the president who quietly got word to his good friend Schulman to ask the question, putting the French issue front and center.

The photographers wait.

Giraud remains standing, smiling tolerantly, head bare in the noonday sun.

General Charles de Gaulle is in no hurry.

And remains seated.

. . .

SUBTLE AS A UNICORN, the towering white Anfa Hotel is an unusual choice to hold a top secret wartime planning meeting. Designed to look like an enormous ship at sea, front lobby located just beneath the rounded prow, she sails atop a small hill near the ocean, so close to the Atlantic that guests hear waves when opening a window. In addition to well-appointed rooms in the main building, enormous white villas behind the hotel offer luxury and privacy. The Allies have commandeered the entire establishment.

British and American leadership have labored here for ten days. Almost every top military and administrative official from Britain and America has traveled to North Africa. A single Axis air strike would decapitate the Allied war effort.

"The President, with debonair disregard for proverbs about eggs in a single basket, took along Chief of Staff General George C. Marshall," says *Time*, which then goes on to list the dozen prominent Americans who have flown to Africa, including "alter ego Harry Hopkins."

Churchill's retinue, allotted second billing in the American publication, is also mentioned by name and title. Despite his two stars, General George S. Patton is not an active participant in "Symbol," as the gathering is code-named. Instead, the general is responsible for providing his peers and superiors with food, rooms, security, and whatever other hospitality they might require.

The conference is therapeutic, a break from the bitter cold winter of Washington and London. Days have been spent in negotiation at the long oval conference table in the Anfa's great room, fifteen meetings in all, charting the shape of the war. Nights are a time of dinner and cocktails with enough revelry that the attendees will recall Casablanca as a grown-up summer camp.

Surprisingly, the conference results in almost total agreement about what comes next. As Churchill hoped, the outcome favors Britain. In particular, it has been reiterated that defeating Germany will take precedence over the war in the Pacific, where both the United States and Britain have suffered enormous losses. President Roosevelt is fond of the term *unconditional surrender* in describing what that victory will look like. This means the nation-by-nation retaking of Europe, not stopping until Berlin is in Allied hands and the Nazi leadership is held accountable for every transgression.

It is also agreed that the Operation Roundup invasion of France scheduled for this year must be scrapped. A cross-Channel attack is still very much on everyone's minds. This is the easiest way to stage a military buildup in Great Britain and ship two great armies the short distance to France. But the Torch landings in North Africa and failed invasion of France at Dieppe last August have shown that 1943 is not the time. The earliest possible invasion of France is 1944. Paris must endure at least one more year of occupation.

Unless . . .

Unless Winston Churchill's Mediterranean strategy pays off.

America and Britain have agreed to begin the assault of Europe's "soft underbelly" with an invasion of Sicily this coming July. Italy is next. Rome by Christmas is possible.*

Only then Paris.

But nobody knows when.

. . .

THERE MIGHT HAVE BEEN a third Frenchmen in Casablanca today who was eager to shake hands in front of the assembled press, all the while coveting recognized leadership of the French people. That individual's name is Admiral François Darlan.

The pro-Vichy naval officer just happened to be in Tangiers to see his ailing son when Operation Torch landed. Sensing an opportunity to quickly end the fighting, General Dwight Eisenhower conveniently ignored America's newfound loyalty to General Giraud. "Ike" offered to name Darlan commander of French forces in North Africa.

In exchange, the admiral would order all Vichy troops to lay down arms.

Not satisfied with such a pedestrian title, Darlan argued with Roosevelt for more power. This disagreement lasted two weeks, during which time the admiral outrageously showed his continuing loyalty to Adolf Hitler by allowing Nazi troops to land in Algiers. In the name of a rapid peace, an increasingly exasperated Eisenhower finally relented, agreeing to Darlan calling himself French high commissioner of North and West Africa. No matter that Darlan was a pro-Nazi collaborator and commander in chief of the Vichy armed forces. "If we collaborate with Germany," Darlan has stated, "that is to say, if we

---

* The eight points of agreement of the Casablanca Conference were to defeat Germany first, funnel more aid to the Soviet Union, capture Sicily, increase American troops and matériel in England, open a supply route into China by retaking Burma, conduct a study of German industrial strength to increase aerial bombing, take total control of North Africa and the Mediterranean, and make Britain responsible for all matters related to the nation of Turkey.

work for her in our factories, if we give her certain facilities, we can save the French nation."

Eisenhower's distasteful concession came to an abrupt end four weeks ago. Just after lunch on Christmas Eve, a twenty-year-old pro–de Gaulle resistant named Fernand Bonnier de la Chapelle fired two rounds from a World War I–era Ruby 7.65 pistol into the high commissioner— one bullet in the chest, another in the head. Admiral Darlan died instantly—and conveniently.

Chapelle is tried in a Christmas Day court, followed that evening by a military tribunal confirming his death sentence. It is a sanguine General Henri Giraud who insists the execution take place as quickly as possible. So it is that, at 7:30 the following morning, Fernand Bonnier de la Chapelle is shot by firing squad in a Tangiers square. Later that day, power reestablished, Giraud succeeds Darlan as high commissioner.

The messy and coincidental assassination is viewed by many as a conspiracy. Indeed, the execution of François Darlan saves the United States and Britain a great deal of embarrassment. Collaborating with a Nazi collaborator is not at all the moral high ground to which the Allies aspire in their war with Adolf Hitler.

Now, Casablanca Conference almost at an end, General Charles de Gaulle reluctantly rises to his feet before the gathered press to shake Henri Giraud's hand. De Gaulle is taller by several inches, his lanky physique casting a sitting Winston Churchill almost completely in shadow. De Gaulle's expedient handshake is brief and hardly warm. Lips pursed. Face tight and strained. Body leaning away from his adversary. Giraud is beholden to the Americans and knows it. De Gaulle depends upon the British more than ever but pretends he does not.

Franklin Roosevelt and Winston Churchill have their shotgun wedding.

Yet, this union can never last.

For almost three years General Charles de Gaulle has owned the hearts and minds of Frenchmen praying for deliverance. And for almost three years the general has remained steadfast to that cause. He has ruled uncontested, a symbol. This raises the question as to whether the general should lead France because he is the best choice or because, so far, Charles de Gaulle is the only choice.

Time will tell. General de Gaulle now has an opponent.

Giraud is everything de Gaulle is not: flashy, charismatic, and even exciting. Men like him attract a following.

This battle to lead France will end soon enough.

And whether it is Charles de Gaulle or Henri Giraud, only one Frenchman can prevail.

51

P aris wears a bull's-eye.

Sixteen minutes out. A golden Sunday. The good people strolling the Tuileries cannot yet see or hear the 133 B-17 bombers flying in tight formation toward a beleaguered City of Lights. The American Flying Fortresses are still fifty miles away. Each Dark Olive Drab No. 41 fuselage bears a name emblazoned just below the cockpit, vestiges from life before wartime: *Bad Check, Holy Mackerel, The Devil Himself, Iza Available, Vicious Virgin, The Witches Tit,* and so on. Each B-17 also carries six 1,000-pound high-explosive M44 bombs. An hour ago, somewhere over the English Channel, bombardiers made their way back past the cockpit into the bomb bay, where they personally armed each explosive by hand.

Nor can the citizens of Paris hear the banter and singing echoing through the Flying Fortresses as excited aircrews close in on the Eiffel Tower and Notre-Dame, utterly thrilled to glimpse these landmarks for the first time in their young lives. And on this gorgeous afternoon without any harassing German antiaircraft fire, and so far no Luftwaffe fighters rising to meet the bombers, that view will be spectacular.

There's nothing special so far about April 4 other than this amazing weather. The people of Paris are just trying to make it through another day. Citizens are starving but not dying, cold to the bone for lack of heat, fearful of venturing outside their homes, terrified of a simple knock on the door, quarantined by fear, hiding Jews in crawl spaces and secret rooms, enduring the closure of more than one hundred Métro stations because the Nazis can't find enough power to run the trains—meanwhile allowing German soldiers to ride public transport for free—and purchasing copies of Jean-Paul Sartre's *Being and Nothingness* (*L'Être et le néant*) not for the philosophy but because it weighs exactly 2.2 pounds and can be used as a measuring weight, since traditional copper kilograms have been appropriated to make bullets.

The Germans still eat well in the city's finest restaurants, leading one officer to describe how something as simple as food feels like military triumph. Captain Ernst Jünger compares the view looking down on the city from the sumptuous confines of the Tour d'Argent restaurant near Notre-Dame as "a kind of diabolical satisfaction, the gray oceans of rooftops under which the starving tried to keep body and soul together. In such times, eating well and copiously gives a feeling of power."

So it is that the entire French population of Paris prays for the merest sliver of relief. Anything.

Yet, going about its business, suffering in silence, Paris is just moments from a thousand tons of death falling from the sky.

. . .

TEN MINUTES OUT.

Base altitude for the bomber formations is 22,000 feet. Groupings of twelve aircraft give one another room in the air by keeping a horizontal distance but also stacking upward five hundred vertical feet at a time. Oxygen masks. Unlimited visibility. No evasive action whatsoever as the heavily laden B-17s level off for what promises to be a milk run.

The French countryside between coastline and capital is bright emerald, like "the green Illinois river valley over which I had trained," in the words of one American pilot. Each plane is 74 feet long with a wingspan of 103 feet and carries not just bombs but an arsenal of machine guns poking at all angles from the top, bottom, sides, and back end of the fuselage to defend against German fighters—indeed, a true flying fortress. The aircrews number ten men, all now dressed in fur-lined leather jackets and thick boots to ward off the high-altitude subzero chill.*

Four minutes.

Today's target is not Paris and certainly not its inhabitants. Each B-17 will drop its six HE (high-explosive) bombs on the Renault armament works in the suburb of Boulogne-Billancourt, where 1,500 German trucks, tanks, and armored cars are assembled each month. The British bombed the plant one year ago but the Nazis rebuilt it, as they will surely attempt to do after today. The secondary target, should the crews not unload over Renault due to enemy opposition or some other unforeseen event, is a nearby Citroën factory. The third and final place to clear bomb bays is the Sotteville railroad marshaling yard in Rouen, on the way home. No one wants to battle German aircraft over the Channel with ordnance in the hold. Round trip flight time is a little over five hours.

Two minutes out.

"Bomb bay open," the bombardier abruptly commands. All interphone chatter stops. The two five-foot-wide doors swing outward, opening a cavernous hole in the bottom of the aircraft. One dizzying

---

* An aircrew comprises the pilot, copilot, bombardier, navigator-radioman, and gunners firing .50 and .30 caliber machine guns. Top speed is 287 miles per hour.

look straight down shows nothing but France four miles below. Hard, cold wind fills the surprisingly narrow fuselage.

Key to the Allies' precision aerial bombardment is a device known as the Norden bombsight, developed in great secrecy during the 1930s. The Norden looks like Rube Goldberg's idea of a movie camera: one lens and many sharp angles. Bombardier and bombsight are positioned all the way forward in the enormous glass nose bubble, allowing an unobstructed view. Ground speed, bomb weight, airspeed, distance to target, and other variables are fed into the Norden's electromechanical computer. The bombardier then places one eye against the lens, allowing him to look straight down onto the target. If his coordinates are off, a needle and ball displayed inside the bombsight remain distant from one another. When those two bisect, the Norden initiates a series of electrical activities that drop the payload automatically. The bombsight is synced to the automatic pilot during those final moments, meaning the real pilot and copilot are temporarily not in charge of the controls.

One minute.

But the true secret to the Norden's precision is the ability of a talented bombardier to make use of the gyroscopically stabilized telescopic sight to drop bombs at just the right instant. Communicating with the flight deck, he instructs the pilots how to maneuver the B-17 into position for optimal accuracy. Every occupation from ditchdigger to surgeon affords room for artistry. The Norden's version is a bombardier improvising a new chord that makes every bomb fall just right.

"Bombs away," comes the command at 12:16 p.m.

"Eggs" drop in small clusters, tumbling end over end toward the Renault factory. Yellow lights flash in the cockpit. It takes forty seconds for each bomb to fall those long miles to earth. Crews return to the interphone in the meantime, watching below for the explosions and smoke indicating a direct hit.

Then it comes. Puffs of gray destruction billowing up from the ground in staccato succession as bombs detonate on target.

Mission accomplished. Time to get the hell out of here. The large bomber crews break into song, "all ten voices roaring into the interphones in unison," Major Allen Martini of the *Dry Martini* will remember.

The revelry ends fast. Scores of German Focke-Wulf fighter aircraft finally take to the sky, chasing the bombers back to the Channel. Four B-17s will not return to base, their crews either killed or parachuting out to be taken prisoner when their aircraft are shot down. Thirty-three German aircraft are also lost.

But the raid is a complete success. Each man has done his job and is rightfully proud of obliterating the Renault factory. Photographs will show a tangle of unrecognizable metal photographed in natural sunlight because the roof is no more.

"American Flying Fortresses in large force pounded and blasted the Renault works," the *New York Times* will report in tomorrow's edition. The *Times* will also state that Vichy French leader Marshal Pétain condemns the attack as "unjustifiable." Pétain goes on to belittle General Charles de Gaulle and General Henri Giraud as "rebel chiefs," a backhanded compliment marking the closest Pétain has come to openly referring to a parallel French government. The Fighting French respond that the speech is "rather clever" while also doubting it was written by the increasingly senile Pétain.

And on the same front page, almost side by side with details of the Paris bombing and Pétain's rant, is an above-the-fold piece about General George S. Patton's tank command successfully battling across Africa alongside former Vichy French forces led by General Giraud. In one week Patton will complete his rise to international fame by gracing the cover of *Time* wearing the three stars of a lieutenant general.

Thus, April 4, 1943, is a quietly remarkable day in the war.

The events are not as stunning as May 10, 1940, or infamous like

December 7, 1941. It's really just another day. Births, anniversaries, and weddings will be celebrated and remembered, just like yesterday and tomorrow. Milestone events in individual lives will also score this calendar date as specific and worth cherishing: hearts broken, virginities lost, odd lumps beneath the skin. Someone will cheat. Someone will find out she is pregnant, perhaps by a German soldier, becoming one of the 50,000 French women who will bear an occupier's child. Someone will tell someone else for the first time that they love them and that person will say "I love you too," instantly marking that moment on this date as an epiphany to remember for eternity.

Even in wartime.

But there's one more thing that makes today special. And it begins with the Norden bombsight.

The glaring deficiency of this wondrous invention is that preference for jazz. The Norden works best when a bombardier improvises a last-minute change of course to correct for wind or weather, or maybe even just a hunch. But this is impossible when bombers fly in formation. The massed "staggered box" style of attack designed by one of aviation's greatest advocates of aerial bombardment, an American colonel named Curtis E. LeMay, requires bombers to approach a target en masse. Deviation is forbidden. Wingtip to wingtip, waves of B-17s level off and drop their explosives in strict formation. The staggered box is genius, ensuring greater success, fewer downed bombers, and more crews making it home alive.

But the staggered box also means that bombs miss.

Thus, April 4, 1943, will be remembered with specificity throughout Paris. One misguided thousand-pounder destroys the Pont de Sèvres Métro station, one mile south of the Renault factory. The Nazis quickly take advantage of the mishap, publishing photos of Parisian corpses lying in the streets.

In one picture, a nun in white habit stands next to a group of police, every one of them just standing there, not knowing what to do about all these men and women who appear to be sound asleep in the middle of the road.

Another mile away, at the Longchamp Hippodrome on the eastern edge of Paris, people run. Everyone is running. No one knows where they are going. Today is the first meeting of this year's Thoroughbred racing season, and suddenly bombs are falling from the sky right onto the grass racetrack, scattering spectators, horses, jockeys, and the many German officers enjoying a Sunday afternoon wager.

Fifteen hundred Parisians are wounded today. *Wounded* can mean a cut on the leg. *Wounded* can also mean the loss of that leg. Or a whole side of the face.

To three hundred and twenty-seven citizens, such distinctions don't matter because they die.

On April 4, 1943.

.   .   .

LIFE GOES ON. There is no other choice. The Americans and British are doing what they must to win the war. Sometimes the line of fire strays into innocents. There is no helping that. The stunned people of Paris regroup, bitter about being bombed by their saviors, elated at the destruction of the Renault factory, and accepting that all of this is their lot right now.

Yet there comes a moment at the end of this tragic day, as Parisians press their ears to the BBC for the five minutes of nightly good news the British allot the French, when it seems for just a moment that April 4, 1943, will also be remembered for filling the city and nation with hope.

The Allies are about to invade. That's what the rumors are whispering. Turning their radios down so low that not even their neighbors can hear—for those friends from whom borrowing a cup of sugar was second nature once upon a time before the war might now be on the Gestapo payroll—Parisians listen for confirmation.

Those hopes are dashed.

Hard.

Like a steel-toe German boot kicking Paris's most tender nether region, on today of all days.

The Nazis are spreading the rumors, listeners are told. Their goal is to flush out members of the Resistance. Germany is even using fake commando raids on their own defenses to trick French resistants into prematurely rising up in revolt.

The Fighting French spokesman scolds Parisians as if speaking to children:

"You will be told about the beginning of Allied operations on the Continent at the very moment they begin."

52

Winston Churchill is prepared to invade.

So is Franklin Roosevelt.

But they disagree as to where and when.

Lunch was civilized: Roosevelt, Churchill, the dying Harry Hopkins, and William Maxwell Aitken—a.k.a. Lord Beaverbrook—the prime minister's close friend and adviser. The ninety-minute affair was held in the quiet privacy of the president's study.*

---

* Roosevelt's study is now known as the Yellow Oval Room. It is located on the second floor of the White House. The name was changed during the John F. Kennedy administration, when the room was altered from a private library and office into a drawing room used for more official functions, such as serving drinks before formal dinners. It is worth noting that the entire White House was gutted and rebuilt during the Truman Administration. The only sections left untouched were the outside walls. Meticulous measurements were taken before the demolition, meaning that the current rooms were rebuilt to within inches of perfectly resembling the originals. So while the shape and location of these rooms are the same, they are not technically the same spaces used by Roosevelt or any previous president.

The Oval Office is now a zoo. Almost two dozen generals and politicians stake out sitting space on the two couches and collection of polished wooden side chairs. Orderlies and aides know better than to stand anywhere else other than along the curved walls. Maroon carpet bearing the Seal of the President. Matching dark drapes. White walls. Polished maple desk and office furniture inherited from former president Herbert Hoover. Roosevelt, arteries turning to concrete from martinis and tobacco, smokes through a long, slender cigarette holder.

Churchill has once again traveled a great distance to discuss strategy with Roosevelt, this time crossing the Atlantic on board the *Queen Mary*. "The ship had been admirably fitted up to meet all our needs. The whole delegation was accommodated on the main deck, which was sealed off from the rest of the ship," Churchill will write of the journey. "From the moment we got on board our work went forward ceaselessly.

"The conference, which I had christened 'Trident,' was to last at least a fortnight and was intended to cover every aspect of the war."

There is a lull in the fighting. Churchill has not journeyed all this way to discuss battle strategy but to position the global chessboard for a next bold Allied move. The prime minister and his chiefs of staff have spent the crossing in endless meetings to prepare for the Americans. President Roosevelt and his staff have been no less busy, holding crucial White House gatherings to divine their own agenda.

Invading France tops the list. The president's primary objective from this Trident Conference is obtaining a British commitment for a cross-Channel invasion in spring of 1944.

Unlike at Casablanca, Roosevelt intends to get his way. If not, the president has made the audacious decision that he will transfer large numbers of American troops to the Pacific, essentially letting Britain once more wage war against Hitler alone.

Africa is conquered. The Afrika Korps nothing but a memory. Thousands of Germans and Italians taken prisoner in Tunisia and Libya traveled to America with Churchill, albeit secured in the *Queen Mary's* hold. Disgraced General Erwin Rommel was not among them; he is now recuperating from his many illnesses in Germany. The most damaging of all is rumored to be "African sickness," as fellow Nazi generals term Rommel's increasingly cynical nature.

The leadership of France is as unpredictable as ever. Charles de Gaulle is soon to relocate his headquarters from London to Algiers, if for no other reason than to keep a closer eye on General Henri Giraud. Roosevelt still wishes to see the British jettison the "bride," as he refers to de Gaulle.

The Soviet Union has beaten back the German invasion, triumphing decisively in January after the horrendous 872-day Siege of Leningrad. There are two great fears about what the Soviets will do next: settle for peace with Hitler and cease fighting, thus allowing the Führer to focus his entire war effort on the British and Americans; or push their armies as far west as possible before the war ends, claiming all that territory for themselves.

There is no good option. Both are grave cause for concern.

The Allied invasion of Sicily will take place this July, that decision having been made four months ago in Casablanca. Italy will follow.

But of all these issues, everything about Trident circles back to the main agenda item.

The Oval Office quiets. Churchill sits to Roosevelt's right hand, on the edge of the Hoover desk, looking out at the assembled brass.

Franklin Roosevelt's voice is always charming though never lacking in steel. He will brook no disagreement with what he is about to say.

The cross-Channel invasion of France known as Operation Overlord will take place in 1944.

The date will be May 1.

Prime Minister Churchill acts quickly, arguing that the soft underbelly should still play a prominent role in this new strategy.

"I replied that as we were now agreed we could not do this until 1944, it seemed imperative to use our great armies to attack Italy," the prime minister will write.

"By patience and perseverance our difficulties were gradually overcome."

But as Winston Churchill well knows, Franklin Roosevelt has won the day. British power is on the wane.

And the prime minister will do everything in his power to stop that slide.

53

General Charles de Gaulle is nostalgic.

It is the general's last Thursday in London. De Gaulle's Carlton Gardens office looks down on the Mall, where the city's residents enjoy a warm spring afternoon. The general is so eager to assume the mantle of authority in a French territory that he does not think much about whether or not he will miss London—as if such an emotion is possible for a true Frenchman. Yet a great deal of emotion bubbles beneath the surface. The historical impact of what transpired here in this city of Yorkshire pudding and the venerated Connaught Hotel—two of de Gaulle's local favorites—cannot be overlooked.

Today is the anniversary of the last moments of the Battle of Abbeville, de Gaulle's final day as a fighting man. It is also nearly three years since the general fled to London. This next move is of equal importance, for the decisive power struggle with General Henri Giraud awaits. De Gaulle is prepared to be brutal.

First he must say goodbye. The general was in disarray when he first sought help from this ancient French foe. The fate of his own family was as unsure as that of his great nation. Yet de Gaulle imposed like a bad guest, taking every advantage of his hosts, fraying every last nerve of Winston Churchill and his British wartime cabinet.

And yet, despite many moments of misgiving, Churchill sticks with de Gaulle. *Friendship* is the last word the prime minister and the general would use to describe their combative alliance. But the many niceties shown this visitor go beyond mere diplomacy. De Gaulle's rise to power would never have been possible without the British prime minister.

Now de Gaulle reveals a side Churchill has never seen. The general pens a simple farewell thank you note:

As I leave London for Algeria, where I am called by my difficult mission in the service of France, I look back over the long stage of nearly three years of war in which Fighting France has accomplished side by side with Great Britain and based on British territory.

I am more confident than ever in the victory of our two countries along with all their allies.

I am more convinced than ever that you personally will be the man of the days of glory, just as you were the man of the darkest hours.

Yours very sincerely,
Charles de Gaulle

· · ·

MUCH LATER, LONG after de Gaulle's departure, Winston Churchill is asked if he believes de Gaulle to be a great man.

"If I regard de Gaulle as a great man?" the prime minister responds incredulously. "He is selfish, he is arrogant, he believes he is the center of the world."

Churchill takes a breath.

"You are quite right. He is a great man."

54

Jean Moulin is late.

General Charles de Gaulle's Resistance organizer approaches the office of Dr. Frédéric Dugoujon with weary trepidation, telltale neck scar hidden beneath a scarf, even on this warm last day of spring. Moulin turned forty-four yesterday. He wears sunglasses. Brown trilby. A sharp gray suit. Moulin's papers claim he is an art dealer from Nice named Jacques Martel. But today he will be addressed only as "Max," his code name.

The resistant enters the three-story stone building with decorative gray shutters on the Place Castellane. Moulin is eager to begin and end today's conference as soon as possible. Eight grown men crowding into a general practitioner's office in the middle of a Monday afternoon is not the cleverest way to conduct secret Resistance business.

Moulin presses the doorbell. Another cause for concern is that this is the building's only entrance and exit. Sudden escape will be impossible if police surround the building.

Madame Brossier, the doctor's maid, allows Moulin inside but mistakes him for a patient. She sends him to a waiting room rather than upstairs, where the meeting's attendees have already waited forty-five minutes—an eternity in Resistance protocol, in which tardiness of even fifteen minutes warns of something horribly wrong.

Moulin takes off his hat and glasses. Sits. Six patients glance at him, then continue waiting their turn.

In a room across the hall, Dr. Dugoujon examines a small child as the boy's mother looks on. Windows open. Summer breeze.

Everything is so normal.

.   .   .

MOULIN ARGUES WITH HIMSELF, unsure what to do next. Standing up and wandering through the house would be too obvious. This roomful of patients with nothing better to do will watch his every move.

So he remains seated.

Like Virginia Hall of Britain's Special Operations Executive, Moulin's success is due to discretion. The results have been overwhelming. Since parachuting into France eighteen months ago, Moulin has founded a new Resistance press and information bureau and a general study committee to discuss postwar France, coordinated radio communications with London that allow the Resistance to speak with one voice, and strengthened the SOE-Resistance bond.

And just one month ago Moulin's signature achievement unified eight different partisan organizations into the National Council of Resistance. The group then held a secret meeting in Paris to vote that Charles de Gaulle be recognized as the true leader of France. This is the boost to Gaullist fortunes for which the general has longed, proving to President Franklin Roosevelt that de Gaulle is the authentic French authority and finally giving the general a real armed presence inside France itself.

Moulin's next challenge will be a new group named the Maquis.

A recent demand from the Nazi government known as the Service du Travail Obligatoire (STO) requires hundreds of thousands of able-bodied citizens to perform obligatory work service in Germany. In time, more than 650,000 French men and women will be conscripted into forced labor. But not everyone obeys the rules. Young working-class citizens are fleeing their homes and hiding out in woods and caves to avoid the STO, striking back at the Germans with independent acts of guerrilla sabotage. They call themselves the Maquis—"shrubland" in English—a reference to their new wilderness homes.

Moulin will get around to the Maquis in his own time. Max is tired. He is certain the Gestapo knows his true identity.

Suddenly, in the street outside, cars screech to an abrupt halt. The sound of slamming doors. Footsteps on gravel.

The cars are black. Citroëns.

Jean Moulin knows without looking.

Shouting. Front door forced open.

Gestapo.

.   .   .

No one has touched Jean Moulin. Not yet.

These final seconds before being taken into custody are the last moments of personal space Jean Moulin will ever possess.

His body is his own.

Moulin is not bleeding or bruised. No place is swollen. His bones are each of one piece. His lungs are not filled with water from a simulated drowning. He has not felt the sudden jolt of pain as a fist out of nowhere punches the side of his head, making his ears ring and eyes see stars. Moulin's fine clothes are not torn. None of his teeth are broken. His testicles are his own private possession, concealed from the world, swaddled in the soft citadel of his undergarments, as far away from electrical current as they will ever be.

Then that moment is past.

It starts with a shove. Up against the wall. Arms grabbed and wrenched. Then that moment when all freedom is lost: handcuffs.

A small man with a pointed face stares at Moulin, not sure if this is "Max" but sure he will find out.

SS Hauptsturmführer Nikolaus "Klaus" Barbie is thirty, handsome, sadistic, and a cat lover who calls his torture chambers "kitchens." Barbie's pale eyes, one torture victim will long remember, are "extraordinarily mobile, like those of an animal in a cage."

Thus begins an epic battle of wills.

The unwritten Resistance rule is that an operative should attempt to hold out for at least two days of torture before divulging any information. This is enough time to change code names and close down networks before the Germans can use that information.

But Jean Moulin doesn't just know too much; he knows everything. Max must never break.

Klaus Barbie, of course, wants answers right now.

Let the pain begin.

55

Jean Moulin knew it might be like this.

Back when he first parachuted into France, then reveled in ten sensual days with his lover before beginning his ministry to rid France of the devil, the resistant knew full well his life could end in this horrible fashion.

Sultry summer night. A busy metropolitan train station near the German border. Boxcar doors sliding open. Steel wheels braking. Big black locomotives rolling into the night. Whistles.

The resistant, broken, is left to die in a railway car all his own: dehydrated, filthy, unconscious.

It is seventeen days since Moulin's arrest. Not one second of that time has been pain-free. Moulin no longer possesses fingernails or toenails. Steel handcuffs around his wrists ratchet tight around radius and ulna—not muscle or tendon, but the bones themselves. Every knuckle is broken, slammed in a door again and again. He has been drowned and revived in an icy bathtub. Hung naked from shackles in front of strangers and beaten the length of his body with a rubber bat.

Electrodes attached to his bare testicles.

A German hand turning up the power.

The Gestapo *verschärfte Vernehmung* interrogation techniques utilized in the first days of occupation are a quaint memory. There are no more rules. Klaus Barbie has beaten Moulin to exhaustion—his own. Eyewitnesses will long remember the Gestapo officer dragging a body down a flight of steps, so exhausted from the labor that he pauses to catch his breath. Barbie favors handcuffs lined with spikes. He breaks teeth by shoving a bottle hard into the mouth, simulates death by firing squad to watch the victim shit his pants, beats children and pulls out their hair before killing them with the heel of his boot if they are Jewish.

But Jean Moulin has not broken. Head purple and swollen, brain so jarred from repeated blows that he lapses in and out of a coma, Moulin never gives Barbie a shred of information. The Resistance will never suffer a security break on behalf of Jean Moulin.

"This man," Charles de Gaulle will write, "still young, but with an experience already formed by his career, was cast from the same mold as the best of my companions. Filled to the brim of his soul with a passion for France, convinced that Gaullism should not just be a struggle for liberation but the spur of a complete renovation, penetrated by the idea that the State was embodied in the Free French, he aspired to great feats."

Not for money. Not for fame. Not for a beautiful woman who might take him skiing in the Alps for ten days of lovemaking—or sit with him here in this deserted boxcar just to cradle his broken body and nurture his tortured soul.

It's for country.

Jean Moulin has done it all for his beloved nation. He loves France the way Charles de Gaulle loves France—a glorious ideal to be cherished and ultimately realized. In Moulin's extreme suffering, he is more Joan of Arc than de Gaulle himself.

And now, worldly body on its way to yet more torture in Germany, Jean Moulin takes one final breath.

Joan of Arc is dead. Jean Moulin is dead.

The time has come for someone else to rescue France.

56

General Charles de Gaulle's archrival wants to be that hero.

Four thousand miles west of the Metz railway yard, General Henri Giraud poses for an Oval Office photo with President Franklin Roosevelt. Giraud in white dress uniform with black tie, a perfect mirror to the light suit and dark tie worn by Roosevelt. The French high commissioner for North Africa stays close to the president on the right, just like in Casablanca, the perfect ventriloquist's dummy.

This photograph will soon grace a full page in next week's *Life* magazine, a step toward fulfilling Roosevelt's hope that the American people will come to see Giraud as the future of France. The president plans for Allied troops to occupy France after the war rather than allow national independence. Roosevelt is grooming Giraud as his chosen leader, in spite of—or perhaps because of—the five-star general's dismal administrative skills.

An hour-long lunch just took place in the White House space

known as the small dining room. Giraud has come to Washington for three days of meetings. Lunch today, meetings tomorrow, late-night cocktails on Saturday before saying goodbye to the most powerful man on earth.

The general's landing in America coincides with the final moments of Jean Moulin's life in that faraway boxcar. Both Frenchmen, in their own ways, seek a free nation. But there are no full military honors or seventeen-gun salute for Moulin. No White House reception.

Giraud receives all this acclaim and more.

But Roosevelt well knows this is a last-gasp effort. De Gaulle has skillfully tightened his hold on France—at the expense of Giraud's personal authority and even the reputation of the United States. General de Gaulle expands his wide base of support by thoughtfully articulating disdain for Vichy sympathizers and a defiant belief in the future of a Free France. The less articulate and less passionate Giraud, in the words of British secretary of foreign affairs Anthony Eden, has "no position at all."

In March, Giraud poked at General de Gaulle during a speech in Algiers, parroting President Roosevelt's argument against de Gaulle's claims of authority. "I am the servant of the people of France. I am not their master," Giraud stated. "The free will of the people alone forms a basis of law."

The *New York Times* ran the full text of the speech alongside a separate article with a Washington dateline stating that "officials" were pleased with the contents of the oratory, which also included Giraud making a connection between the French struggle and the American people by quoting Abraham Lincoln's Gettysburg Address.

The presence of *Life*—bastion of all things American—today in the Oval Office would seem to be a boon to Roosevelt. But the magazine is instead taking a defiant stance in favor of Charles de Gaulle.

"Those who understand France are profoundly disturbed by General Giraud's visit," reads a lengthy editorial that runs alongside today's photograph of the president and his presumed ruler of France. "The White House and the State Department are up to their ears in French politics, and their persistent aim has been to build up General Giraud at the expense of the other great French leader of our time, General de Gaulle."

The editorial continues:

"The result is that U.S. foreign policy toward France is now a matter of personalities, based on Mr. Roosevelt's dislike of a single man . . .

"De Gaulle has become a living symbol of freedom for millions of Frenchmen. Many of them never heard of him before. But for them 'de Gaullism' represents the only possible creed that can redeem France from the shame of her defeat."

Advantage, de Gaulle.

57

Winston Churchill is doing America's bidding.

The prime minister sits up in bed. The *Queen Mary* plows through the same North Atlantic waves once traveled by the *Titanic*, though with a slightly different routing of Scotland to Halifax in six days. Churchill's stateroom is "spacious," in his own words, allowing Brigadier K. G. McLean and two staff officers to set up an easel and large map at the foot of the bed stretching almost from one side of the cabin to the other.

Spacious, indeed: walls of exotic wooden veneer cut from rare trees grown throughout the British Empire, natural sunlight through two rectangular portholes to Churchill's right, two toilets, a bathtub, sitting room, kitchen, and a multitude of storage closets hidden inside every nook and cranny in the space-saving nautical way. Churchill is once more en route to meet with President Roosevelt, preferring the *Queen Mary* because it is literally fast enough to outrun a U-boat torpedo.*

And, unlike an airplane, the ocean gives the prime minister time to think.

Each day of this passage is spent studying "the problems we were to discuss with our American friends, the most important of these was, of course, Overlord," in Churchill's words. Friends or not, those problems always seem to go America's way these days.

Casablanca was a high moment for Churchill and Britain. The Trident Conference was not. Franklin Roosevelt turned control of the war in America's favor during those two weeks in May, and the "friends" grow more in charge every day. Winston Churchill knows he must go along and is doing his best to be a compliant ally, hence his deep interest in this Operation Overlord briefing. Churchill will learn enough that when the time comes and key decisions must be made, his awareness of all things Overlord will help him lobby for his generals and their tactics. In this way, as always, the prime minister will be arguing for Britain.

Yet subservience stings.

Churchill clings to power as he begins to slide off the stage. Two issues remain at the forefront of his personal plan for how the war should play out. Churchill never takes his eye off of Italy and his "soft underbelly" theory. Britain's long maritime presence in the Mediterranean lends a sentimental nationalist stripe to this strategy.

And Churchill refuses to back down on the subject of General Charles de Gaulle. The Fighting French movement is growing stronger by the day among French Communists and trade unionists. In a recent meeting with his war cabinet, Churchill was informed that

---

* One prewar Cunard line brochure described the *Queen Mary* as the "ship of beautiful woods" for its use of rare species from around the British Empire. It is estimated that fifty-six varieties of wood were utilized, including many now extinct.

America's prestige in France is at an all-time low, mostly due to President Roosevelt's attitude toward de Gaulle. Not only does breaking with the general reduce Britain's influence on a postwar France, but with the will of the French people hitched more and more to de Gaulle, obeisance to America's contrary position is a clear sign to the world that Churchill and his nation are weak.

Thus, Italy and de Gaulle.

And that is enough. It needs to be. It's all Churchill has anymore.

The prime minister drinks his morning eye-opener as Brigadier McLean briefs him in clipped sentences about Operation Overlord. Planning is proceeding briskly. This morning marks the first time Churchill is being presented with the entire scope of the invasion, which includes troop strengths and ships required to put the force ashore. Churchill finds the level of detail "precise," reveling in such minutiae.

With the exception of one issue: landing site.

"The choice narrowed to the Pas de Calais or Normandy," Churchill will write. "The former gave us the best air cover, but here the defenses were the most formidable, and although it promised a shorter sea voyage this advantage was only apparent."

Instead, the assembled officers suggest, Normandy might be considered the best option.

"Normandy gave us the greatest hope," the prime minister enthuses.

"The seas and beaches were on the whole suitable, and were to some extent sheltered from the westerly gales by the Cotentin peninsula. The hinterlands favored the rapid deployment of large forces."

Churchill also believes a Normandy attack would fool the Germans. He notes the sandy beaches are perfect for landing craft and dismisses the "concrete forts and pillboxes" of Adolf Hitler's Atlantic Wall as useless unless the Germans are also willing to place a sizable force on the beaches to slaughter the Allies as they land.

Churchill will long remember the decision to land at Normandy:

"Here was the front on which to strike."

58

Erwin Rommel builds the new resistance.

The Nazi resistance.

The field marshal's personal train stops for the night on a rather mundane siding in this simple rural station. The Spartan stopover on Denmark's Skanderborg–Skjern line offers no reason for Rommel and his generals to venture outside their luxury transport into the brisk Danish air. Dinner is to be followed by a few relaxing hours in the car reserved for maps and planning.

Thus, the true beauty of Silkeborg is lost on the field marshal in the early darkness of this northern latitude. Were it daylight, Rommel and his staff might be gazing out upon one of the most picturesque cities in central Denmark, surrounded by lakes and woodland, triggering that lobe of the field marshal's brain that sees topography as a puzzle, calculating the best places to position an army and ensure battlefield victory.

For Rommel has literally come to Denmark to study the lay of the

The Atlantic Wall

ATLANTIC WALL
1942–1944

land—and how he can alter Europe's hills and folds from pastoral paradise into impenetrable death zone.

The field marshal is healthy, jovial, and revived for the first time in years. He just spent ten days at home with Lucia, where they celebrated twenty-seven years of marriage. It offered the field marshal a chance to spend time with Manfred, soon to turn fifteen and be conscripted. Now Rommel is surrounded by handpicked officers with whom he can speak his mind, not a member of the SS or Gestapo among them. Most of these men served under him in Africa. They know that Rommel is falling out of favor with the Führer. Yet they do not care. Their loyalty remains stalwart.

But every man knows this is Rommel's last chance.

Hitler is tasking Field Marshal Rommel with construction of the Atlantic Wall, a 4,000-mile coastal defense from Norway down to the Spanish Pyrenees. Hitler originally ordered construction to begin in 1941 as a response to British commando raids. This was followed up by a second directive in 1942 stating that the entire Atlantic coast be turned into a series of 15,000 defensive positions.

But progress has been dismal. With Allied invasion of the French coastline likely imminent for 1944, the Führer revitalizes the project by putting his best man in charge. The clock is ticking. Winter weather makes an invasion impossible right now, but that will change come spring. Erwin Rommel has six months to accomplish what has not taken place in three years.

Rommel is a pariah. The people of Germany still worship the Desert Fox, but his failure to win in North Africa is a stain on his military record. Enemies among the Nazi high command chortle at his downfall, long jealous of Rommel's fame and all too happy to see the field marshal relegated to a posting more suited to a construction engineer than a master tactician.

Even Adolf Hitler is sensitive to Rommel's plight. For Africa might have been won if only the Führer had listened to Rommel. And Hitler knows this. He has belatedly apologized for his failure to heed the field marshal's warnings. It is also coming to light that the Italian high command was complicit in Rommel's downfall, concealing enormous quantities of fuel from the Afrika Korps in a fit of pique because the Desert Fox was loath to take orders from Mussolini's generals.

But what is done is done. Hitler considered sending Rommel into the Italian or Greek theaters but had a change of heart. And ordering Rommel east to fight the Soviets—still 1,000 miles from Berlin but advancing every day—would meet stiff political resistance from commanders in that theater.

Hitler's diplomatic and ingenious solution is the Atlantic Wall. No general has waged war longer against the British, French, and Americans. Rommel knows not just Allied tactics but those of individual generals. This gives him prescience in figuring when and where an invasion will take place and how it will proceed once troops are ashore.

Thus, this unlikely journey. Rommel and his staff are now assessing the current state of the Atlantic Wall, from the Danish coast down to Brittany. Landing an army south of the Breton coast would be an act of enormous stupidity, so Rommel keeps his focus narrow.

The origins of this plush luxury train are unknown, but a clue can be found in the Cyrillic writing in the parlor car, with its two sleeping chambers. There is also a dining car, conference car, and elaborate cabin for the field marshal with a large master suite. The bathroom features an unusual bell for those using the toilet, which greatly amuses the field marshal and his staff.

Rommel has only just begun planning but he imagines a "death barrier" six miles deep up and down the coast. Mines, anti-invasion barriers at low tide, sharpened stakes, and flooded fields to thwart gliders and paratroopers. He will pay the French well to build these defenses, guaranteeing construction crews enough francs that they will put financial happiness before patriotism.

Hitler believes the Allies will attack at Calais, the shortest distance from Britain to France.

Rommel agrees.

And the strength of the Atlantic Wall will reflect that certainty.

59

T he Allies attack the soft underbelly.

And it isn't soft at all.

Six hundred commandos of the First Special Service Force climb hand over hand up a towering limestone cliff one hundred miles south of Rome. Winter has come early. Faces are blackened by shoe polish. The orders are clear: Speak only in whispers. Better not to speak at all.

And don't look down.

Each American and Canadian on this wall tonight has prepared himself for death or capture, burning all personal letters and wearing no identification but dog tags. Rifles, heavy packs laden with ammunition and grenades, twelve-inch V-42 combat daggers sheathed to each hip, combat boots instead of climbing shoes.

The Forcemen are "lumberjacks, forest rangers, hunters, Northwoodsmen, game wardens, prospectors, and explorers," in the words of Lieutenant Colonel Robert Frederick's original recruiting poster.

Many of the volunteers were already in the military, given the choice between joining this new unit or spending the war in a stockade. One year training in the Montana wilderness has molded this American and Canadian band into an elite fighting force capable of waging war in the most extreme conditions.

Frederick is a thirty-six-year-old West Point graduate who spent the early part of the war as a glorified clerk with a reputation for extreme personal fitness. No one was more surprised than the colonel when General Dwight Eisenhower ordered him away from desk duty to build an irregular fighting force. In typically nonchalant fashion, the lean, dogmatic Frederick made his first parachute jump in slippers.* And while his small stature and meticulous attention to detail make the colonel a different breed from the roughnecks he recruited to the Forcemen, their devotion is complete.

In time, even Winston Churchill will praise Frederick's greatness.

But first there is the matter of capturing this peak known as Monte la Difensa.

Spread out across the rock face directly below the German position, fingers numb and muscles exhausted, these "special forces" scramble upward in absolute silence.

. . .

WINSTON CHURCHILL's "soft underbelly" theory appears correct.

But only for a short while.

The Allies are not fighting the Italian army, as Churchill so dearly hoped after the British routed them in Egypt. Italy is effectively out of the war, having ousted the Fascist regime of Benito Mussolini in July.

---

* Frederick had a firm policy that any man refusing to get parachute qualified would be transferred out of the unit. Rather than seek his own exemption because his new pair of special parachute boots had yet to arrive, the colonel wore bedroom slippers to qualify. "You jumped?" his intelligence officer asked incredulously in an August 1, 1942, phone conversation recorded by a War Department stenographer. "Sure," Frederick responded, "what the hell."

But the German army has filled that void, rushing troops to the Italian Peninsula. The fighting is a bloodbath.

Operation Baytown, as the September 3, 1943, Allied invasion of Italy is known, saw British troops face token resistance as they crossed the Strait of Messina from the newly conquered Sicily to the Italian mainland. Led by General Sir Bernard Law Montgomery, hero of El Alamein, the British Eighth Army made landfall and sped north, virtually unopposed.

Six days later, the U.S. Fifth Army landed three hundred miles north at the port of Salerno. Theirs was a far more daunting German welcome. The Fifth was almost thrown back into the sea. But after two weeks of intense fighting, and substantial help from Montgomery's advancing British Army, the Americans finally moved northward up the Italian boot.

The Fifth Army is led by General Mark Clark. At forty-seven, the rangy, trim Clark is America's youngest two-star general. There is no love lost between Clark and his compatriot, the renegade genius Patton, the victor on Sicily. Patton is a patriot who would never root for Clark to fail here in Italy. It would be enough satisfaction if Clark were to get bogged down in a stalemate. Yet there is a definite rivalry between the two. Patton believes Clark lacks the stomach great generals need to dominate the battlefield, a notion Clark is trying very hard to prove wrong.

Few men can match Patton for daring, but Clark is every bit Patton's equal in vainglorious self-promotion. Photographers are allowed to take Clark's picture only from the left, which he considers his best side.

Clark's German opponent is the brilliant Field Marshal Albert Kesselring, commander of the Tenth Army. At fifty-seven, this career soldier has commanded forces in Poland, France, Russia, and the Battle of Britain. He is one of the most popular generals on either side, nicknamed "Uncle Albert" by his troops and praised for wily tactical genius by his Allied opponents.

Superior manpower and supplies favor General Clark and the Allies. Yet Kesselring has terrain and the elements on his side. Realizing Germany lacks the resources to wage war the length of the Italian Peninsula, Adolf Hitler originally ordered a complete withdrawal from all but the upper regions of the country. The Führer decreed that the Wehrmacht would draw their defensive line north of Rome.

Kesselring disagreed. He argued that the mountainous terrain south of the Italian capital is perfect for waging a defensive war. The field marshal promised Hitler that a small number of German troops could effectively tie up a much larger Allied force for at least nine months. Kesselring is not often wrong, a tactician every bit the equal of fellow field marshal Erwin Rommel.

Hitler relented.

Kesselring's confidence is based on simple fact: the Italian Peninsula is just 150 miles wide, narrow enough for a savvy commander to establish defensive positions across its width. The Barbara Line is the name given to the first of Kesselring's strongpoints. The steep terrain offers no place for tank warfare. Allied transportation and troop movement must go through the low valleys. By placing artillery atop mountain summits, Kesselring also controls the bottomland in between. Every Allied movement is met with devastating bombardment.

But the Barbara Line can only hold so long.

This is also a part of Kesselring's strategy.

Just when the Barbara Line is sure to crumble, Kesselring orders his men to fall back to a second series of peaks. The soldiers become construction workers, wielding crowbars, sledgehammers, and explosives to carve fortifications and caves out of solid rock to form a string of independent and interlocking fortresses across the Italian mountaintops.

This new position is known as the Winter Line.

And Monte la Difensa is the vital link in this chain of peaks.

Yet winter is coming. Severe rains are turning rural dirt roads into quagmires. Muddy rivers rage, impassable. Nonetheless, beginning on November 5, American troops attack Monte la Difensa as British troops struggle up the fortified slopes of a parallel peak nearby named Monte Camino.

Allied failure is total. Kesselring has placed the 15th Panzergrenadier Division atop Monte la Difensa. Once known as the 15th Panzer Division, these hardened soldiers were part of Field Marshal Erwin Rommel's vaunted Afrika Korps. For twelve days the 15th Panzergrenadier Division slaughter the Fifth Army. Allied corpses line the muddy forest paths of Monte la Difensa, each man a victim of Kesselring's brilliant strategy.

But Monte la Difensa must be taken. It is the "gateway to Rome" for Allied war planners, blocking any advance toward the Italian capital. Capturing the Eternal City will not imply that the Allies have conquered all of Italy, but the symbolic significance of occupying the capital city of an Axis power cannot be understated.

In the minds of many, particularly British prime minister Winston Churchill, Rome is the ideal location to enjoy Christmas dinner.

On November 22, 1943, a desperate General Clark orders the highly trained yet untried First Special Service Force to capture la Difensa. On paper, conquest looks impossible. The Germans are too entrenched, too sophisticated, and too ready, weapons zeroed in on the thin network of trails that constitute the only obvious path to the summit. Lethal cross fire awaits any army foolish enough to enter that killing zone.

Which is why the Forcemen now climb the opposite side of the mountain.

60

The Forcemen stand atop Monte la Difensa.

Perfect quiet. Germans doze, hidden in the rocks like hunters waiting for a stag. The morning watch huddles over small fires. Breakfast smells. Thin snowfall. Mountain shale. Darkness.

Forcemen fix bayonets and creep along narrow paths. More and more men haul themselves up onto the summit. An order is passed in whispers and hand signals: no gunfire until sunrise.

A sentry stumbles into their midst. Throat immediately slit. Shoved off the cliff.

First blood.

So far so good.

Then someone kicks a rock.

Forcemen dive for cover, pressing flat behind chunks of shale. But there is no place to hide. The 15th Panzer Division fought at Bir Hakeim, responding to the French breakout by lighting up the desert night with phosphorus flares. These veteran fighters now do the same atop Monte la Difensa, an automatic reflex bathing the Forcemen in the same bright red-green glow.

Sunrise has come early. Time to open fire.

Luck is with the Forcemen. The German guns are aimed the wrong way, still waiting for an attack from the opposite slope.

That changes.

Quickly.

Most German soldiers fire the K98k bolt-action rifle, which can be fitted with a sniper scope for precision. Others fire the lightweight MP 40 "Schmeisser" submachine gun. But it is the Maschinengewehr 42 that truly commands the mountaintop. The MG 42 is a twenty-six-pound, tripod-mounted, air-cooled machine gun now swiveling 180 degrees to fire 1,200 rounds a minute at the Forcemen.

"It was a terrible weapon," one American private will remember. "Muzzle flashes blinking at me, but there wasn't much I could do at the time. I never saw so many flashes in my life."

Just two months ago, as the 15th Panzergenadier Division retreated up the Italian Peninsula, a small group of their soldiers tried to rape a local girl as she peeled vegetables in her family's garden. Her uncle stepped from the house and shot one soldier dead, then fired again, wounding a second German. Desperate, uncle and young niece fled into the mountains.

The 15th went house to house through the town of Bellona the next morning, dragging every male villager into the local square. A priest was pulled from the altar as he said Mass. Monks were arrested in the local monastery. The Germans randomly selected fifty-four innocent victims to avenge the death of one rapist soldier. These men and boys were taken to a quarry, lined up on the edge of a cliff, and slaughtered with the same MG 42 machine guns now firing atop Monte la Difensa.*

A similar horrendous drop may soon await the Forcemen.

---

* Bellona still commemorates the martyrs' deaths each October 7.

The clatter of machine guns, rifles, and smaller submachine guns melds with the thunder of exploding grenades. Much too loud to hear right. Forcemen stranded in the open make easy targets. Hidden MG 42 fire ricochets off rocks, spraying splinters of shale.

The Forcemen strip their dead friends of weapons, ammunition, and those precious V-42 killing blades. Fighting becomes hand-to-hand. The enemy is no longer a distant apparition but real flesh-and-blood human beings, just as wet and cold and desperate to stay alive. Stabbing and strangling and doing whatever else it takes to kill becomes intimate.

Panzergrenadier fighters grow desperate. Many hold up their hands in surrender, only to reach for their weapons and open fire when unsuspecting Forcemen step within range.

From that moment on, the Forcemen adopt a policy they will follow for the remainder of the war: no surrender.

"Some of the guys were shooting German prisoners, but hey, that's the way it was," one Forcemen sergeant will remember.

"They were the enemy."

. . .

THE ALLIED STRATEGISTS are wrong: Monte la Difensa is not the gateway to Rome. Despite the British also capturing nearby Monte Camino, Hitler's Winter Line stands strong, its many other Apennine peaks uncaptured.

In the words of the Führer, Kesselring's defenses will "mark the end of all withdrawals."

No retreat. No surrender.

And Rome must never be taken.

61

I t is now officially Christmas.

And Winston Churchill is closer to death than Rome.

Christmas morning. Four hundred miles due south of Monte la Difensa. Floor-to-ceiling French windows covered in blackout curtains. The prime minister wears a bathrobe, slippers, and a special blue silk dressing gown emblazoned with golden dragons. Allied commanders in full uniform sit all around, everyone listening as the invalid Churchill lobbies his desperate new strategy.*

It is three months since the invasion of Italy. Capturing Rome by Christmas has not happened. Enraged by "the stagnation of the whole campaign on the Italian Front," Churchill now makes his case for a

---

* Among them are Dwight Eisenhower, Air Marshal Arthur Tedder, General Harold Alexander, General Walter Bedell Smith, General Alan Gordon Cunningham, and General Henry "Jumbo" Wilson.

second invasion of Italy, an audacious attack behind the Winter Line to finally take Rome.

The plan is known as Operation Shingle. When first conceived by Churchill, the amphibious assault on a beach known as Anzio was at first deemed a perfect "end run" around the German defenses by General Dwight Eisenhower, supreme commander in the Mediterranean. Ike was so confident in its success that he made plans to move his headquarters from Tunis to a palace in Rome after the first of the New Year.

But Shingle was canceled one week ago. Fifth Army commander Mark Clark made the decision. Eisenhower seconded it. The German defenses are too strong. Brutal winter sleet and snow are causing just as many casualties as the battles themselves. Hands are too frozen to pull a trigger and feet too frostbitten to march. German fighters no longer kill from mountaintops by lobbing down artillery fire—such a waste of precious shells. Better to let the Americans and British crawl close in the heavy snow and shoot them dead at short range.

There are many reasons Eisenhower, chain-smoking unfiltered cigarettes across the table from the prime minister, has changed his tune about Shingle. Politics are among them: the American aligning himself with President Roosevelt's favored invasion of France rather than extended fighting in Italy. But Ike is also an accomplished strategist. He now believes thousands of Allied soldiers will die on the Anzio beachhead. The landing zone lies on a flat plain extending inland to Rome. There will be no protection from the full might of the German army.

Boyish one year ago, the balding fifty-three-year-old Eisenhower has been drastically aged by the pressures and sleeplessness of wartime command. To the disappointment of Churchill, who longed for a British general to lead the Allied invasion of France, Eisenhower has been selected to take charge of Operation Overlord next May. Adding further insult, Eisenhower believes Churchill's "soft underbelly" argument borders on delusional—and is determined to turn the Allied focus from Italy to France as soon as possible.

"The prime minister and some of his chief military advisers still looked upon the Overlord plan with scarcely concealed misgivings," Ike will later recall. "Their attitude seemed to be that we could avoid the additional and grave risks implicit in a new amphibious operation by merely pouring into the Mediterranean all the air, ground, and naval resources available."

So Eisenhower fights back. It is not lost on Churchill that Franklin Roosevelt and Joseph Stalin would never spend eight hours on Christmas Eve pleading with their generals about strategy; both would simply demand to be obeyed. But Churchill's personal power is slipping, as is that of his once-mighty nation. U.S. troops are flooding into England, overwhelming the British with the immense scale of their force. It is America that now controls the pace of war in western Europe. On the other side of the continent, the Soviets are turning the tide, slowly pushing back the Germans. Tenuous though it may be, Italy and the Mediterranean is Britain's only hope to assert itself as an equal Allied partner.

Yet politicians in Washington and London are clamoring for a quick end to the war—which, to many, means a focus on France. More insulting, Adolf Hitler publicly gloats that Rome will never fall into Allied hands. Churchill, as ever, refuses to concede. Tonight the prime minister will argue for as long as it is necessary, with whoever he needs to convince, in order to win this argument.

Eisenhower is equally insistent, stating bluntly that the landing force will suffer "annihilation."

Every officer in the room knows what this means.

Churchill and Eisenhower have a strong relationship. This villa in which Churchill has lain in bed for two weeks is Ike's personal residence. The stop in Tunisia was meant to be short. Instead, fever, lower-lobe pneumonia, and atrial fibrillation have made Churchill Eisenhower's indefinite houseguest.

Eisenhower has gone to great lengths to keep the prime minister comfortable. When U.S. Army personnel assigned to serve as waiters failed to behave graciously toward the British leader, a furious Eisenhower had each man flown back to Algiers in the cramped hold of a B-17 bomber.

And yet at Christmas, of all times, Eisenhower uses the most damning word—*annihilation*—to voice his fears about an invasion planned by Winston Churchill.

The generals in this room were educated at the military academies of Sandhurst and West Point. They have made a career of studying how battles are won and lost. They have watched friends and classmates die because powerful men made stupid decisions. To them, *annihilation* is synonymous with personal grief—and one of World War I's biggest debacles.

It was the infamous battle known as Gallipoli, an amphibious assault very much like what the prime minister is proposing in a new guise as Operation Shingle. More than 550,000 men died or were wounded.

And Winston Churchill planned that invasion.

. . .

"MERRY CHRISTMAS," exults Churchill as he leaves the assembled generals and shuffles off to bed. It is almost 1:00 a.m. Operation Shingle is reapproved. General Eisenhower has recused himself and allowed Churchill to make the final decision. Within a month, thousands of British and American forces will land on Anzio's beach and sprint to Rome.

"It will astonish the world," Churchill confides to British general Harold Alexander. Before going to sleep, Churchill writes an urgent message to Franklin Roosevelt, cajoling for landing craft.

The prime minister sees it clearly now—the capture of Rome and glorious redemption from those who doubt his strategy. The cross-Channel invasion of France will become of secondary importance. If all goes well, the Allies will fight from Rome to Paris long before it is necessary to launch Operation Overlord.

To his daughter, Sarah, the prime minister is even more confident: "The war is won."

Winston Churchill thinks it will be easy.

But as the prime minister well knows, the only easy day in this war was yesterday.

TAKING PARIS

62

General Dwight Eisenhower was right.

A chaplain. A bugler. A lone ambulance parked on broad, flat beach. Mourners wearing the caduceus. Curtiss P-40 Warhawks in formation above, not here for the funeral, just vectoring inland toward German artillery positions.

Boasts from German radio that the Allies will be pushed back into the Mediterranean are temporarily forgotten. For now. The annoying German propaganda leaflets dropped onto Anzio gloating about the hopeless Allied situation are set aside. As are the thousand other irrational thoughts and rumors constituting a day in the war.

It is time to grieve.

For now.

Annihilation takes on many meanings—and that slaughter has not yet happened. But by any definition Winston Churchill's Operation Shingle is verging on fiasco. The Allies landed almost 40,000 men on this shoreline two weeks ago. Instead of racing the thirty short miles to Rome, British and American forces advanced absolutely nowhere. Churchill is insistent the fighting continue, even arguing for the postponement of Operation Overlord with his war cabinet so fighting in Italy can be "nourished and fought until it is won."

That will take a long while. Anzio and its neighboring oceanfront town of Nettuno are now lined with a city of olive drab tents and foxholes dug into sand. There are no great fortifications or towering historic walls rising up to protect the Allies as they hunker in the open—just a long stretch of flat Italian beach that grows even smaller when the tide rolls in. It is everything to survive another day, praying that a quarter-ton round from Germany's Anzio Express artillery doesn't score a direct hit on your position. The most fearsome of the German artillery pieces is the Krupp K5, a gun so large it must be hauled into battle on a railway car. "Anzio Annie," as it is nicknamed by the Allies, possesses an eighty-three-foot barrel capable of precisely launching a five-hundred-pound shell thirty-five miles.

This is not a battle of small-arms fire or bayonets—not yet—but an engagement of enormous artillery pieces firing from a dozen miles away and fighter aircraft making war in the Great Above.

Among the Allied soldiers is Second Lieutenant Ellen Ainsworth of Glenwood City, Wisconsin. The twenty-four-year-old nurse is part of the 56th Evacuation Hospital, tasked with providing immediate care for the wounded and dying. This collection of doctors and nurses has been together since March 1942, when the unit first assembled at Fort Sam Houston in San Antonio, Texas. Their job is building hospitals from nothing, whether it be setting up the operating theater in an olive drab tent or an abandoned warehouse. Then they wait for the shelling to start and the inevitable onslaught of stretchers, ready to make use of the stockpiles of bandages, medication, and those ominous containers marked "whole blood."

The 56th has served in Algeria and now Italy, moving up the Boot as battlefields push north: Paestum, Avellino, Dragoni, Calvano, and now Anzio. The doctors and nurses are a tight unit, enduring the same mud and cold-to-the-bone misery as frontline soldiers. They take their fun where they can find it. The 56th celebrated the wedding of nurse Lieutenant Ruth Gifford to an Army Air Corps officer this past Christmas. There was a dance. Carols. Drinking.

Four weeks later the 56th landed at Anzio. On January 30, the unit received its first patient from the Operation Shingle landings. Within the next thirty-six hours, 1,129 more injured soldiers were admitted. Minor casualties were evacuated by ship. The rest went into surgery right here on the beach.

Lieutenant Ellen Ainsworth is known for singing well and often, so proud of where she's from that she taught her fellow nurses the Wisconsin fight song. Ainsworth enjoys a drink and a smoke and a dirty joke. She is calm under fire. She doesn't have a favorite form of good luck, so she carries them all: rabbit's foot, four-leaf clover, a Saint Christopher medal, hot dice.

A special bomb shelter was built for the nurses just a few days ago, but the lieutenant refused to enter during the nightly German shelling. "Everyone will be killed if a bomb hits that shelter," she told a fellow nurse. This would mean there will be no one to take care of the wounded. "I'll take my chances elsewhere."

So Ainsworth is unprotected on the night of February 12. German flares light up the sky during the heaviest bombardment anyone can remember. An antipersonnel bomb finds Ellen Ainsworth, white-hot steel slicing open her chest. The piece of shrapnel the size of a quarter does not scare her. She has seen far worse and knows her odds. But her thoracic cavity is pierced and air enters the body through the chest instead of the lungs. In medical parlance, Ainsworth suffers a sucking chest wound.

Lieutenant Ellen Ainsworth remains calm. She informs the attending surgeon that her blood pressure is a steady 130 over 80.

But the small metal fragment not much bigger than her Saint Christopher medal is already working its way down into her intestines—literally burning its way into Ainsworth's soft underbelly.

Infection spreads over the next few days as the lieutenant's organs become septic. "Don't worry," she tells fellow nurse Lieutenant Avis Dagit, who chokes back tears at the tangle of tubes sprouting from the arms and nose of her good friend. "I'm tougher than anything Jerry can throw at us."

Ainsworth adds: "Was anyone else hurt?"

"You're the only one."

"Thank God," the young lieutenant replies.

At 1000 hours this morning, after four days of decline, Lieutenant Ellen Ainsworth of Glenwood City, Wisconsin, youngest of three siblings, impassioned belter of "On, Wisconsin!," dies.

Her face is pale gray as she takes her last breath.

Ainsworth's young body is dressed in a brand-new uniform she was saving for a special day. Two green army blankets are wrapped around her corpse. She is lifted into the back of the ambulance now surrounded by mourners on Anzio Beach.

Taps concludes.

Second Lieutenant Ellen Ainsworth is driven away from the beach to a cemetery filling each day with Anzio casualties, there to be buried thousands of miles away from Wisconsin.*

The sounds of war never stop: thunder and whistle of artillery salvos, the high whine of finely tuned fighter engines, shovel blades pressed hard into the sand for digging new foxholes.

The mourners go back to work. Someone says Ellen would have wanted it that way.

Someone always says something like that.

---

* Ainsworth is buried at the Sicily-Rome American Cemetery in Nettuno, near Anzio: Plot C, Row 11, Grave 22.

Two things are certain as the hospital tents take on more wounded and those bright new white ribbons of gauze and precious vials of whole blood find a body:

Rome isn't happening anytime soon.

And this isn't the way to Paris.

63

The restless woman with one leg steps back onto French soil.

Virginia Hall hurries off the beach. A dark moon bequeaths the sky to more distant lights: the Big Dipper, Cancer, the blazing silver of Venus. The tang of tide pools is right beneath her foot but from the darkness comes the smell of coastal pines and the honey scent of thrift growing wild and pink. That's where Hall is headed. This Breton coastline has the highest tidal rise in Europe. The risk of being caught between pounding waves and rocky cliffs is a true threat. So she hustles. There is absolutely no time to savor what can only be called a homecoming.

Yet the truth is close enough to be an emotion: this is France.

British Motor Gunboat 502's three Paxman VRB diesel engines rumble offshore, already charting a course back across the Channel to the Royal Navy base at Devonport. Hall can no longer hope for rescue if this landing was spotted by coastal German sentries.

But Hall is not alone. American Henri Lassot, code-named "Aramis," is undertaking his first mission. The erstwhile painter trips while scrambling ashore and grumbles about the treacherous footing, forcing Hall to lift him to his feet. Lassot is a man, so officials in London have deemed him the team leader despite Hall's unrivaled experience. Lassot is sixty-two and white-haired, a natural for his cover as an aging Frenchman.

Normally, Lassot and the thirty-eight-year-old Hall might be pretending the role of father and daughter. But Virginia Hall looks not one day younger than her new partner.

It was not the twenty days she spent in Spain's Miranda del Ebro concentration camp after crossing the Pyrenees that added years to Hall's face. Nor has the recent decision to transfer from the British SOE to the new American Office of Strategic Services (OSS) aged her face and added girth to her hips. This choice was made out of a desire to return to operational duty rather than spend the remainder of the war as a training officer in Britain. On the surface, this would appear impossible. Hall's cover is beyond blown. Klaus Barbie and the Gestapo have not yielded in their determination to have their day with her and Cuthbert. And the Limping Lady is still famous enough that any Frenchwoman in her late thirties walking with a hitch in her gait is immediately suspected of being Virginia Hall.

It is for all these reasons that the restless woman with one leg has made the drastic decision to change every aspect of her appearance.

The willowy, athletic Virginia Hall is gone. She no longer appears thirty-eight. No elegant shoes or trim slacks. She has never been one to show her teeth when smiling, preferring a bemused upturn of the lips, but even if she did, there is now a good chance she will never do so again.

The woman shuffling quietly up onto the coastal bluff wears her hair in a tight gray bun. Wrinkles line the corners of her eyes and mouth. Hall's beautiful white teeth, polished by the very best advances in American dentistry, are now filed and stained into the unbrushed nubs endured by France's rural poor; even her golden fillings have been removed and replaced by less expensive French tin. Every article of Hall's clothing is designed to make her look heavy and slow, from thick wool skirts to sweaters heavy enough to conceal her Colt .32 pistol. French Jewish refugees in London have vetted her teeth and clothes for authenticity. Cuthbert is still very much a factor in Virginia Hall's gait, but she has lost the limp, training herself to waddle like a slow old woman. To add yet one more degree of authenticity, Hall does not wear shoes. Instead, her feet are clad in footwear known as sabots, carved from a single block of wood.

Now she must walk twelve miles to the train station in Morlaix.

Hall and Lassot each carry a suitcase. Hers conceals a Type 3 Mark II transceiver, allowing Hall to send and receive Morse code messages from London. She carries a half million francs, quite a sum for a woman pretending to be a peasant. Hall's wooden leg, radio, money, and that telltale American pistol strapped to her hip are the sort of contraband that no number of filed teeth can explain.

Yet there is no place Virginia Hall would rather be. The Allied invasion of France is just weeks away, and Virginia Hall is here to coordinate the Resistance. In what will surely be the riskiest operation she has ever undertaken, Hall will separate from Aramis and find work as a simple country milkmaid, radioing information about German troop strengths and locations, working with the French underground to coordinate espionage.

The restless woman with one leg knows this means squalor, filth, and long days with no friends. Her only company will be the cows she milks and takes to pasture.

But this is the life she chooses.

The glamorous life of a secret agent.

64

APRIL 15, 1944
LA ROCHE-GUYON, FRANCE
DAY

General Erwin Rommel tours his Atlantic Wall from dawn to dusk.

But not today.

Rommel's black Horch 770k Tourenwagen convertible with its sloping front fenders, polished hood ornament, and robust padded seats remains in the garage on this cold and overcast Saturday. The damp is no good for his lower back and yesterday there was a coastal whirlwind: splendid and stormy Brittany for breakfast, then Saint-Nazaire, inland to Angers and Le Mans before returning to this palatial headquarters château outside Paris. Rommel sat in the front passenger seat, as always, reading the road maps to direct his driver, the dedicated Corporal Karl Daniel.

Security here at the Château La Roche-Guyon is formidable, befitting the field marshal's necessity to the Third Reich: black wrought-iron gates, sentry boxes, perimeter pillboxes, antiaircraft batteries, and even hidden escape tunnels. The château is just as impressive, a sprawling eighteenth-century manor house with a surprise around every corner: tapestries, chandeliers, gardens, and its own observatory.

Rommel enjoys his day of rest amid this luxury, pleased but not content. Thoughts of Allied invasion are ever on his mind. "We'll only have one chance to stop the enemy," he has confided to an aide, "and that's while he's in the water . . . struggling to get ashore . . . for the Allies, as well as Germany, it will be the longest day."

The field marshal devotes his genius to making that happen.

Most frustrating, despite the Führer's promises to give him complete backing in developing the Atlantic Wall, Rommel struggles to convince Adolf Hitler that positioning panzer divisions along the coastline will save Germany. An invasion force—even one with superior Allied airpower—would be hard-pressed to defeat such a mobile armored force designed to feint, attack, and hide. If Rommel must play defense, then the panzer, so central to the field marshal's tactical thought process, must never be far away.

So far this argument is in vain. The Führer prefers to hold tanks in reserve, fearful of the panzers being pinned down on the day of invasion.

Rommel scoffs inwardly at this notion: a great tank commander is never pinned down.

Yet the field marshal's restless tactical mind is undeterred, already turning the Atlantic Wall from façade into fortress. He has won the argument on many other strategies that will save the Third Reich. Thousands of laborers—Germans and French alike—wade into the cold Atlantic each day to imbed anti-invasion obstacles below the surf line. Rommel's innovations are genius, such as ten-foot "Belgian gates" along entire beachfronts to block landing craft and tanks. "Rommel's asparagus" are sharp wooden posts designed to shred the hulls of landing craft. "Ramps" angle steel blades from the water to slice ships and men. "Tetrahedrons" are steel pyramids with sharpened edges as anti-tank defenses. And six-foot steel "hedgehogs" litter the beaches like an oversized game of jacks.

Thousands of these terrors cover every beach in France, and all are topped with land mines.

Each obstacle prevents Allied soldiers from stepping onto dry land. For men lucky enough to wade out of the Atlantic breakers onto the sand, barbed wire, more mines, and steel-reinforced concrete bunkers concealing machine-gun nests await, each weapon sweeping the beach in a perfect field of fire.

Rommel does not keep these inventions a secret. Reporters and newsreel crews are invited to join him on his inspection visits. The field marshal is always captured at his jaunty best, that easy grin, tightly cinched leather jacket, and the Knight's Cross against his throat.

Today, Rommel is in a jovial mood but not entirely relaxed. He spends the afternoon analyzing Luftwaffe reports about Allied air activity along the coast and patterns of enemy minelaying in the English Channel. No detail is too small for the field marshal.

Evening brings the arrival of a new staff member. Rain falls through the Seine Valley as Generalleutnant Hans Speidel's chauffeured sedan pulls into the château courtyard. This burly and bookish forty-six-year-old intellectual is to be Rommel's new chief of staff. Speidel is from Swabia, like Rommel, allowing for an ease of conversation that does not often exist in the company of the more arrogant officers of Prussian birth. Speidel also wears a Knight's Cross.

Rommel and Speidel have known each other for two decades, so the conversation is more about catching up than the task at hand. War is their business. So Speidel is unsparing in his opinions about the many defeats the German army now endures. The cynical "African sickness" still festering within Rommel makes a comeback as he listens, still believing he should have defeated the Allies in the desert. This Atlantic Wall is a chance to make things right, yet once again Rommel is being second-guessed, not allowed to completely pursue his own tactics. Defeat will be appended to his good name. Rommel retires for the night feeling alone and isolated.

"What will history say in passing its verdict on me?" Rommel writes in his journal before going to bed. *Me* is underlined. "If I am successful here, then everyone else will claim all the glory—just as they are already claiming the credit for the defense and the beach obstacles that I have erected.

"But if I fail here," Rommel concludes, "then everybody will be after my blood."

65

General George S. Patton is being relieved of command.

Just across the English Channel from where his rival, Erwin Rommel, also fights for his livelihood, Patton stands at attention in the office of General Dwight Eisenhower, summoned to hear his fate. Ike will note that Patton is "resplendent as always in his get-up. He wore very shiny highly polished cavalry boots; his riding trousers were perfectly creased and immaculate; those two ivory-handled pistols were hanging in holsters at his waist; the left chest of his tunic was laden with ribbons; his shiny steel combat helmet bore three stars in front."

Patton's hunger for the fight has never been greater. His skills as a commander and leader never more honed. Now, one month before

---

* Patton and Eisenhower told differing versions of this story, with the date set for either May 1 or May 3.

what should be the biggest battle of his career, his life as a soldier is about to vanish—all because he can't keep his mouth shut.

A cigarette smolders in Eisenhower's desktop ashtray. As supreme commander for the Allied invasion of Europe, Ike relies on cigarettes and cowboy novels to take the edge off, yet his stress grows with each passing day. The greatest buildup of men and material in world history is taking place in Britain. More than 160,000 Allied troops will land on the Normandy beaches.

And Ike is in charge of it all.

Every aspect of planning falls on General Eisenhower's shoulders— including its ultimate success or failure. It is not enough that he frets about soldiers and planes and ships. Patton also weighs heavily on Eisenhower's mind. The general's impulsivity and theatrics have created a rift between these two old friends. Whether it be Patton slapping a hospitalized soldier for cowardice in Sicily or the most recent infraction, alluding to a postwar future in which Britain and America rule the world at the expense of the Soviet Union, Patton's impulsive antics are a distraction to the Allied cause.

Winston Churchill shrugged when he heard of the general's comments about the Soviets to a women's group in the English town of Knutsford, stating that Patton was "only speaking the truth." The prime minister understands that Patton's words were offhanded and meant to be witty. No one knew a reporter was present.

But these are sensitive times. American generals can't be dictating global foreign policy. U.S. Army Chief of Staff General George C. Marshall, Eisenhower's boss in Washington, demands Patton's resignation.

Ike now hands Patton three telegrams, one at a time. The first is Marshall's demand for Patton to be fired and sent home.

Patton reads the telegram. He is shaken but not surprised.

The second is a shock. This is Eisenhower's response to Marshall, stating, "If I am not considered capable in wartime of handling problems of my own efforts and troops, I can no longer properly continue to command in these posts. I therefore propose to accompany General Patton to the United States."

The third telegram is Marshall backing down.

"Regarding Patton, the decision is yours."

Eisenhower knows Patton's depth of emotion. Despite his reputation as "Old Blood and Guts," the general wept openly when a young aide was killed by a German bomber in North Africa—even cutting off a lock of the young man's hair and kissing him on the forehead before the desert burial, then writing a personal letter home to the officer's mother, an old family friend from California.

Yet, on the other hand, Patton openly encourages his men to grease their tank treads with the guts of their enemies.

No one can predict what General George S. Patton cares about.

So nothing prepares Eisenhower for what happens next.

"He started to sob," Ike will long remember of this moment. "Since he was so much taller than I, he put his head on my right shoulder and continued to sob. Then his helmet fell off and bounced on the floor."

Patton immediately stops crying. He bends down and picks the polished helmet off the floor and places it back on his head.

Then Patton starts sobbing all over again.

This is too much for Eisenhower, who collapses onto his office couch in laughter.

"George couldn't even cry without his helmet off," Eisenhower will recall. "Imagine that."

Ever the soldier, Patton remains at strict attention, weeping, eyes forward and chin rigid, even as his longtime friend laughs.

Eisenhower finally stops giggling.

"I expect, George, from now on that you will please keep your goddamned mouth shut. When it is time for you to speak, I will tell you," Ike scolds.

"I intend to use you to the fullest—you will have every opportunity to get into all the combat you ever dreamed of," he adds.

Executing a perfect salute, Patton turns in an about-face and marches from Eisenhower's office.

On to France.

66

General Charles de Gaulle announces the invasion of France.
And he's doing his best to be happy about it.

De Gaulle strides through the Portland Place doorway, standing tall to make his presence known. Everything about the BBC studio is familiar: recording room, microphone, small engineer's window. The general has made French history here and is determined to do so again. "The giant figure of the general blocked the entrance door. His face was set. One glance told me that he was in his grimmest mood," one British official will remember. De Gaulle's handshake is limp, for him a sign of disdain instead of weak masculinity.

It is two days since de Gaulle returned from Algeria to England and was informed for the first time of the D-Day landings. As with Operation Torch, the general was not allowed to know beforehand. A military band played "La Marseillaise" as he landed at RAF Northolt. A note from Churchill welcomed de Gaulle, inviting him to pay a visit to Portsmouth, where the prime minister has traveled by train to witness the great Allied armada gathering for invasion.

General Eisenhower also greeted de Gaulle, even in the final minutes of Overlord planning. Ike considers de Gaulle a friend. "He's a character," Ike will comment about the general. "Now, he and I were never Charles and Ike—not like with Winston, for example. Winston and I, why, we were just as warm as personal friends could be under the circumstances. De Gaulle never was that. He never had time, for one thing, and for another, he's rather remote. I think he believes his position requires it. He tries to create this feeling of remoteness, of mystery—or you might say mystique—and that whole business. But . . . there was also a good feeling, not only of respect and admiration, but of a very measurable degree of affection."

.   .   .

BY THE TIME Charles de Gaulle woke up in his luxury room at the Connaught Hotel this morning, thousands of Allied soldiers were already dying on the beaches of Normandy, their first steps on French soil undone by Field Marshal Erwin Rommel's Atlantic Wall. Everything works: Rommel's asparagus, hedgehogs, ramps, and the tetrahedrons.

Almost everything: Rommel's request to position panzers near the beach was never approved.

Which is why his Atlantic Wall is failing.

As every great military leader from Julius Caesar to Ulysses S. Grant has proven, numbers win. A land mine can only explode once. The 156,000 Allied troops assaulting Normandy's beach defenses in the first wave of the invasion are overwhelming the Wehrmacht forces and Rommel's wall, scrambling ashore like a massive horde of heavily armed and extremely belligerent tourists as they set foot on French soil for the first time, British, Americans, and Canadians determined to kill as many Germans as possible while awaiting the order to advance on Paris.

But as de Gaulle well knows, no French troops are currently fighting in France.

Ironically, the Fighting French are nine hundred miles southeast and entering Rome, having endured 30,000 casualties in the Allies' Italian Campaign.

. . .

EVEN AS Charles de Gaulle now stands in this cramped BBC recording studio, Winston Churchill rises three miles away, then addresses the House of Commons.

Churchill rambles on for ten minutes about the liberation of Rome.

No one wants to hear it. The D-Day landings are a cause of "intense excitement" in Parliament, as Churchill notes. Even the most jaded politicians are hungry for word of this morning's invasion. The prime minister does his best to keep tension high, the legendary speaker convincing himself he is keeping his audience on "tenterhooks" about Rome. But Churchill has stood in this room too many times and delivered so many addresses that he innately senses the temperature of his audience. The growing lack of interest is palpable. Churchill slowly shifts his oratory to Normandy, sharing what few details he is allowed by intelligence restrictions. Commons is soon in his thrall.

Rome is yesterday's news.

. . .

GENERAL DE GAULLE alerts the people of France that hope is finally on the way—as if the Allied landing is planned, executed, and under the command of General Charles de Gaulle. He stands with uniform dry and hair neatly combed, as far from the salty air, gritty sand, and bloody death of Normandy as any man can be.

This does not matter. It is the idea of the invasion that the French people must know about, just as it was the idea of France that kept him going when all seemed lost.

"The supreme battle has begun," de Gaulle begins. He holds a handful of notes but speaks extemporaneously, defying British demands that he present them with a copy of his full speech before going on the air.

"It is of course the battle of France—and the battle *for* France. France is going to fight this battle furiously. She is going to conduct it in due order.

"The clear, the sacred duty of the sons of France, wherever they are and whoever they are, is to fight the enemy with all the means at their disposal."

. . .

DE GAULLE'S RECORDED words echo across France six hours later. The Resistance knows the time has finally come. The citizens of Paris finally breathe, looking forward to a day without occupation.

That day will not come tomorrow.

But it is definitely coming.

. . .

DE GAULLE SPEAKS directly to the Resistance.

"The orders given by the French government and by the French leaders it has named for that purpose are to be obeyed exactly," the general says in the radio message, referring to himself, the organized Resistance leadership set in place by Jean Moulin, and the works of operatives such as Virginia Hall, now widely regarded as the top commando in all France. Her success is legendary and the Gestapo's Klaus Barbie has not relented in his search. But her daily coordination of Resistance attacks on German ammunition dumps, telephone lines, bridges, and railroads grows bolder and more destructive with every passing day.

"The actions we carry out in our enemy's rear are to be coordinated as closely as possible with those carried out by the Allied and French armies," de Gaulle continues.

"Let none of those capable of action, either by arms or by destruction or by giving intelligence or by refusing to do useful work for the enemy, allow themselves to be made prisoner. Let them remove themselves beforehand from being seized and from being deported," de Gaulle reminds his people, audaciously suggesting death—even suicide—before dishonor.

"The battle of France has begun. In the nation, the empire and the armies there is no longer anything but one single hope, the same for all.

"Behind the terribly heavy cloud of our blood and our tears here is the sunshine of our grandeur come out again."

. . .

WINSTON CHURCHILL NUMBERS the speech among de Gaulle's greatest, calling the delivery "remarkable."

France agrees. Ten days later, General Charles de Gaulle returns to his homeland, stepping ashore on Norman beaches now under complete Allied control. Winston Churchill has arranged this visit without informing President Franklin Roosevelt.

De Gaulle travels inland to Bayeux, where the local people are shocked to see the great general in person and greet him like a returning hero.

"The inhabitants were overcome by a kind of stupor which exploded into cheers and tears," de Gaulle will write in his memoirs. "Women were smiling. Men held their hands out to me. We went our way together, overwhelmed and fraternal, feeling our patriotic joy, pride, and hope surging up from the abyss."

Yet, to the American leadership in Washington, even now the general's authority over France is still in doubt.

"De Gaulle will crumble . . . British support of de Gaulle will be confounded by the progress of events," President Franklin Roosevelt predicts to Secretary of War Henry L. Stimson.

"Other parties will spring up as the liberation goes on and de Gaulle will become a very little figure."

. . .

GENERAL CHARLES DE GAULLE does not remain in France. Not yet. He flies home to Tangiers. Triumphal entries do not take place in the Norman countryside.

That parade must wait for Paris.

67

General Erwin Rommel drives back toward Paris.

The field marshal has been warned not to take the main road. It has also been suggested that Rommel journey back to his château in a less conspicuous form of transportation than his beloved Horch.

But since D-Day Rommel has spent all day, every day, on the go. The splash of luxury provided by his gorgeous black sedan makes the two hundred and more daily miles bearable. Top down. Warm summer weather. Poplar stands and roadside drainage. If it weren't for the flaming hulks of panzers, German trucks, and the inevitable smell of burning flesh, this might be a pleasant drive through the Norman countryside.

---

* Despite the similarity between the name of this small town in the Calvados region and that of British field marshal and Rommel nemesis Bernard Law Montgomery, there is no connection. The village is named for an eleventh-century French nobleman loyal to William the Conqueror, Roger de Montgomery.

Rommel strives to contain the Allied invasion to the coast, six weeks after the breaching of his Atlantic Wall. But everything about the German situation is *Scheisse* and the field marshal grows more and more comfortable saying so. In a lengthy report intended for the eyes of Adolf Hitler, Rommel the day before yesterday wrote of the impossible situation in Normandy. He cites specific figures about casualties, Allied destruction of the railway system, and the unceasing amount of men and matériel arriving from England.

"In these circumstances we must expect that in the foreseeable future the enemy will succeed in breaking through our thin front," Rommel concludes the grim page-long summary. "The unequal struggle is approaching its end. It is urgently necessary for the proper conclusion to be drawn from this situation."

Rommel wisecracked about the missive when running into an old Afrika Korps colleague this morning, telling Lieutenant Colonel Elmar Warning that if Hitler does not heed his warning to retreat, "I'm going to open up the western front. Because only one thing matters now: the British and Americans must get to Berlin before the Russians!"

But there is nothing more Rommel can do today. So he heads for the peace and quiet of his château, two hours' drive from the fighting.

The late-afternoon sky is bright but growing dim, a time of day when Serengeti lions and RAF fighter pilots prefer to do their hunting. Corporal Daniel drives the Horch, Rommel navigates, and two young officers along with a sergeant tasked specifically as a lookout for enemy aircraft ride in the spacious rear bench seat.

Feldwebel Hoike, as the sergeant is known, does his job. Shortly before 4:30 he spots two British Spitfires dropping to treetop level for a strafing run. Rommel has not followed suggestions to trade the Horch for a much less conspicuous *Kübelwagen*, but he has taken the precaution of a side road to heart. Under normal circumstances, when a large caravan of troops clogs a larger thoroughfare, this is sound advice. But right now the field marshal's black convertible with its top down and five occupants clearly dressed in German uniform is the only target on this farm road.

There is no escape.

The Spitfires stitch the country highway with 20mm cannon rounds. At Bir Hakeim, the British called this "sport." They still do. Corporal Daniel attempts to swerve, but the road is barely wider than one lane. Rommel's driver is hit. Corporal Daniel will lapse into a coma, live for several hours, and die.

The three men in the back seat are fine. Scared. Adrenaline coursing. Banged up. But fine.

Erwin Rommel is not fine.

The Horch skids. No one is driving anymore. The field marshal turns at the last instant to stare at the attacking Spitfires, stalwarts of the Empire, camouflaged fuselages, robin's-egg blue underbellies, and two cannons in each wing firing rounds powerful enough to pierce panzer armor.

Rommel's head slams hard into the windshield as the Horch crashes into a ditch, shattering his skull in three places. The left side of his face is all but destroyed as the field marshal is launched from his seat into the middle of the road.

The Desert Fox has fought his last battle.

And soon the Führer will order his death.

68

General Dietrich von Choltitz has orders from the Führer.

The new military commander of Paris awakens in room 213 of Le Meurice, a luxury hotel smack in the heart of the city. Blackout curtains. Red-carpeted hallways. Breakfast of marmalade, black coffee, and four slices of toast delivered by longtime aide Corporal Helmut Mayer.

This is the general's first morning in charge. A garrison of 25,000 soldiers is now at his beck and call. Choltitz has absolute control of absolutely everything in the City of Lights. Food, women, fast cars—all are his for the asking. In the history of mankind, very few individuals have been able to make that claim. The citizens may be suffering right now—starving, angry, praying for relief—but to be ruler of Paris is to be sovereign lord of the finest pleasures life has to offer, a most wondrous joy indeed.

On this warm summer morning, that man is Dietrich von Choltitz, a forty-nine-year-old monocle-wearing career officer with a budding heart condition and the sudden awareness that he has a conscience.

Thus, rather than greeting the day awash in joy, General von Choltitz is wrapped in gloom.

The general has just traveled by train and automobile from Adolf Hitler's headquarters in faraway East Prussia, the Wolfsschanze—the Wolf's Lair. The differences between that remote utilitarian bunker and gay Paree could not be more remarkable. Choltitz has been everywhere in this war: accepting the surrender in Rotterdam, enduring the bitter siege of Sevastopol, and most recently fighting in Normandy. He thought he had seen and done it all.

Then came his meeting with Hitler.

Von Choltitz now awakens in a room overlooking the Louvre and Tuileries and tries to make sense of his new moral compass.

It is nine hundred miles from the Wolf's Lair to Paris. Plenty of time to work through the memory of his visit with Hitler. The two met in a windowless cement bunker. Choltitz was jarred by the Führer's feeble appearance. "I saw an old, bent-over, flabby man with thinning gray hair—a trembling, physically demolished human being," Choltitz will write.

But that fragile exterior was set aside as Hitler launched into a rambling dissertation on his life and career that ended with the Führer venting his rage about a recent assassination plot. "He spoke in a bloodthirsty language with froth literally coming out of his mouth. His entire body trembled. Sweat was running down his face," Choltitz adds.

General Dietrich von Choltitz is a faithful soldier and follower of Hitler, a career officer with a paunch and reputation for completing a job at all costs. He has taken part in the persecution of Jews and kept his mouth shut about it.

But as he stood in the pale artificial light of the remote bunker, Choltitz realized the war was lost. Hitler ranted about a new weapon technology that would turn the tide of the war but it was clear that the

Führer's grasp on reality was slipping. "I saw in front of me someone who has lost his mind. The fact that the life of our nation was in the hands of an insane being who could no longer judge the situation or was unwilling to see it realistically depressed me immensely," the general will lament.

But Choltitz had no choice but to stand and endure the harangue.

Hitler finally got to the point.

"Now," the Führer barked. "You are going to Paris."

More bile as Hitler derided the soft lifestyle of soldiers stationed in the city.

"You will stamp out without pity any uprising by the civilian population, any act of terrorism, any act of sabotage against the German garrison," Hitler rants. "For that, Herr General, you will receive from me all the support you need."

Choltitz now faces a cruel choice as he begins his first day as commander of Paris. He can either follow Hitler's order to defend the city at all costs, which will eventually mean the destruction of any resources of which the Allies can make use: power plants, fuel depots, water supply, and even the picturesque bridges across the Seine.

Or Choltitz can defy those orders, save hundreds of thousands of lives, prevent the sort of lengthy siege that destroyed every city block in Stalingrad and reduced its residents to cannibalism in order to stay alive.

All he has to do is surrender.

The war is almost lost. Surrender would be simple. The French did it so easily four years ago.

Yet, there is a consequence.

Thus, the heavy gloom that has settled over General von Choltitz.

Should he defy Adolf Hitler, the Nazis will enact a policy known as the *Sippenhaft*. This brutal practice of punishing relatives for the actions of a family member was originally invoked during the Middle Ages.

Sippenhaft means that if Choltitz violates the Führer's direct order and surrenders Paris intact, his wife, Huberta, their two daughters, Maria and Anna, and infant son Timo will be executed.

General Dietrich von Choltitz must make his decision soon.

The Allies are coming. Time is running out.

69

Paris is uneasy.

It's hot. The sort of day when the air is thick and sweat makes bedsheets stick and finding a beach feels like the most wonderful idea in the world. Which is precisely how Paris spends this holiday known as the Feast of the Assumption: beach umbrellas along the Seine, swimming, bathing suits, splashing, fishermen with bamboo poles on shaded banks, lovers strolling the shore.

The Germans are swimming too. But not in the Seine. The city's pools are for occupiers only. The enemy is older these days, the Fatherland running out of good men. So it's middle-aged reservists with their beer bellies splashing in the *piscines* rather than the strapping young bucks with the hard bodies who used to sunbathe in their underwear—now either dead, in POW camps, or fighting somewhere west or east. This new breed of Nazi brings the weight of mediocrity and age. Paris notices. Paris bridles. Paris is less frightened of the occupiers than ever before.

So there's something new in the air today, unspoken electricity making everyone just a little more on edge than usual. Today marks the Virgin Mary's ascent into heaven, but the undercurrent in Paris is a different form of uprising.

The Allies are coming, but who knows when?

It is time for the Germans to leave.

Yet the closest Allied troops are still a hundred miles from the city. That could take weeks.

So Paris is taking matters into its own hands.

The police have gone on strike, joining the railway workers who have refused to show up for work the past three days. There is talk of a general strike that will immobilize the entire city.

But the Germans are fighting back.

On this very day, new German commander Dietrich von Choltitz disarmed the city's 20,000-man police force. More than 5,000 weapons have been seized.

And trains still head east. Today, 1,654 male and female prisoners are being bused from Fresnes Prison to a railway siding in the suburb of Pantin, where SNCF employees are still reporting for work. The prisoners are being loaded into boxcars for the journey to the Buchenwald and Ravensbrück concentration camps. The railway cars and local air reek of large animals and dung, because these boxcars normally ship beef and pork from the Pantin stockyard next door.

The men and women enduring standing-room-only conditions in this glaring heat are not only Jews and resistants but also 168 Allied fliers shot down over France. These *Terrorflieger*—"terror fliers"—are being denied the basic rights of all prisoners of war. They are scheduled to be executed upon arrival.

Nothing in Paris feels normal right now. The dogs and cats have all been eaten. Citizens live on elm, linden, and ash leaves from public parks. Electricity and gas are shut off for hours at a time.

The Germans have wired every bridge for detonation.

One thing is certain: the Allies are coming.

But maybe not soon enough.

70

General Charles de Gaulle is about to drown.

And it's his own fault.

"England? Never!" the general insists. The view outside his circular window on his Lockheed Lodestar, the *France*, is of the English Channel on a stormy day. Low clouds. No sunshine. One hundred yards visibility. And as de Gaulle has just been informed, no petrol in three of the aircraft's four fuel tanks. The *France* circles off the southern tip of England, waiting for an RAF fighter escort to ensure a safe flight across the Channel to Normandy.

But the Spitfire has missed the rendezvous. Lodestar pilot Lionel de Marmier insists he must turn back and land in England—or ditch in the Channel.

"Tell Marmier," de Gaulle emphatically informs his orderly—there is more uprising in Paris with each passing day and de Gaulle is eager to take control of the city—"I will land only in France."

The pilot has his orders. Marmier aims the aircraft due south.

At more than 200 miles per hour, the ninety-mile crossing from southern England to the Cotentin Peninsula takes almost half an hour.

The two-man flight crew sweats every minute of the ordeal, but de Gaulle is far more concerned with getting to Paris. The French countryside finally comes into view. The gas needle dips below empty. A landing spot must be found immediately among the small farms and country roads. Marmier has no idea of his location. One of the pilots passes a map back to de Gaulle.

The general looks out the window. He scrutinizes the topography. "Here," says the general, stabbing a finger at a site east of Cherbourg.

Marmier checks the map against his current coordinates.

De Gaulle is correct.

As Marmier lands on the small local airstrip, the red light on his cockpit control panel indicating just two more minutes of fuel flicks on.

Charles de Gaulle is back on French soil.

Barely. But he is here.

And this time the general intends to stay.

71

General Dwight Eisenhower plans to bypass Paris.

And Charles de Gaulle intends to change his mind.

The supreme commander stands in the map tent at his forward headquarters. The roar of propellers fills the night as de Gaulle's refueled *France* lands in a nearby field. The light spatter of raindrops on canvas beats tattoo as Ike scrutinizes maps showing the approach to Paris. Impromptu wooden floors prevent him from standing in the mud. Eisenhower has watched with approval as de Gaulle has taken leadership of the French people, so deft in his maneuvering that General Henri Giraud is now just a footnote.* Ike quietly defies President

---

* "Here and there were some little unpleasant scenes, but the fact is that it was only before Giraud made clear his distaste for politics and then accepted without question de Gaulle's pre-eminence in the political field. Giraud wanted to command French troops in the field—that's what he really wanted to do. Well, of course, it didn't really work out in the long run and finally Giraud disappeared from the scene," Eisenhower will later remember.

Franklin Roosevelt in his backing of de Gaulle as the next leader of France. But he knows that de Gaulle has flown here to pick a new fight—this time with Eisenhower.

"This man and I have always been very good friends, although the start of our relations was not a really promising start," Eisenhower will say of de Gaulle, adding that their 1942 meetings in London were soon overshadowed by their deepening friendship during their time in Africa the following year.

But Eisenhower is nervous when he hears French being spoken outside his tent on this rainy evening, signaling the impending arrival of de Gaulle. Despite his lofty title as supreme commander of the Allied Expeditionary Forces, Ike finds himself intimidated by the force of de Gaulle's personality.

"After all, I was commanding every damn thing on the continent—all the troops—and all that de Gaulle could count on: troops, equipment, every damn thing supplied by America," Eisenhower will note. And he knows that none of that matters to General de Gaulle. It doesn't help that the Frenchman towers over him, almost six inches taller. Eisenhower is afraid he will buckle to de Gaulle's demands and reminds himself not to "get committed to Paris."

Neither man can possibly know that Adolf Hitler issued an order today stating that Paris is to be a *Schwerpunkt*—strongpoint—to be defended at all costs. This certainly means another Stalingrad.

But both de Gaulle and Eisenhower are well aware that fighting between the Germans and the Resistance is escalating. A group known as the Comité de Français de Libération Nationale is fomenting insurrection. Paris police are also rising up. German snipers are shooting back. De Gaulle wants to charge in and take control of this insurrection, and Eisenhower thinks that's a stupid idea that could sucker Allied forces into months of street-to-street fighting.

De Gaulle steps into the tent. He is freshly shaven, having borrowed a razor to clean himself up before this very important conference.

Ike walks de Gaulle through easel after easel of maps, showing Allied troop positions in comparison with the Germans. The point of Allied strategy right now, Eisenhower reminds the general, is to defeat the German army. Should the Allies get stuck in a prolonged battle for Paris, the Wehrmacht will escape to reload and rearm to fight another day. The smart move is to ignore Paris and race toward Germany. The war could be over in six months. Taking Paris means bringing the Allied advance to a dead halt. This could extend the war at least one year.

De Gaulle argues back. The uprisings in Paris are largely workingmen, who favor the French Communists. There are 25,000 armed citizens under authority of the French Communist Party. Should they take control of the city, there will be dire repercussions when the war is over and these same partisans align themselves with the Soviet Union instead of America and Great Britain. De Gaulle fears his own government will be ignored and shoved aside if he does not get to Paris as quickly as possible to assume the mantle of authority.

De Gaulle's argument is political. Eisenhower's is tactical.

Ike does not back down.

So General de Gaulle pivots, presenting an alternate strategy. The French 2nd Armored Division under the command of General Jacques-Philippe Leclerc is currently in France, serving under General George Patton and his Third Army. De Gaulle threatens to give the order for Leclerc to peel off and take Paris single-handedly.

Eisenhower tenses but does not take the bait. The 2nd Armored, Eisenhower will later recall, "couldn't have moved a mile if I didn't want it to, and it wouldn't have."

Ike turns de Gaulle down flat.

General Charles walks back to his plane, alone and lost in thought.

"Where is General Leclerc?" de Gaulle asks, finding an aide, already making plans to ignore Eisenhower.

The general has waited four years to take Paris. He will not come this close and be denied.

72

George S. Patton has no interest in taking Paris.

The general is exhausted. The last two weeks have seen his Third Army punish the enemy, racing across France so fast that he needs a personal airplane to direct the battles. Most recently, Patton's army very nearly encircled the Germans in what will become known as the Falaise Pocket. He did not succeed but won the battle decisively before the enemy snuck away through a gap in the Allied lines. The fields of western France are piled with thousands of dead from both sides. An estimated 50,000 Germans have been taken prisoner but just as many have gotten away.

So Patton is relieved to finally get a moment's rest. No sooner does he close his eyes than he is summoned on important business. The general is in disarray as he carefully picks his way through the grove of poplars encircling his temporary headquarters. A faint poacher's moon is the only light. Patton's hair is uncombed and uniform shirt

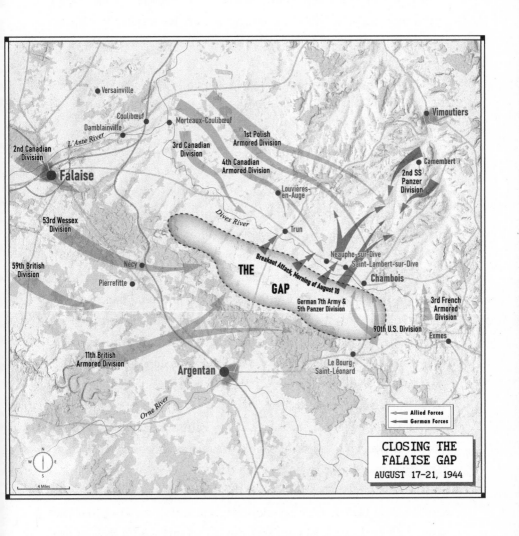

Versainville

Coulibœuf

Damblainville

Morteaux-Coulibœuf

L'Ante River

2nd Canadian
Division

Falaise

3rd Canadian
Division

4th Canadian
Armored Division

1st Polish
Armored Division

Vimoutiers

Camembert

2nd SS
Panzer
Division

Louvières-
en-Auge

53rd Wessex
Division

Dives River

Trun

59th British
Division

Nécy

Pierrefitte

Neauphe-sur-Dive

THE
GAP

Breakout Attack, Morning of August 10

Saint-Lambert-sur-Dive

Chambois

3rd French
Armored
Division

German 7th Army &
5th Panzer Division

90th U.S. Division

Exmes

11th British
Armored Division

Argentan

Le Bourg-
Saint-Léonard

Orne River

Allied Forces
German Forces

**CLOSING THE
FALAISE GAP**

AUGUST 17–21, 1944

N
W   E
S

4 Miles

untucked. Arriving at a large olive drab tent, he pulls back the heavy canvas flap and steps into the thin illumination of lantern light.

Three men wait inside. Everyone is speaking French. Two wear uniforms. The third is a thirty-nine-year-old Communist resistant with a receding hairline wearing a dirty rumpled suit. His name is Roger Cocteau, code name "Gallois." The Parisian has traveled far and risked his life to be here.

"Excuse me," Patton says in casual French—"*Pardon*." He does not introduce himself. "I've been sleeping. OK. I'm listening. What's your story?"

As intelligence officer Colonel Robert F. Powell, one of the men in uniform, already knows, Cocteau has quite a tale to tell. The resistant has made it his mission to convince General Eisenhower to liberate Paris. Cocteau has crossed through German lines and nearly gotten shot in his quest. Paris is rising up. Small-arms fire, bonfires, barricades. The people are starving, now more than ever. The Normandy landings and subsequent destruction of French rail lines have choked off all access to food. What little arrives in the capital is hoarded by the Germans. Now the people are rebelling and Resistants are coming out of hiding to wage gun battles in the streets with the occupiers. The bloodshed will be enormous if the Allies do not step in soon.

The words rush out of Cocteau, rehearsed since he fled Paris days ago. Patton does not interrupt.

"You're a soldier and I'm a soldier," Patton tells the Frenchman when the saga is complete. "I'm going to answer you as a soldier."

Patton tells Gallois that his job is defeating Germans, "not capturing capitals." Racing across France requires all the gasoline the Allies can muster. Taking Paris would mean allocating some of that precious fuel to the city. In addition, the U.S. Army would have to feed the 3.5 million citizens of Paris—an extraordinary task, considering that all those rations would have to be driven two hundred miles by truck from the Atlantic Coast. In Patton's estimation, the Resistance should take full responsibility for starting the uprising—and finishing it—themselves.

Patton extends his hand and wishes Cocteau well.

But the general's answer is no.

A stunned Roger Cocteau remains in the tent as Patton steps back into the night. Energy whooshes out of him as he is overcome by exhaustion and rejection.

. . .

GEORGE S. PATTON stands alone in the dark, pausing on the way back to his cot. As a historian and believer in reincarnation, the general sees war from an unusual perspective, believing he been present at many battles in past lives. This campaign across France is new for him, despite forty years in the Army during this current lifetime and all those battles from ancient times. Instead of just being a commander, he is a conqueror, knowing full well that history will judge him by his battle strategy and the benevolence or ruthlessness shown to the vanquished.

The failure to close the Falaise Pocket and prevent the escape of those thousands of German soldiers was a crushing disappointment to Patton. But in that failure he now sees an opportunity that will transcend this day and this month and even this war. All those escaping Wehrmacht soldiers will be waiting when the U.S. Army gets around to chasing them. This opens the smallest of strategic windows, allowing the Allies to assist the insurrection in Paris before moving on.

As a man who speaks French, once lived in France, and proudly spouts a personal motto based on French audacity, Patton has a deep affinity for this country and its people. From the basement meeting in a Louisiana high school that pointed him toward armored combat and the command he now holds, the arc of the general's life these past four years points firmly toward the opportunity now before him.

Long after historians stop writing about his march to the Rhine, General George S. Patton will be immortalized for taking Paris.

. . .

ROGER COCTEAU HAS nowhere to go. He still sits in the tent with Colonel Powell and his fellow officer, a resistant named André Babois. There is nothing to talk about.

Suddenly, General Patton steps back into the tent holding a bottle of champagne and glasses.

"Are you ready to take a long voyage?" Patton asks, pouring a toast for everyone in the tent.

Upon draining his glass, Cocteau is driven to meet General Omar Bradley, a man who might be able to change Eisenhower's mind about Paris.

The time is 3:30 a.m. when Patton goes back to bed, taste of champagne still on his tongue, once again proving there's no telling what George S. Patton will care about.

73

Dwight Eisenhower is changing his mind.

The supreme commander is up early. Morning songbirds are just starting to trill. A cup of coffee—first one of today's twenty. The first cigarette of today's three packs. Eisenhower sits at a small wooden field desk looking at a letter from Charles de Gaulle, restating his arguments about Paris. He has also had discussions in the last twenty-four hours with General Omar Bradley about the Frenchman sent his way by George S. Patton.

This morning's *London Daily Herald* is stating that Franklin Roosevelt and Winston Churchill will tour Paris once liberation occurs, also mentioning that Charles de Gaulle *may* be allowed to join them and "probably have the place of honor."

To Eisenhower, this just isn't right. He will do everything in his power to help de Gaulle succeed. Although he has not said so, Eisenhower holds the same fondness for Paris as George Patton, having lived there in the fashionable 16th arrondissement for fourteen months in the late 1920s. He learned to read and write French during that time.

It is 10:30 when Eisenhower meets formally with General Bradley to discuss the Paris situation. Bradley relays information from his chief intelligence officer, Brigadier General Edwin Sibert, who debriefed Roger Cocteau at length: "If we don't get to Paris in a couple days there's going to be an awful slaughter."

In addition to Bradley, Eisenhower speaks with General Marie-Pierre Koenig, hero of Bir Hakeim, now fighting with the Allies in France.

Then, still not certain Paris is the smartest tactical maneuver, Eisenhower writes a small note to chief of staff General Walter Bedell Smith.

"It looks now as if we shall be compelled to go to Paris," Eisenhower writes, in effect giving the formal order.

74

The French are on the move.

One hundred and twenty-two miles to the Champs-Élyées. The 2nd Armored Division under the command of General Jacques-Philippe Leclerc hits the road at first light. Two hundred Shermans, 16,000 men, and more than 4,000 more vehicles and artillery pieces. This long column of men with their machines has never been so excited about rapid forward movement.

Today they're going home.

Some of these soldiers are so close to loved ones that they can pick up the phone and call. But for others Paris is more spiritual, the ideal of freedom so often encouraged by Charles de Gaulle. To see the tricolor flying from the Eiffel Tower will be an emotional first for these men.

Not since Bir Hakeim has an army been so diverse. Frenchmen, Arabs, Africans, and even Lebanese, Chileans, and Mexicans. Gaullists and former Vichy fighters. Spanish Civil War veterans. Former

POWs captured in 1940 and now finally getting the chance to make it right. And the most hallowed of these men, the survivors of Bir Hakeim. General Leclerc is a nobleman with the surname of Haute-clocque who adopted the nom de guerre of Leclerc to prevent his family from suffering. Leclerc comes from a hereditary line of soldiers dating back to the Crusades. He is described by American observer Colonel David K. E. Bruce of the OSS as "tall, spare, handsome, stern-visaged and a striking figure."

The 2nd's diversity is underscored by their shared goal of Paris. Nothing else in the war matters. The people of France have grown used to the sight of Americans, British, and Germans, but these long columns of French soldiers are the first sign that the nation is truly being liberated.

Entire villages pour out to greet the advancing columns. World War I veterans stand at attention, saluting, wearing all their medals. Women throw flowers—and themselves. Tank crews and infantry alike are given every imaginable libation.

And these are only the country roads. The men of the 2nd can't imagine what Paris will be like. It's so easy. No enemy fire. A cakewalk.

The people of Paris know the French are coming. A large band of journalists, including American Ernest Hemingway, travels the same route. Each is eager to be the first reporter in Paris. The BBC is already announcing that "Paris is free!" and King George VI has already sent a congratulatory telegram to Charles de Gaulle, whom he came to know well during the general's London years.

By day's end, Paris is just twenty-five miles away. The long journey on the road earns a celebration from the men of the 2nd Armored Division, who happily make use of the cognac, wine, beer, champagne, Armagnac, and every other potent potable tossed or handed or delivered with a kiss from a young maiden in every village along the way.

But tomorrow will not be so easy.

The Germans are not done fighting.

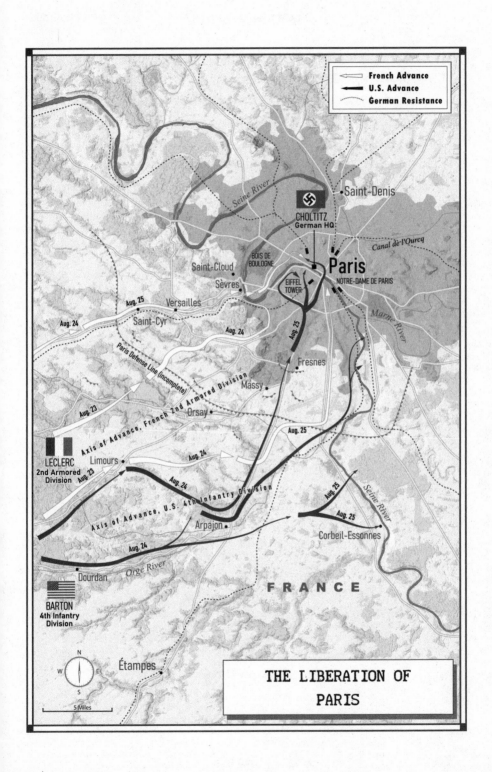

THE LIBERATION OF
PARIS

. . .

"The defense of Paris is of decisive military and political significance," Adolf Hitler messages General Dietrich von Choltitz. "Its loss would tear open the whole coastal front north of the Seine and deprive Germany of bases for very long-range warfare against England.

"Historically, the loss of Paris always means the loss of France . . .

". . . Paris must not fall into enemy hands except as a field of ruins."

75

Paris is impatient.

A lone Piper Cub light aircraft circles the city. The aircraft has no weaponry and has become the preferred mode of transportation for Allied generals wishing to quickly traverse the French countryside. This particular plane is in the service of General Jacques-Philippe Leclerc. No one on the ground knows that. But the sight of a plane with American markings and no intention of bombing or strafing is a source of curiosity to everyone below.

The 2nd Armored Division pushed off eight hours ago. But the crowds lining the roads are even larger than yesterday. Even in the driving rain, they stand along lanes lined with oak trees, cheering and crying and rejoicing without reserve.

German resistance is equally passionate. The fighting is in skirmishes instead of set-piece battles, but fierce enough to see seventy-one French soldiers killed and more than 140 tanks and vehicles destroyed.

A note written on burlap and weighted with lead is dropped from the Piper, now flying over the brown stone headquarters of the Paris police near Notre-Dame.

"*Tenez bon*," it reads, "*nous arrivons.*"

"Hang on. We're coming."

.   .   .

GENERAL LECLERC PHONES German commander General Dietrich von Choltitz to discuss surrender terms. Choltitz can think only of *Sippenhaft*. For the sake of his wife, daughters, and an infant son, he must not give the appearance of surrendering too easily.

Choltitz tells Leclerc that now is not the time.

.   .   .

THE FRENCH ARRIVE at 9:22 p.m.

Finally.

Warm evening sun bathes Paris on a day that began overcast and gray. Following the same path through the Porte d'Italie, a gate in the city wall once used by Napoleon on his own campaign to take Paris, lead elements of the French 2nd Armored Division pour into the city.

The Nazi occupation is almost over.

Almost.

.   .   .

IN THE DARKNESS, a lone church bell rings.

It is the bourdon, Emmanuel, all fourteen tons pealing low in F sharp. A dozen policemen, watched closely by gargoyles, pull the rope in Notre-Dame's belfry.

More bells. Churches throughout Paris, the first bells anyone has heard since June 1940. Then, from the cathedral at Sacré-Coeur, the nineteen-ton Savoyarde—the largest bell in France, so enormous that the sound can be heard almost ten miles away—begins to toll.

.   .   .

THE AMERICANS RUMBLE into town the next day. This is the special calendar date to be forever tied with liberation: August 25, 1944. Sherman tanks and infantry of George S. Patton's 4th Armored Division pour into the city. They are clearly not French, but the outpouring of affection from Parisians is no less than that for their own countrymen.

The 20,000 Germans in Paris are now finding ways to leave. The civilian uprising is a motivator; seemingly innocent men and women randomly surprise German soldiers on the streets with a shot to the head. German snipers open fire from rooftops, but only for a time. Soon, the German exodus is almost complete. No one detonates a single bridge on the way out. General Dietrich von Choltitz offers his surrender. He makes it look like he has no choice—because he doesn't. Angry crowds greet him as he exits the Meurice, now a prisoner of war. Corporal Mayer, the general's aide, has packed a valise with a spare uniform that his commanding officer might wear in captivity. The bag is wrenched from Mayer's hand by the mob, then ripped open, its contents greedily pilfered. Von Choltitz watches in amazement as a woman waves his uniform trousers with the red stripe running down the seam as her new souvenir. And then the general is driven off in an armored vehicle, his fate still uncertain.

General Dwight Eisenhower monitors the situation from a distance. George S. Patton is already pushing on to Germany.

Winston Churchill cheers.

Charles de Gaulle enters the city in a chauffeured limousine late in the afternoon, already planning a long, defiant march down the Champs-Élysées to show his authority tomorrow. Leclerc's 2nd Armored Division will line the route, starting at the Arc de Triomphe with the relighting of the eternal flame. This will be the consolidation of power and realization of a dream he has clutched in his fists for so long.

De Gaulle is France.

But the liberation is about Paris.

The people rejoice. These reserved, isolated, sometimes haughty citizens celebrate like never before. Soldiers are inundated with affection. Jewish residents rip off their yellow Stars of David and hand them to the Americans as thankful souvenirs. French soldiers lucky enough to hail from Paris find their families, stepping through a front door and hugging an astonished mother who hugs back so hard and strong that these men will talk about the moment the rest of their lives.

Impromptu singing of "La Marseillaise." Alone and in huge crowds. Voices big, tears now flowing in every corner of the city. Corks popping as champagne saved for this moment explodes into the sky. Dancing. Delirious lovemaking.

More champagne. More everything.

No one's waking up early tomorrow.

And the flags, of course. The Nazi swastika is ripped down throughout the city. Tricolors hidden four years beneath floorboards and in crawl spaces now drape over balcony railings and wrap like shawls around men and women wandering through the streets, unafraid. Even when the few remaining German snipers take stupid last-minute pot shots, firing into crowds as a final display of Nazi arrogance, the people of Paris walk uncowed down familiar boulevards, delirious with joy that the City of Lights is theirs once again.

By the end of the day, the people of Paris can look to the Eiffel Tower and see their flag—the emblem of *Liberté, Égalité, Fraternité*—fluttering in the breeze.

Paris has been taken.

And now taken back again.

Vive le France.

AFTERWORD

GERMAINE TILLION, the French resistant betrayed by Father Robert Alesch, spent a year in the Paris prisons of Fresnes and La Santé. On October 21, 1943, Tillion was deported with her mother, **Émilie,** to the all-female Ravensbrück concentration camp outside Berlin. Amazingly, Tillion continued her ethnographic studies, observing the behavior of guards and fellow prisoners. She secretly wrote an opera to keep up her spirits. Émilie was gassed before the war ended, but Germaine Tillion survived. Tillion wrote extensively about the war once she returned to Paris, and resumed her ethnographic studies in the Middle East and North Africa. Germaine Tillion died on April 18, 2008. In 2014, it was announced by French president François Hollande that Tillion's body would be buried at the Pantheon along with great French heroes dating back to the Revolution. Her family did not wish to disturb her remains, so dirt from her burial site occupies a place of honor at the Pantheon. Tillion, said Hollande, "incarnated the values of France when the country was beaten to the ground."

. . .

CHARLES DE GAULLE went on to a long and successful career as the leader of the French people. De Gaulle served for two years as head of the provisional government of France following World War II. He later served as prime minister from 1959 to 1969, then president for the next ten years. De Gaulle died in 1970 at the age of seventy-nine.

. . .

WINSTON CHURCHILL WAS voted out of office after Allied victory in Europe but before the end of World War II. However, he was once again elected prime minister in 1951, serving four more years. Churchill died in 1965 at the age of ninety. Revisionist historians now believe that his "soft underbelly" strategy for attacking the European continent was a sound policy and might have succeeded, given greater Allied support.

. . .

GENERAL GEORGE S. PATTON fought to the very last days of World War II, famously pushing his troops as far east as possible to halt incursion by troops of the Soviet Union into those territories. Patton was a passenger in a car hit by a truck just one day before returning home at war's end. He was paralyzed and died soon after in Germany.

. . .

FIELD MARSHAL ERWIN ROMMEL was implicated in the July 1944 plot to kill Adolf Hitler. Given the choice of suicide followed by a state funeral or a public trial that would surely result in torture and execution, Rommel took a cyanide pill in October 1944.

. . .

GENERAL DWIGHT EISENHOWER went on to serve two terms as president of the United States. He kicked his three-pack-a-day cigarette habit, passing away at the age of seventy-eight in 1969.

. . .

VIRGINIA HALL WAS decorated by British king George VI and American president Harry S. Truman for her brave undercover work. It is widely believed that much of the success of D-Day is owed to her intelligence reports and sabotage of German defenses with the French Resistance. Hall subsequently served in the Central Intelligence Agency. She died in 1982.

. . .

THE MEMORY OF JACQUES BONSERGENT lives on. Following the war, the Lancry Métro station in the 10th arrondissement was renamed in his honor. Bonsergent is buried in his hometown cemetery at Malestroit in Brittany.

. . .

COLONEL FABIEN, A.K.A. PIERRE GEORGES, was captured and tortured by the Nazis in 1943 but escaped. He died the following year when a mine exploded while he was leading a Free French fighting unit against German forces during the Battle of the Bulge. It is now common in France to name streets in towns with Communist leanings for Colonel Fabien. The Colonel Fabien Métro stop is under the Boulevard de la Villette, on the border of the 10th and 19th arrondissements.

. . .

THE BATTLE OF BIR HAKEIM is remembered as one of the great French moments of World War II—and, indeed, French military history. The Bir-Hakeim Métro stop is an elevated platform in the 15th arrondissement, just a ten-minute walk south of the Eiffel Tower.

. . .

GENERAL JACQUES-PHILIPPE LECLERC—a.k.a. Jacques-Philippe Leclerc de Hauteclocque—was the French representative to the Japanese surrender on board the USS *Missouri* at the end of World War II. He was killed in the crash of a B-25 bomber flying over Algeria on November 28, 1947. The general is interred in the crypt at Les Invalides in Paris.

. . .

JEAN MOULIN'S ASHES were interred in the Pantheon in Paris on December 19, 1964. As with many French heroes, a Métro station has been named in honor.

. . .

THE HUSBAND AND wife French refugees who appeared in *Casablanca*, **Marcel Dalio** and **Madeleine Lebeau**, went on to have lengthy film careers. The couple split up during the filming of *Casablanca*, with Dalio citing "desertion." Dalio died in Paris in 1983. Lebeau lived long enough to become the oldest credited cast member of the film. She died in Spain in 2016 after breaking her femur in a fall. Madeleine Lebeau was ninety-two.

. . .

FATHER ROBERT ALESCH was arrested after the war and placed on trial. Germaine Tillion witnessed the proceedings. The priest was found guilty and shot by a firing squad on January 25, 1949.

ACKNOWLEDGMENTS

Writing is a solitary profession, but no book is possible without the inspiration from those who have gone before, the encouragement of peers, and the patience of loved ones. There comes a moment in each book when the research and writing make the process feel very much like drifting alone on a boat into the middle of a vast lake, knowing that the world waits on the shore but the time to paddle back and reconnect must wait until the last word is written. The lonely drifting is a vital part of the process. It's hard and necessary. But it is the friends and loved ones who make it all worthwhile.

Here's the short list of those who made *Taking Paris* possible.

Much thanks to David Cornwell (nom de plume: John le Carré), James Salter, Michael Herr, and Jim Harrison—inspirations all. Gone but certainly not forgotten.

To my editor, the very patient, calm, and thoroughly professional Brent Howard. *Taking Paris* is a parallel history of World War II, a wander that was supposed to be just the story of June through August

1944. That's the book Brent bought and the book I intended to write. But then the issues of context started nagging at me and the next thing you knew, we were going all the way back to May 1940. Thus, this book was very late and I am forever thankful to Brent for allowing me the extra time to get it right.

To Bill O'Reilly and Makeda Wubneh. Thanks for everything. It's such an easy throwaway line, but in this case I mean it with all sincerity.

To Evan Bell and Yifan Yang, for crunching the numbers.

Brian Sobel did me an enormous service by reading with an historian's eye, gently suggesting that the narrative did not require many of the earlier stylistic mistakes I insisted upon making.

Chris Noonan is that rarest of individual: a lifelong friend. Smart, tough, and funny. You should the give the writing game a try, Shithead.

To my incorrigible brothers in the Tough Guy Book Club: JC Abusaid, Mike Brough, Mark Burkhardt, John Burns, Gregg Hemphill, John Herold, and Alan Mariconda. Thanks for enduring friendship, lively conversation, endless ballbusting, and indulging me with feedback from early pages to finale.

There are not enough words to describe my thanks and affection for the great Eric Simonoff. His contact name in my phone is "Super Agent." I mean that in every sense of the word. Eric's friendship and career guidance is the sort of profound relationship every creative person should be lucky enough to enjoy.

Finally, to Calene and the boys—Devin, Connor, and Liam. I do nothing to deserve your love. I drift away on that boat into the middle of the lake with every book I write. The lawn doesn't get mowed. Christmas lights stay up until February. My attempts at conversation revolve around historical trivia I've come across during the day's work. But you continue to wrap your arms around my messy, impulsive, and often unwashed self to remind me that I am, indeed, a nerd and a history geek—and that's cool. You are my sunshine.

NOTES

I wrote a lengthy explanation of the methodology behind my research process for *Taking Paris* but after giving it a long thought I ended up hitting "delete" and starting over. This is a book that could not have been written before the digital age. Thanks to COVID, there was no travel, no libraries, no archives, no museums, no battlefields to walk—map in hand, imagining the feints and parries as men fought and died. I am sometimes not sure if I am a writer who travels or a traveler who writes, but removing the actual road trip from the creative journey completely changed what it means to research a work of history.

Everything was done online. Everything. I had no choice. Digitized newspapers like the *New York Times* and the *Times* of London literally took me back in time, and online databases such as (and I'm just picking one of the many priceless sources of information at random) George Washington University's Churchill appointment calendars made it possible to see the handwriting, style of paper, and intensity of the prime minister's day. YouTube showed me detailed videos of long-ago battlefields in Africa and Europe, the sights and sounds of Paris being liberated, and a marvelous video about life inside a Char B1.

Google Earth allowed me to see images of the places United Airlines could not fly me. Countless other Google searches told me about plants, artifacts, church bells, and the thousands of other details that go into writing history. When one cannot go to Paris to hear the bells of Notre-Dame, listening to the deep peal of the bourdon is as simple as an online search. Try it. Completely enchanting. I'd sometimes write about Paris with the sounds of the bells of Notre-Dame ringing through my office. Puts you right there.

As a journalist, I spent a decade covering the Tour de France long ago, so many of my recollections about the sights and smells of various towns and cities came from notebooks filled with observations from those years. One particular morning in Paris during those years, I left my room early for a run through the streets of the city. But while the streets were empty, the sidewalks were filled with thousands of spectators waiting for the bike race. In a burst of inspiration, I went back to my hotel and retrieved my press pass. I had the privilege and thrill of flashing my press pass to the gendarme and climbing over the metal barricades holding back the fans, there to run alone up the empty cobbles to the Arc de Triomphe. It was spectacular. Needless to say, being able to travel on foot through a roadway normally teeming with cars gave me the unique perspective of running in the footsteps of the Armistice Day protesters, the Nazi occupiers, and Charles de Gaulle himself.

Finally, more than ever, I leaned on the scholarship of others: Julian Jackson's *De Gaulle* and his other works about wartime Paris; Hanna Diamond, Jean Edward Smith, William Manchester, Sonia Purnell, and more than a hundred other authors whose books formed tall piles surrounding my desk like a defensive perimeter; an infinite list of Google books that provided a telltale fact or two, as well as the secondary and sometimes tertiary Google searches to verify that data. And if you are looking for the most in-depth work about the taking of Paris, please read *Is Paris Burning?* by Larry Collins and Dominique Lapierre. Written in 1965, the authors had the enormous good fortune of interviewing the many participants in Paris on that historic day.

Finally, I hope you have enjoyed this journey. Let's do it again soon.

INDEX

ABOUT THE AUTHOR

Martin Dugard is the *New York Times* bestselling author of several books of history, among them the *Killing* series, *Into Africa*, and *The Explorers*.